COBBETT IN IRELAND

George Dawson

William Cobbett by Daniel Maclise

COBBETT IN IRELAND

A
WARNING TO ENGLAND

Edited by Denis Knight

LAWRENCE AND WISHART
London

Lawrence and Wishart Limited
39 Museum Street
London WC1A 1LQ

This edition first published 1984
© Denis Knight, 1984

This book is sold subject to the condition that it shall not, by way of trade or otherwise, be lent, re-sold, hired out or otherwise circulated without the publisher's prior consent in any form of binding or cover other than that in which it is published and without a similar condition, including this condition, being imposed on the subsequent purchaser.

All rights reserved. Apart from any fair dealing for the purpose of private study, research, criticism or review, no part of this publication, may be reproduced, stored in a retrieval system, or transmitted, in any form or by any means, electronic, electrical, chemical, mechanical, optical, photocopying, recording or otherwise, without the prior permission of the copyright owner.

Photoset in North Wales by
Derek Doyle & Associates, Mold, Clwyd
Printed and bound in Great Britain by
The Camelot Press Ltd, Southampton

Contents

ILLUSTRATIONS	8
ACKNOWLEDGEMENTS	9
PREFACE	11
FOREWORD BY GEORGE SPATER	15
INTRODUCTION	19
A BIBLIOGRAPHICAL NOTE	29

CHAPTER 1
Intended Visit to Ireland *Political Register*,
26 July 1834 — 31
'I Will Say What I Have to Say at Dublin ...'
PR 2 August — 34
'Before This Register Leaves the Press ...'
PR 13 September — 35
'It May Happen That Some Gentlemen ...'
PR 13 September — 36
'All The Way Across From Normandy ...'
10 September — 37
'The Turnips and Grass Have Been Equally
Fine ...' 10 September — 38
'M'y Voici ...' 14 September — 39
Letter I to Charles Marshall 22 September — 43

CHAPTER 2
To Daniel O'Connell 23 September — 49
Speech by Mr Finn, Member for Kilkenny, and
Address by Mr Nevin Welcoming William
Cobbett to Ireland, With William Cobbett's
Reply *PR* 27 September — 52
Letter II to Charles Marshall 27 September — 59
To Mr Smith, Printer 27 September — 63

To the Members of the Meath Club 28 September	64
To Mr John Dean *PR* 4 October	65
My Proceedings in Dublin *PR* 4 October	67
'To Correspondents' *PR* 4 October	75

CHAPTER 3

To the Citizens of Kilkenny 30 September	79
Letter III to Charles Marshall 1 October	81
To Lord Althorp 4 October	84
To the Kilkenny Weavers *PR* 11 October	86
To the Citizens of Waterford *PR* 11 October	88

CHAPTER 4

Letter IV to Charles Marshall 6 October	92
To the President of the United States of America 8 October	96
To Lord Radnor 12 October	98

CHAPTER 5

Letter V to Charles Marshall 17 October	120
Reply to the Industrious and Labouring Classes of the City of Cork *PR* 25 October	126
To the Earl of Radnor 18 October	129
To the People of Salisbury 19 October	141
Burning of the Parliament House 20 October	142

CHAPTER 6

Answer to the Parish Priest and Other Inhabitants of the City of Kilmallock 19 October	145
Letter VI to Charles Marshall 25 October	147
Burning of the Parliament House 25 October	153
To the Sensible and Just People of England *PR* 8 November	157
The O'Connell Tribute. To Mr Staunton of the *Morning Register* 29 October	164
To Mr Staunton 31 October	165

CHAPTER 7

To the People of Salisbury 3 November	171
To Lord Althorp 3 November	173
Letter VII to Charles Marshall 4 November	182
Mr Cobbett's Lecture on Repeal 8 November	186

CHAPTER 8
  Address to the Gentlemen of Dublin   8 November   209
  Letter VIII to Charles Marshall   10 November   212
  To the Earl of Radnor   216
  To Lord Althorp   10 November   218
  The Cobbettites   12 November   227

CHAPTER 9
  Letter IX to Charles Marshall   15 November   230
  To the King's Servants   16 November   236
  Turning Out the Whigs   19 November   242

CHAPTER 10
  To the People of Oldham   21 November   245
  Letter X to Charles Marshall   25 November   257

APPENDICES
I   Dedication, to the Working People of Ireland
       PR 5 April   259
II   Repeal of the Union   *PR* 17 May   261
III O'Connell's Welcome to Mr Cobbett
       11 September   284
IV Address From the Trades of Ireland to the People
       of England   *PR* 27 September   287
V   Address of the Citizens of Kilkenny to Mr William
       Cobbett, MP   *PR* 11 October   289
VI Address of the Manufacturing and Operative
       Weavers of Kilkenny   *PR* 11 October   292
VII Garden and Field Seeds   *PR* 8 November   294

INDEX   298

Illustrations

William Cobbett by Daniel Maclise — *frontispiece*

Letter from William Cobbett to his printer-cum-publisher, Oldham — 12

House of Commons, 1833 by Sir George Hayter, detail showing William Cobbett and Daniel O'Connell — 51

Grand Parade, Cork — 121

Custom House, Limerick — 150

Page from *Cobbett's Weekly Political Register*, 29 November 1834 — 256

Acknowledgements

We are grateful to the Houghton Library of Harvard University for permission to reproduce the letter from Cobbett to Oldfield, and to the National Portrait Gallery, London for permission to reproduce a detail from *House of Commons, 1833* by Sir George Hayter.

Preface

In the autumn of 1834 William Cobbett visited Ireland for the first time. By midsummer in the following year he had died, at Normandy Farm, Ash, six miles from his birthplace at Farnham. Writing from Limerick in October to Charles Marshall, the 'most able and the most skilful' of his farmworkers, Cobbett had promised him that at the end of his travels in Ireland he would publish 'a little book with the following title: *Ireland's Woes: A Warning To Englishmen*.' Alternatively, in a letter to Oldfield, his associate-cum-publisher in London, it was to read: *The Sufferings Of Ireland: A Warning To England*', addressed to 'The Industrious Classes of England.'

On his return to England in November with the manuscript of another little book, *Legacy to Labourers*, again a gift to Charles Marshall and the labourers of England, the Member for Oldham was flung straightway into the continuing and bitter struggle against the hated measures of the Poor Law Amendment Bill enacted in the summer by the Whig administration. A dissolution of Parliament, a general election early in the new year (Cobbett and John Fielden were returned unopposed for Oldham), the urgent campaigning, late sittings at Westminster, family unhappiness and failing strength, all these obliged him to postpone the writing of his cherished 'little book' on Ireland. Cobbett's death in June put the seal on that postponement.

In this way Cobbett's Irish book, still-born, was to remain forgotten until G.D.H. Cole in his classic *Life of William Cobbett*, published in 1924, mentioned it in his final chapter. Then, six years later, Cole and his wife Margaret, in their beautifully-researched gathering up of all the *Rural Rides*, including the tour of Scotland, reproduced Cobbett's ten remarkable letters to his farm-servant, all but the last of which

Mr. Oldfield   Dublin, 30. Sep. 1834.

Dear Sir,

1. I am preparing for publication a work under the following title.

"The
"Sufferings of Ireland
"a
"Warning to England.
or
"The horrible state of the Irish People, proved by undeniable
"facts, collected on the spot, during an extensive Tour,
"in Ireland, in September and October, 1834.
"Addressed to
"The Industrious Classes of England

"By Wm. Cobbett M.P. for Oldham.

"Published in Numbers,
"Price 6.d
"N.o I.
"London,
"Printed, &c &c."

2. I will not, if I can avoid it, publish this work on <u>my own account</u>, as <u>bookseller</u>; but will <u>sell</u> the thing to some one, if I can; and, I hope, to you.

3. The terms that I propose are these: 1. To begin publishing on Saturday, the 22 Nov.
    2. To publish every succeeding Saturday.
    3. To publish 10 Numbers in the whole.

Letter from William Cobbett to his printer-cum-publisher, Oldham were written from Ireland.

What I have been able to trace of Cobbett's book, from accounts in the Irish newspapers, from his lectures in Dublin, from the frequent addresses of the citizens, journeymen and trade unionists of the towns he visited, and from his answers, from surviving letters in manuscript kindly put at my disposal, and above all from the hardly-faded pages of his *Weekly Political Register*, I have brought together.

In this pleasant task, I am signally indebted to George Spater for his generosity in making available to me while he lived in Sussex his fine library of first and rare editions of Cobbett; for his kindness in putting at my disposal manuscripts of Cobbett's correspondence from Ireland; and for reading through my notes and making some suggestions. I am indebted to many others. To Mrs Molly Townsend of the William Cobbett Society for the friendly encouragement she has given me in undertaking work in her own Irish field; to Professor Hywell D. Lewis, of Normandy Park, Normandy, for answering my inquiries about Cobbett's farm; to Mr Brendan O'Cathaoir, of Bray, Co. Wicklow, for his discovery of the rare text, in the *Pilot* newspaper, of Cobbett's extraordinary and never-republished lecture on Repeal. My thanks are due to the director of the National Library of Ireland; to the staff of the Farnham Library, and librarians of the Brighton Area libraries and the University of Sussex, and to Mr Hunt of the Oldham Libraries, Art Galleries and Museums.

I am grateful to many others for their help; to Richard Stanton, of the University of Sussex, for the benefit of his wide and concerned knowledge of Irish history; to Diana Turner; to my family, especially to Nora, Simon and Peter for providing space for Cobbett and Ireland in house and conversation over the past two years. With this help, and after a silence of 150 years, I offer what I can of Cobbett's own book back to his readers.

Denis Knight,
Piboulède, October 1983

Foreword
by George Spater

Ireland. A nation capable of siring a Jonathan Swift, an Edmund Burke, an Oliver Goldsmith, a Richard Brinsley Sheridan, an Oscar Wilde, a Bernard Shaw and a James Joyce, could not fail to be of interest to William Cobbett.

When he was a boy of eleven or so he spent the whole of his small fortune, three pence, for a copy of Swift's *A Tale of a Tub* which, in his own words, 'produced what I have always considered a sort of birth of intellect.' Swift became a model for Cobbett's literary style.

For at least the first decade of Cobbett's life as journalist he was a follower of Edmund Burke ('this great man ... the profoundest of statesmen'), and although Cobbett later formally disavowed any allegiance to Burke's conservative principles, there always remained, as inconsistent as it may seem, a deeply-seated conservative strain underlying Cobbett's radicalism which owed a great deal to Burke's philosophy.

Cobbett read much, perhaps most, of Goldsmith. He knew by heart the four hundred-odd lines of *The Traveller*. A quotation from that poem appeared on the title page of Cobbett's first book, published anonymously in 1792, and Goldsmith was quoted again and again by Cobbett for the rest of his life.

Sheridan was briefly admired by Cobbett as a member of the Whig opposition with whom Cobbett was associated early in the 1800s, but from about 1803 Sheridan became a favourite target for Cobbett's biting wit; first because Cobbett found him shallow, and later when it became clear that Sheridan had no intention of acting in accordance with his publicly professed libertarian views. On Sheridan, as on others, Cobbett wielded his shillelagh with all the skill of a native Irishman.

Cobbett's involvement with the Irish was not limited to the great literary names of the period. Cobbett admired and, in return, was admired by the dashing Lord Edward Fitzgerald, Cobbett's Major in his soldiering days, who was killed during the Irish uprising of 1798.

Cobbett befriended the Reverend Jeremiah O'Callaghan, an Irish Catholic priest expelled from his living for refusing to give last rites to a parishioner guilty of lending money at interest. O'Callaghan, after many adventures, went on from Cobbett's household to become a hero of American Catholicism, 'the apostle of Vermont' where he built the first Catholic church in Burlington, the state's largest town.

The famous Irish wit, John Philpot Curran, Master of the Rolls in 1806 and member of the Privy Council, visited Cobbett in Newgate when the journalist was imprisoned during 1810-12 for criticizing the brutal flogging of English soldiers. Peter Finnerty, the Irish journalist, was an intimate friend of Cobbett as was, for a time, the half-demented Daniel French, Irish barrister and classical scholar who stupidly created a crisis in the Cobbett family by repeating a suggestion (wholly unjustified) that Cobbett had engaged in 'unnatural propensities' with one of his male employees.

And finally, Cobbett fought and made up and fought again and made up again, Irish style, with the great Daniel O'Connell, 'The Liberator', who declared during a period of amity that Cobbett was 'one of the greatest benefactors of literature, liberty and religion'.

These Irish friendships were only a small part of the story. From almost the beginning of his spectacular career as a journalist in England, Cobbett had enrolled himself as a sympathizer with the Irish cause, although he remained a member of the Church of England all his life. In 1803 he published the 'Juverna' letters condemning the English administration in Ireland and was promptly prosecuted by the government for libel. He criticized the corruption that secured Ireland's acceptance of the Union with England in 1800. He attacked Protestant prejudice in his *History of the Protestant 'Reformation'*, a best seller of 1824-6, when it was published in parts. He was a long-time leader in the fight for Catholic Emancipation, a war finally won in 1829, which enabled Irish Catholics to serve in the House of Commons. He proposed the elimination of the Protestant hierarchy in Ireland, both civil and clerical. He fought to relieve Irish Catholics from paying tithes for the support of the Protestant church, snorting at the suggestion of William Wilberforce that the Irish Catholics could be converted to Protestantism.

Cobbett had desired to visit Ireland long before he managed to do so in 1834. When he arrived at last he was hailed as 'statesman, politician, moralist, political economist, grammarian, historian, gardener and farmer' and as a writer surpassing Swift in 'purity, simplicity, in clearness and cogency'. This Irish welcome, in which the egotistical Cobbett possibly received all the honours he thought he deserved, was a glorious capstone to his career, for when he left Ireland in November 1834 he had but seven months to live. How like Cobbett, and how symbolic of the English attitude towards Ireland, that Cobbett's ten published letters from that country, describing what he did and saw there, should be addressed to 'Charles Marshall, Labourer', one of Cobbett's employees on his farm in Surrey, who could neither read nor write.

George Spater,
White River Junction, Vermont
15 September 1983

Introduction

'Tussy must look through Cobbett some time, to see what he has on Ireland,' Marx wrote to his friend Engels in 1869, at the time of the Fenian campaign in England. Marx's daughter had just returned from a visit to the Wicklow Mountains, Killarney, Cork and Dublin with Lizzy Burns and Frederick Engels; and now the two young women, along with Tussy's sister Jenny, were stronger devotees than ever of the Irish cause. If Eleanor looked, or even began to look, we do not know. If she did, the task was certainly a daunting one. For Cobbett had first mentioned Ireland as far back as 1795, when he published in Philadelphia his *Bone to Gnaw for the Democrats*, with its patriotic growl at the United Irishmen. He continued to write on Ireland, with added warmth from the time of his friendship with John Philpot Curran in 1812, throughout the life-span of *Cobbett's Weekly Political Register* until his death in 1835.

Nowhere, however, in the glances towards his boyhood days in Farnham which he scatters through the *Rural Rides*, *Adventures of Peter Porcupine*, and in his journal of *A Year's Residence in America*, does it seem that Ireland was talked of at the 'Jolly Farmer' inn, the house where he was born. That the Irish were 'the wild Irish' to his village seems the sum of his remembrance; and it is likely that the first Irishman he met was the Captain in the West Norfolks who enrolled him at Chatham, when the young recruit thought he was entering the Marines. But Cobbett does tell us how as a boy he would listen sometimes as his father raised his voice over the American War of Independence. Seated with his rustic customers around the inn table, George Cobbett would berate the King's government and warmly defend the colonial rebels. Cobbett's father, grandfather, and doubtless his forebears, had some of them been peasants, some day-labourers. Such radical thoughts as stirred the air seem never to have been much below the surface among the endangered peasant class in the latter half of the eighteenth century, and were to blaze out furiously after the Napoleonic wars, and again in the 1830s. They did not die out until the peasant-yeoman class was quietly put to death in the ebb-tide of the Chartist 1840s, when survivors not dragged into the 'Wen' of London and the manufacturing towns became wage-labourers on the new squires' farm-estates, or agents and servants in their country houses.

Modern conservatives, more especially those who prefer to view themselves as belonging to 'no party' in the manner deprecated by Swift, have chosen to depict Cobbett the young man as a Conservative, *sui generis*; and to think of the older man, the radical near-republican Cobbett, as a Conservative by nature, but gone astray. If there is to be found a grain of truth in this, the harder, nearer grain must surely be that Cobbett was peasant-born, peasant-bred, and all his life retained the memories and fought for the objects of the peasant class. The politics of the peasant are to keep himself in being, and his land within the family. He seeks stability, in face of the permanent surprise of crops and weather: so that the peasant class is revolutionary, or conservative, in the measure that it is being stamped on or supported. In Cobbett's lifetime, the one hope of stability for the small yeomen and the labourers (their interests were hardly separable), lay in what had happened in the American colonies. To an even greater extent it lay in what had happened – and was still to happen – in republican France.

When William Cobbett, not yet thirty, returned from the Loyalist colony of New Brunswick with a Sergeant Major's cane in his knap-sack and a letter of commendation from his commanding officer Major Lord Edward Fitzgerald (who was shortly to be killed in the rising of 1798), he was strictly no more a Tory than a radical. He was a peasant turned soldier:

> To the army, to every soldier in it, I have a bond of attachment quite independent of any *political* reasonings or considerations. This partiality I have always retained. I like soldiers, as a class in life, better than any other description of men. Their conversation is more pleasing to me; they have generally seen more than other men; they have less of vulgar prejudice about them; to which may be added, that, having felt hardships themselves, they know how to feel for others.

In his breast there lay the conviction, hotly felt, that it was his duty on his fellow-soldiers' behalf to bring to justice dealers in corruption in the army stores, and in particular to press charges against four of his regimental officers, of profiteering on the men's flour and fire-wood rations.

When the honourably-discharged Sergeant Major discovered on the road to the regimental headquarters in Portsmouth that counter-charges were being prepared against him of having 'drunk to the destruction of the House of Brunswick' in the Sergeants' mess, and that in pursuing his own charges he was hazarding his liberty and, possibly, his life – in the event of a military flogging – he and his newly-wed Anne Reid made a sudden dash for the French coast. But in York Street, London, he had already deposited with the Whig publisher Ridgway the manuscript of an explosive pamphlet, *The Soldier's Friend*, or it is possible Cobbett posted it from France.

This first of Cobbett's published writings was a defence – the authorship of which he was to deny for many years – of the soldier's rights as a citizen under common law, whose services were in fact paid for, not by the Crown, but (Cobbett had by now read Paine's *Rights of Man*) by the 'sovereign people' in their parliament. The pamphlet delivered a well-aimed blow at peculation in high places; it cited the fact, admitted by the Secretary of War in the Commons, that unauthorized deductions were customarily made from the soldier's pay-book. On its title-page Cobbett had chosen, significantly, the accusing line from Goldsmith's *The Traveller*, 'Laws grind the poor, and rich men rule the law.' It was a theme which, in due course, he was to make his own. Of army officers, Cobbett declared:

> The world is often deceived in these jovial, honest-looking fellows, the officers of the army; I have known very few of them but perfectly well knew how to take care of themselves, either in peace or war ...

The *Soldier's Friend* in seeking to visit on its officers, or on

> some of them at least ... shame and punishment for the divers flagrant breaches of the law committed by them

and for their manifold, their endless wrongs against the soldiers ...

reached out beyond the army. Seamen at the time of the Nore and Spithead mutinies distributed within the fleet a twopenny reprint; and in *A Review of the Reports made by the Naval Commissioners: by a Society of Gentlemen* (27 July 1805), Cobbett was expressly (though ridiculously) charged with having brought about the Nore mutiny. More to the point perhaps, a soldier now turned writer had fired his first shot – though from the safe enough distance of a village in Artois – as an investigative, obdurate and trouble-making journalist.

Cobbett decamped to the village of Tilques, near St. Omer, (so he later admitted from America)

> full of all those prejudices that Englishmen suck in with their mother's milk, against the French and against their religion: a few weeks convinced me that I had been deceived with respect to both.

He had met everywhere among the peasants there with 'civility ... and hospitality in a degree that I had never been accustomed to.' Writing from near-revolutionary Philadelphia as an Englishman fallen among rebels who spoke English but thought French, he recalled that he had found the people of Tilques

> excepting those who were already blasted with the principles of the accursed revolution ... to be honest, pious, and kind to excess.

He set himself to learn French, no doubt from those not so accursed, 'romped' innocently with a youthful instructress in her language, and was on his way with Nancy to visit Paris when he heard that Louis XVI had been deposed and his Swiss Guards murdered. The wheel of revolution was turning swiftly. War with England, the Cobbetts must have realised, was inevitable. The honeymoon couple turned aside for Le Havre, and aboard the American sloop *Mary* took sail for New York.

Plough-boy, soldier, now a married man without a job, Cobbett at thirty took to teaching French to Philadelphians and English grammar to the Girondist *émigrés*. A patriotic English exile in the heady jacobin atmosphere of the 'city of brotherly love', it was perhaps to be expected that he should spring to a defence of the world he had grown up with in his youth: the well-trodden bounds of field-labourer, yeoman farmer, respected squire and king. It must have been almost by instinct he picked up his single-stick to defend time-worn values, and wielded it 'as an Englishman and as a calf of John Bull' against a whole new world of ideas: French, American, and now, reactively, the 'infamous' Tom Paine's. It was not long before he was hurling *A Bone to Gnaw*, and then *A Kick for a Bite* at Philadelphian democrats, and *The Bloody Buoy* at republicans and admirers of the French Revolution.

Such early ventures in the near-virgin field of American political journalism – a field he was to make virtually his own – piled up steadily over his eight years in the United States until they filled twelve volumes of the *Works of Peter Porcupine*. It was an animal with an unpleasantly sharp quill; Paine, Priestley, Dr Rush, every species of presumed Jacobin, revolutionist and other 'systemist', Jefferson's anti-federalist democrats and 'true' republicans, and even Hamilton's almost pro-British, conservative Federalists, all were brought under the scrutiny of the Porcupine's savage pen. Under the spit-and-polish of this astonishingly literate ex-soldier, his 'quill' had in fact achieved a cutting edge all the more painful to its victims because it was driven home with such candour and good humour. 'I have endeavoured to make America laugh instead of weep,' Cobbett congratulated himself. Whether it was matter for laughter or tears, Cobbett had successfully defended, at least in his own eyes, the tranquillity of the Vale of Farnham and the whole of England, against the earthquakes of revolution in France, and rebellion and democracy in America.

Seen under these aspects – and they were seen so by King and government in London – an independent anti-British republic in America was one thing, and danger enough. Irish independence was quite another. Irish republicanism to boot, the dreams of Wolfe Tone and the poems of William Drennan, these were for Cobbett in this period things unheard of, barely comprehensible. In the second part of *A Bone to Gnaw for the Democrats*, in 1795, he had attacked the 'Proceedings' of the United Irishmen's Dublin club; and in his *Detection of a*

Conspiracy, Formed by the United Irishmen, published in the course of the insurrection, he roughly dismissed the rising of the United-men, when Catholics, Presbyterian dissenters and Episcopalians fought as Irishmen to achieve an independent nation. Within two years of 1798, Cobbett, stung by $5,000 damages awarded against him in a libel action brought by Dr Benjamin Rush, the controversial practitioner of blood-letting, left for England, exulting,

> I depart for my native land, where neither the moth of democracy nor the rust of federalism doth corrupt, and where thieves do not break through and steal five thousand dollars at a time.

So in midsummer 1800, we find Cobbett with Nancy and two children on the high seas bound for Falmouth. He was not to know – and might hardly have believed it – that when he next set foot on American soil it would be as a 'levelling' and even 'insurrectionist' fugitive from British government. He was to be by then a notorious, even the leading Radical spokesman of the labourers and journeymen. Charges were thrown at him, then and later, of inconsistency. And yet Cobbett was not so much doubling on his tracks, as discovering new routes, sometimes by forced marches, to his beginnings.

Cobbett arrived in England, appropriately enough, at the very moment when the democracy of the Dublin Parliament had never been more moth-eaten, nor that of Westminster more rusted and corruptly absolutist. He arrived in London when, in the sober estimate of G.D.H. Cole

> ... the Act of Union was being forced by all manner of bribery and corruption, and half-promises of Catholic Emancipation to follow the Union were being made, with Pitt's consent, to the Irish Catholics.

It was at the very moment when, as if to round off the tale, thieves in collusion in London and Dublin, and in the Catholic hierarchy no less than within the two Protestant Parliaments of landlords, broke through to seize from Ireland the seat of legislative independence she had enjoyed since 1782.

Westminster and Dublin had between them legislated

Ireland out of existence. Under the Union contract her separate identity, language, wealth and commerce were from then on to be subsumed in England's. Her laws were to be enacted by the Imperial Parliament of which the Irish representatives, in permanent minority, would be powerless to act without Whig or Tory support. A proposal was eventually made that Ireland should be called West Britain.

The Act of Union engineered by Pitt to pull Ireland away from the American path to independence, or the direct French road to a revolutionary republic, opened the modern chapter of England's relationship with Ireland. The 'Unionist' road England was to pursue led through Catholic Emancipation in 1829 to the great Repeal agitation of Daniel O'Connell, and its collapse at Clontarf. It led through the Famine of 1845-9, Fenianism, Parnell and the Home Rule movement; and in our own century, by way of the Ulster resistance to Home Rule, the Easter Rising and the Civil War, to the dismemberment of Irish nationality and the retention of six of the nine counties of Ulster within a diminished but still 'United' Kingdom. It has led to the renewed general national movement in our own day for Irish solutions to Irish situations: for forms of self-government and independence for all the people of Ireland, viewed by Marx's daughters, then by James Connolly as the ground on which to build a socialist republic. But for Cobbett, plainly, the path lay beyond the horizon, and lies outside the scope of this introduction.

For Cobbett, for O'Connell, for the Reform and Chartist movements, the efforts of the Irish in Ireland with their compatriots in England to advance emancipation, repeal, reform and trade union organisation, were inseparable from the struggles of the English working people. They flowed from or were linked with the condition of Ireland since the Union. Nor, on the larger scale, could seven centuries of England's relationship with Ireland escape accountability. Seven centuries, firstly of feudal, then, after Cromwell, of marauding bourgeois forms of conquest and land-seizure, had battered Ireland's Celtic clan-society out of shape, and at last out of existence. The communal ownership of land, and almost every vestige of related social attitudes and structures were dissolved by sword and annexation. The once free native cultivators and herdsmen of the socially-held cattle-droves, were to be beaten down into the dependence of tenants-at-will. The will was of foreign landlords; the land was now engrossed and privatised property, theoretically at the discretion of the English Crown.

Seven such centuries, brought to a grim climax by the younger Pitt's war-measure of 1800, had laid down a field of force which English radicals and reformers, though with the best credentials and intentions, entered at their cost. They are noticed to enter it at their cost today. The field of force, although disrupted, remains. In Cobbett's case, the elderly man who, before he died, wished to see Ireland with his own eyes and meet the people where they lived, was nevertheless such an Englishman. The man who had given the greater part and main strength of his life to the cause of the working people could not but enter Ireland as a foreigner. For all his integrity, goodwill and great popularity as a co-worker with O'Connell and the foremost scourge of the English government, Cobbett while in Ireland was inevitably in some sense an emissary from the nation which had annexed her politically, was exploiting her economically and occupying her militarily.

Cobbett was, of course, aware of this. It is evinced in the forthrightness and considerable tact of his public lectures and addresses. Never, perhaps, was he made more immediately aware of it than when, on the road to Fermoy, his eyes were 'blasted by the sight of three barracks for foot, horse, and artillery.' Here stood the evidence that English law and order had not been recognized in Ireland as lawful, and had never in practice been orderly. He knew that Ireland, even in the year of the Union, had been administered under martial law imposed by statute; and that since that year she had been governed under 'ordinary' forms of English law for fewer years than the fingers on his hand. He knew that in the year before his visit, the Tithe War had attracted the curfews of Westminster's Suppression of Disturbances Act, which called for all offences to be tried by courts-martial. He had come to understand very well that Irish 'lawlessness' and 'violence', its 'wildness' as it had been viewed in Farnham and throughout England, was in actuality the denial and negation of English order imposed by arms. And that it was, above all else, a social reaction against those English property-laws governing the possession of land by some, its dispossession for others.

More than this, and of more immediate concern to Cobbett

because it presented more urgent dangers to the labourers in England, he had the evidence all about him that landlordism was running wild in Ireland. His warning signals, sent through such landed aristocrats as Althorp, his friend Radnor, and directly to his Oldham constituents, were of course intended for the broad working-class readership of the *Register*. Those he sent to Charles Marshall were addressed directly to the English labourers and small farmers paying rent and poor-rates.

Cobbett was concerned that if English and Anglo-Irish landlords were to succeed in imposing an unfettered will over Irish society, the landlords and industrialists in England would not be slow to follow suit. Such restraints as had been placed on the landowners in England, through the working of class compromises reflected in custom and law, were absent from the social wilderness of conquered Ireland. The visible evidence that English laws of property supposedly transposed to Ireland had escaped social control, was daily presented to Cobbett in terms of unimagined poverty; of pauperism unrelieved except by private charity; of rack-rent or eviction, emigration or starvation. (The Irish Poor Law provisions of 1838, cosmetic and inadequate as they were, were undoubtedly brought in through Cobbett's earlier agitation.) Cobbett made plain his fear that if absolutist powers were not defeated in Ireland they would little by little slip over into England.

'I defy any man to show that injury can be done to Ireland in any way whatever, without that injury recoiling upon England,' Cobbett had said in May. With all the energy and resources at his command, and with something of a premonition of his own shortness of time, Cobbett now warned that the 'gallon-loaf' whig monetarists in the offing, Brougham and his 'coarser-food' band of Malthusian economists who had recently fastened the Poor Law Amendment Act on the backs of the labourers and town workers, were poised to set up an ascendancy of unblemished 'laissez-faire' dictation by the market, within a grand Whig-Tory coalition of the landlords with the factory-owners. 'Look sharp, then!' Cobbett warned the English labourers, 'The LANDLORD here takes away from the Irish farmer rent, poor-rates, wages, and all, and thus reduces the whole to beggary.'

Engels's shrewd remark to Marx, that 'Irish history shows

one what a misfortune it is for a nation to have subjugated another nation,' contained a force which Cobbett had already appreciated. The oppression in England of the labourers and working people generally could not effectively be resisted, and certainly could not be overthrown, while it flourished without restriction and fully armed in Ireland.

'It is the whole *state* of Ireland; it is the *system of* governing Ireland that ought to be changed!' he had exclaimed in what turned out to be the disastrous, famine-haunted spring of 1807. In the autumn of 1834, many potato-failures on, and under the shadow of the Great Starvation still to come, he could but lend this conviction new force, fire and understanding. It was not to be for Cobbett, it need hardly be said, to effect materially that 'Great Change' he had long sought and worked for. That was to be a task for the hands of the Irish working people, and for theirs alone.

A Bibliographical Note

Writers on Cobbett who have placed an emphasis on his interest in Ireland have been, at least in England, somewhat few and far between. They include, in the order in which their books appeared: E.I. Carlyle, *William Cobbett* (1904); G.D.H. Cole, *Life of William Cobbett* (1924); John W. Osborne, *Cobbett: His Thought and Times* (1966); George Spater, *William Cobbett: The Poor Man's Friend* (1982); and M. Townsend's analysis of Cobbett's writings on Ireland *'Not by Bullets and Bayonets'* (1983).

Books on aspects of Irish and Anglo-Irish history dealing mainly with Cobbett's period and the nineteenth century make up a formidable and rapidly increasing library. Those listed below are necessarily a limited, somewhat selective choice. Others are given in the notes.

Paul Bew, *Land and the National Question in Ireland* (Dublin, 1977) – also, *Les Fénians et l'Indépendance de l'Irlande* (Paris, 1981)

Andrew Boyd, *The Rise of the Irish Trade Unions* (Dublin, 1972)

J. Butt, *The Irish People and the Irish Land* (Dublin, 1867)

James Connolly, *Labour in Irish History* (Dublin, 1910)

John Davies, *Historical Tracts* (London, 1786)

P. Beresford Ellis, *A History of the Irish Working Class* (London, 1972)

J.L. Hammond, *Gladstone and the Irish Nation* (London, 1938)

F.S.L. Lyons, *Ireland Since the Famine* (London, 1971)

Oliver MacDonagh, *Ireland: The Union and its Aftermath* (London, 1977) also, *States of Mind: A Study of Anglo-Irish Conflict 1780-1980* (London, 1983)

Patrick O'Farrell, *England and Ireland since 1800* (Oxford, 1975)

P.S. O'Hegarty, *A History of Ireland under the Union* (London, 1952)

Charles Townshend, *Political Violence in Ireland: Government and Resistance since 1848* (Oxford, 1983)

Cecil Woodham-Smith, *The Great Hunger* (London 1962 & 1981)

CHAPTER 1

Political Register, 26 July 1834.

Intended Visit to Ireland

I have resolved to see this country with my own eyes; to judge for *myself*, and to give a true account of it, as far as I am able, to the people of England. I am resolved to go, as if to a country about which I had never said a word. I have, now, for two sessions of Parliament, listened to such contradictory statements, coming from gentlemen of unimpeachable veracity, that it is impossible I should not desire to have the evidence of the facts before me. It is impossible for me to disbelieve all the statements made on either side. In short, I have a desire to know the real truth; and if I cannot get at it by seeing the country, very few men can. I have seen the claims of the Irish people to *free trade* granted. The want of that was then the burden of complaint; next, *Catholic Emancipation*[1] was to heal every wound: it was granted to an extent never called for, and that has failed. The existence of *tithe*[2] and of *church-rates*[3] was next the great scourge of Ireland; the latter have been abolished, and the former has been so far extinguished as hardly to be a bone of contention; yet the discontents and troubles are as great as ever. I have, ever since the year 1812, or thereabouts, contended for a *legal provision for the destitute* in Ireland: I am satisfied that nothing but that can make that fine and populous country what it ought to be; but I have a desire to know whether this my opinion is well founded. I fear that, if Ireland continue in this state of alienation from England for many years longer, very great dangers will arise from it, especially in case of war with the United States of America, which must come first or last; and few things would give me so much happiness as to see that danger completely and for ever rendered impossible.

It will be my duty, while in Ireland, to inculcate my own opinions relative to the remedy for the evils of that country; and in doing this, I must be clear from the influence of any consideration whatever, relative to the opinions of others.

For this reason, and in order to keep myself clear of all bias; in order that I may discharge this duty in the manner which becomes me, it is my resolution *to be present at no public dinner*; to be a guest in the house of no gentleman in that country;[4] but to go from inn to inn, and to mix, as much as I can, with persons in the middle rank of life, and to see as much as I can of the real state of the working people of the country. I know that to refuse invitations is disagreeable; but this I shall undergo, rather than suffer myself to be committed in any conversations, or to be biassed on the one side or the other, in the smallest degree. I will go to no public meeting whatsoever, in-doors or out-of-doors. If I find it convenient, and likely to be useful, I shall proceed precisely as I did in Scotland, avoiding, by all means, in so inflammable a country, to meddle with any question in which the utterance of my opinions might be likely, in any degree whatsoever, to widen the breach which now so unhappily exists. I am aware that a feeling of gratitude to me exists in the breasts of all Catholics. I wish them to remember, however, that I am a Protestant of the church of England myself; and I here repeat to them what I said to DOCTOR DOYLE, *that the 'History of the Protestant Reformation' was simply the effect of my desire to do justice, and no more than justice, to the character and religion of those, our own forefathers, who built the cathedrals and the churches.*[5] If they bear this in mind, and after this abatement think me worthy of their thanks, it is very well; but I wish to be clearly understood as entitled to them on no other condition. My desire is, to see such a state of things as to make me believe that England (in which name I include the whole kingdom) will *always be*; not only for my lifetime, but always, the greatest country in the world; and I would not give a straw for any effort that did not include that object. I do not desire to see the form of government changed; but, let what will come, '*let England be the greatest, the happiest country in the world.*' That has been my ruling passion ever since I arrived at the age of serious thought. I fear that it will not be so, without a perfect reconciliation between this country and Ireland. I believe (though the belief may be vain) that my going to Ireland at this time may have a tendency to ensure that object, and therefore to Ireland I will go.

Precisely *when* I shall start, or to what place I shall go first, I have not yet made up my mind. Probably immediately after the prorogation of Parliament I shall commence this tour, relative to which I shall have other opportunities of stating particulars.[6]

Political Register, 2 August 1834.

'I Will Say What I Have to Say at Dublin ...'

I will say what I have to say at DUBLIN, and in every town in Ireland that I go to; and the hectoring and abuse of people like these speechmakers and writers will not make me believe that a country which pours out food for a considerable part of the inhabited world, does not contain its fair share of *men of sense*. Many gentlemen that I have known, and that I yet know, they being Irishmen, have said to me: 'Come and see Ireland with your own eyes: you will find as many men of sound sense and judgment there as in any other country of like population.' I believe this; at any rate, I am resolved to try it in a few weeks if I have life and health ...[7] At any rate, I have a right to go, and go I will.

Political Register, 13 September 1834.

'Before This Register Leaves the Press ...'

Before this *Register* leaves the press, I shall, I suppose, be in Ireland; whither I shall go entirely alone, determined to show that I want no protection, assistance or counsel, notwithstanding I am going amongst those whom I, before I quitted my home, called the 'wild Irish'. It is high time that my more immediate countrymen should be wholly disabused in this respect. I have laboured with great zeal, industry, and energy, in order to disabuse them. It was, indeed, considering my capacity for the task, no more than my duty to do this. To God, who gave me that capacity, I was always answerable for the performance of this duty; but now, when a most excellent portion of those[8] whom I have disabused have clothed me with the power of taking part in the making of laws to govern this long-oppressed and calumniated people, it is tenfold more my duty, in spite of all the obstacles which I may have to encounter, to obtain that certain information with regard to this people, without which, I must, at best, be proceeding from hearsay. These expressions of feeling for Ireland, I would not now put upon paper, if I had not been putting them upon paper, and in stronger terms and epithets, during the whole course of the last seven-and-twenty years.

Political Register, 13 September 1834.

'It May Happen That Some Gentlemen ...'

It may happen that some gentlemen may wish to see my crop of corn at the farm, or to see some other thing belonging to my rural management. They will find the farm in the care of Mr JOHN DEAN,[9] who will be ready, at all reasonable times, to show them, or tell them, any thing and every thing about it. According to present appearances he will be harvesting the corn about the middle of October; and any of those gentlemen who have requested of me to be permitted to go and see it, will do well, perhaps, if they continue in the same mind, to go about that time. One thing they will not see there, nor in any part of the neighbourhood round about; namely, *labourers living upon potatoes and salt*; and that no accursed Scotch quack; no barren rig of a woman, who sucks up taxes by writing against those who pay the most of them;[10] this is a thing that none of these devils will ever see in the county of Surrey, and especially in the tithing of Normandy.

NORMANDY FARM[11] is five miles from GUILDFORD, six miles from FARNHAM, seven miles from GODALMING, across the Hog's-Back; eight miles from BAGSHOT; thirteen miles from CHERTSEY; and, on every one of these roads, you go over commons and greens, and through a region of cottages, not one inhabitant of which is there who would not perish rather than be reduced to potatoes and salt.

NB An Irish gentleman who left some French books on agriculture for me to read, is informed that the books are at BOLT-COURT,[12] where they are ready to be delivered to him; that I have not had time to look into but one of them; that I am as much obliged to him as if I had had time to profit from his goodness; that it is great good luck that restores to him his books; and that, if he will be advised by me, he will never again lend me a book which he is not prepared to take leave of for ever; not that this is proper, and not that I like that it should be so; but that it is completely impossible that it should be otherwise.

Political Register, 13 September 1834

'All the Way Across From Normandy ...'

Maidenhead, 10 September 1834.
All the way across from Normandy to this pretty and clean town, which is in Berkshire, the crops of grass and turnips are very fine: finer than I ever saw them in my life. Over this whole stretch of country, the land is very *light*, and a great part of it exceedingly *poor*; but, even on these miserable lands, where, to break up and cultivate is really an invasion of the rights of the grasshoppers, the efts, and the lapwings (black plovers or pewits), the grass and turnips are good. The *grain crops* have been large and excellent; and the *apples* every where abundant and unusually large. The *grapes* (in the quantity of which Surrey, I verily believe, surpasses Champagne) are now nearly ripe in many places; and the crops are prodigious. At one house, in the parish of Farnham, there are, against the dwelling-house, against the hop-kilns, and against other buildings appertaining to the farm, grapes I should think which will weigh *half-a-ton*; many of the branches will weigh from 3 to 5 or 6 pounds. Looking, yesterday morning, up one side of my farm-house, seeing it covered with fine grapes, and seeing the ground below, up to the wall itself, covered with Cobbett-corn, the stalks loaded with ears and nearly ripe; thus looking and seeing, and turning round and seeing Warnborough farm-house, at only a mile from me, I said to myself, What but the *devil*, or *female infatuation*,[13] could have induced Birkbeck[14] to traverse the seas, and after them the wild mountains of America in search of rich land! The *latter cause* is the greatest demolisher of men's sense; Satan may be overcome, and the party assailed left at large, but for the latter there is no remedy short of a razor, a rope, a millpool, a madhouse, or *almost starvation*.

Political Register, 13 September, 1834.

'The Turnips and Grass Have been Equally Fine...'

Birmingham, 10 September
The turnips and grass have been equally fine all the way along, except in some of the thin soil in Oxfordshire, where there is never any grass, and where, I suppose, the turnips are never good.

This is a year of *real plenty*. The hops at Farnham (and, I suppose, in the other hop counties) exceed all that I ever saw before, both in quantity and quality. This town and its environs are always delightful to all those who are fit to live; that is to say, to those who admire the most beautiful scenery accompanied with the most fertile lands; for those who are insensible to these are mere lumps of flesh and skin and bone, not coming within the confines of humanity. In my rambles over this world, and always with my eyes open, I, seeing so many spots to admire, and to thank God for having made, had almost forgotten the spot first trodden by my then little feet. But now, being planked down, for the rest of my life, within 6 miles of that spot, and having frequent occasions to go thither, and to view it in all its bearings, I am convinced, that it is the very finest spot that God, in his goodness, ever made. ARTHUR YOUNG, after making an agricultural survey of England, decided that the space from Farnham to Alton was the finest and richest *ten miles* in England.[15] He must have begun eastward at Bourne Mill;[16] else it is only *nine miles*; and then I join with him in opinion; for here is everything: coppices, trees, corn-fields, meadows, hop-gardens, orchards, gardens, flowers, neat houses covered with grape-vines, a people (though they do go to bed a little late) well fed, well dressed, and able to work.

Political Register, 20 September 1834.

'M'y Voici ...'

NORTH WALES

Holyhead, 14 September 1834.
M'y voici, agreeably to my promise, intending to be in Dublin tomorrow evening, 15 September, as I at first proposed.

I came by the mail from Birmingham (150 miles in fifteen hours), and a pleasanter coach to ride in I never saw, and it was as fine a day as eyes ever beheld: its rival has just commenced, for the sun in all his glory is just rising, and darting his beams over the waters, which divide and subdivide the little strips of land which constitute this part of this little Island of Anglesea.

The turnips and grass exceedingly good all through Shropshire, and as long as there were any turnips. About OSWESTRY they wholly ceased; and we got amongst mountains, which grew worse and worse, more and more mere rocks; those rocks more and more craggy; those crags more and more hideous; till, at last, I actually shut my eyes, in order not to see them any more; unfortunately for my taste, the moon came and followed up the sun, so that even night gave me no deliverance. What a contrast with the spot that I left last Tuesday evening! There they were gathering in the ropes of hops; and there the grapes (white and black) were hanging on the sides of all our houses, while on two sides of mine, the Cobbett-corn plants were standing close up to the walls, loaded with ears of corn, nearly fit to gather in! Never was a truer saying, than that, 'One half of the world does not know how the other half lives.'

Of 'Welsh cattle', I have seen, in my time, hundreds of thousands. They now go over Normandy Common in droves of a thousand, or more, in a drove, on their way to the fairs in Kent and Sussex, where they are great favourites; and, if kept to a proper age, they make very fine oxen and very good milch cows, whole dairies of which are to be seen in those counties and in the weald of Surrey. I have now seen the *beginnings* of these cattle. These mountains have, generally, little plots, or strips of earth, on their bases, or in the narrow valleys that wind about amongst these endless heaps of ugly rock. These plots grow grass, and that grass is excellent. On one of these you see a little stone house, not a tenth part so big as any one of ten thousand *individual stones*, that lie by the side of the road. Somewhere near this little stone house (with a window about as wide as your hat), you see a little hay-stack, containing, perhaps, a ton; and thatched and bound over with bands in such a manner as to tell *what sort of weather* it has to stand. Then, somewhere about the place, you see a little black cow or two, and one or more weaning calves, about the size of a Newfoundland dog. These, according to the capacity of the owner, are sold to the *drovers* or *jobbers*, at one, two, or three years old. As they increase in age they move on towards England, and towards that food which is not to be had at their homes; and thus they come off at last, two, three, or four years old, to work, to be fatted, or give milk, and fat calves, in the south of England, where they cannot be *raised* with profit. Hence the herds of fine oxen, with which I have seen the rich marshes in Kent and Sussex covered over; and hence the fine teams of oxen, which plough and harrow and roll no small part of these lands at the foot of the South Downs. If one of those careful and laborious and frugal Welsh women, who raise these cattle, could see one of her diminutive calves become a fat ox in PEVENSEY LEVEL; or if she could see six or eight of them in the wealds, drawing a timber carriage with ten tons of weight upon it, what would be her surprise!

'Dear is that shed to which his soul conforms,
And dear those rocks which lift him to the storms.'

Upon my soul, Dr. GOLDSMITH, I do not believe you here. He *bears* them, to be sure; they are his *lot* and his *all*; he knows of nothing better; but, you shall never persuade me, that they are as *dear* to him, that he has so much *pleasure* in contemplating them, as the Sussex chopstick has in contemplating his neat garden, his border of flowers, his grape-vine-covered cottage, and all the appurtenances of his dwelling-place. No; nor have these arid scenes the effect of inspiring frankness and generous feelings, as scenes of fertility and plenty have. The *habit* of setting a high value on things of little value is very good to form a prudent man, an usurer, or a miser; but not good to form a frank and generous man. And in support of this my *philosophy* I appeal to the Americans, who never know, or think of, *want*; and who scorn to disguise any sentiment that they entertain; who will speak of their pecuniary embarrassments without the least reserve; who will confess even to their deficiency in courage, if it exist; and whose hospitality and disregard of its affects on their property are notorious to all who know them. Merciful and kind to their deadliest enemies; and brave and patriotic as any portion of God's creation! Curious, too, that natives of all other countries *catch the character* when they go thither. It is *the absence of the fear of want*; it is that *plenty*, which God has said shall be at once the source and the reward of virtue: and, while these facts stare us in the face, a set of hard-hearted villains, bred in the arid and beggarly parts of the north, are hatching projects to reduce the people of the south to '*a coarser sort of food*'!

Be that as it may, however, I have, for *my part*, no idea of *picturesque beauty* separate from *fertility of soil*. If you can have *both*, as on the banks of CLYDE, and on the skirts of the *bays* and *inlets* in Long Island, then it is delightful: but, if I must have *one* or the *other*, any body may have the *picturesque beauty* for me.

The *people* in Wales are just what we see the milk-women in London. Low in stature, but strong; generally light in their dress; and not filthy in their houses. The young women have small round faces; very fresh coloured; very *pretty*; but it is all *hard*; it is *solid*; it may, in a picture, be *prettier*, perhaps; but it is not *like* the assemblage of softness and sweetness that you see in the faces and in all about the girls in Sussex and Kent. Such appears to be the difference between the effect of rearing cattle and of eating them when fat.

From the beginning of Warwickshire I have not seen a grape-vine against a house. They grew *rare* in Berkshire; only *here and there one* in Oxfordshire; but, after that, they wholly disappeared. In 1826, travelling on horseback, I breakfasted on grapes and bread, from Kent to the skirts of Gloucestershire, on the wolds of which they quitted me. And at 'Lidiard Tregoose' (Lidiard *tres grose* or *very big*) in Wiltshire, I had them from the side of the little public house, finer than I ever saw them from a glass grapery. This want, added to the want of flowers in labourers' gardens, and this added to the dull uniformity of the surface of the fields, makes these grass countries truly dismal to one who comes from the endless variety and bustle of a country of *agriculture*; besides the reflection (and one for a *statesman* it is), that these same grasslands, if subjected to the plough, would produce *more meat, cheese and butter, wool and hides* than they DO NOW, and *bread too*, to eat with the meat, cheese, and butter, and backs to wear the wool, and feet to wear the hides. NOT more *rent* to the landlord! But, more food and clothing; more wages to labour, and more riches and power to the commonwealth. What, then, I would pass a *law*, would I, to prevent this excess of pasturage? If I would, I should not be in want of a *wise precedent* in the laws made by our wise ancestors; but, I would not; I would proceed by *indirect means*; I would make it the *interest* of the parties to act as I wished.

Political Register, 27 September 1834.

To Charles Marshall, Labourer, Letter No.I

Normandy Tithing, Parish of Ash,
County of Surrey.

Dublin, *22 September 1834.*

MARSHALL,

   I have this morning seen more than one thousand of working persons, men and women, boys and girls, all the clothes upon all the bodies of all of whom were not worth so much as the smock-frock that you go to work in; and you have a wife and eight children, seven of whom are too young to go to work. I have seen the *food* and the *cooking* of the food, in a LARGE HOUSE, where food is prepared for a part of these wretched people. Cast-iron coppers, three or four times as big as our largest brewing-copper, are employed to boil *oatmeal* (that is, *ground oats in water*, or *butter-milk*, or *skim-milk*); and this is the food given to these poor creatures. The *white cabbages*, the *barley-meal*, the *pot-fat*, the *whey*, and the *butter-milk*, which George[17] boils daily for our little pigs and their mothers, is a dish, to obtain a mouthful of which, thousands of these people would go on their knees. Marshall, you know how I scolded Tom Denman[18] and little Barratt[19] and your own son Dick,[20] on the Saturday before I came away, for not sweeping the *sleeping-place* of the *yard-hogs* out clean, and what a strict charge I gave George to fling out the old bed, and give them a bed of fresh straw every Saturday. Oh, how happy would thousands upon thousands in this city be, if they could be lodged in a place like that roughest hog-bed! I this morning saw a *widow*-woman and her four children, in the spot where they had slept; on *their bed*, in short. George remembers my looking over at the sows and their sucking pigs, and at the two youngest calves, just before I came away; and that I told him to keep them in that nice condition all the time that I should be away. Now, Marshall, this poor widow and her little children were lying upon a quantity of straw not a twentieth part so great as that allotted to one of the sows and her pigs; and if I, on my return, were to see, as I am sure I shall not, the straw of the calves as dirty, and so broken, as that upon which this widow and her children were lying, I should drive George out of the house, as a slovenly and cruel fellow. And this, you will observe, is the case of thousands upon thousands of persons; it is the case of whole streets as long as the main streets of Guildford and Farnham. Your pig-sty and Turvill's pig-sty,[21] and the sties of other labouring men, are made by yourselves, with posts and poles and rods and heath, and your supply of straw is very scanty, and compels you to resort to *fern* and *dead grass* from the common: but, and now mind what I say: I saw Turvill's pig-sty the day before I came off, and I solemnly declare, in the face of England and of Ireland, that Turvill's two hogs were better lodged, and far better fed, and far more clean in their skins, than are thousands upon thousands of the human beings in this city; which, as to streets, squares, and buildings, is as fine a city as almost any in the world! The LARGE HOUSE, of which I have spoken to you above, is called the MENDICITY. The word *mendicant* means *beggar*, and the word MENDICITY means *beggary*. So that this, which was formerly a nobleman's mansion, is now the *house* of *beggars*. From this house there are sent forth, every day, begging-carts, drawn by women, who go from house to house to collect what is called 'broken victuals'. These carts are precisely, in shape and in size, like my *dog-hutches*, except that the begging-carts have a sort of *hopper* at top to put the victuals in at, and a locked-up door at one end, to take the victuals out of. Now mind what I am going to say: the bones, bits of rusty bacon, rind of bacon, scrapings of dishes and plates, left cabbage, left turnips, peas, beans, beets, and the like odds and ends, that Mrs Kenning[22] throws into our *hog-tub*, form a mass of victuals *superior in quality* to these *mendicity-collections*; and in proof of which I state the following facts: that the carts, when they come in, have their contents taken out and examined by persons appointed for the purpose, who separate all that can become food from the mere rubbish and filth, that is, by servants at the houses, tossed into the carts among it; and a gentleman has, in evidence given by him before commissioners here, stated, that out of *seventy odd hundred weight* taken out of the carts the examiners found *only nine hundred weight* that could by *possibility* become human food, the *bones* in these nine hundred weight not being included!

The real statement is this:

In twenty-two weeks the begging-carts collected: 273 cwt
Of this, unfit for any use: 175cwt.

98 cwt.

When the bones and other uneatable things were separated from this there remained, applicable as human food: 9 cwt

So that these poor women, in these twenty-two weeks, actually dragged to this place 273 hundred weight of stuff very little better than that which forms an ordinary town dunghill!

Now, Marshall, I address this letter to you, because you are the most able and the most skilful of my labourers, though all of you are able and good. You cannot *read* it, I know; but, Mr DEAN will read it to you; and he will, some evening, get you all together, and read it, twice over, to you all. I will cause it to be printed on a slip of paper, and cause copies of it to be sent into all the parishes round about our own.

You will, perhaps, think, that the *land* here is not like that at Normandy. Indeed, it is not; for one acre here is worth four of that; the grass here is the finest that I ever saw in my life; six acres of it worth more than my twenty acres; and, when I go home, I shall be happy indeed to find my MANGEL WURZEL and SWEDISH TURNIPS (about which we have taken so many pains) any thing like so good as those which I saw growing here, raised, too, *from seed bought of me.* Here are as fine beef and oats in abundance. The causes of this strange state of things, I have come hither to endeavour to ascertain, and to offer to this suffering people my opinions as to the remedies that ought to be applied.

But, Marshall, I hope that none of you will believe that I lay the state of the Irish working people before you, with a view of making the unfortunate amongst you *patient* under a refusal to give *you relief* according to the ancient law, which our forefathers left us as our best inheritance.[23] Just the contrary is the view, with which I have written this letter. There are certain savage villains, who are urging the Government and the Parliament to adopt measures to compel you to live on 'COARSER FOOD' than that which you now live on; and, in short, to reduce you to the state that I have above described the Irish working people to be in; and I write this, that you may all see what that state is, and that you may be on the watch for any thing that these villains may recommend to be done against you, and that you may be ready to plead and to stand by *the law* against the recommendations of those barbarous monsters, who are seeking to live in idleness and to fatten on your toil.

Besides, it is the duty of you all to wish and to endeavour to better the lot of those Irish sufferers; and, as I shall hereafter show you, you can do much, if you will. People of property are just as kind and charitable here as they are in England: they subscribe large sums of money to prevent this misery: but there wants T H E   L A W, the *Christian* law, the *holy* law of England, which says that no human being shall, on English ground, *perish from want*. How there came not to be P O O R - L A W S here, as well as in England, I have not now time to explain to you. But here there are none; and you see the consequences. MANCHESTER has about the same number of people as Dublin: in the former the poor-rates, it is calculated, hardly surpass the *subscriptions* in Dublin: yet, misery such as is here, is wholly unknown in Manchester. It is *the law* that does all; that law, which has so long been the greatest glory of England; that law which the base Scotch negro-drivers (not the *Scotch people*, who hate them as cordially as I do) are now recommending to be destroyed; but which law, it is our duty to maintain, and, not only to maintain for ourselves, but to cause to be extended to these our fellow-subjects of Ireland.

I hope that you and your family are quite well, and that the Scotch villains will never be able to take from you the bacon and bread that you bring for your breakfast, and to put cold potatoes in your satchel in their stead.

I remain,
Your master and friend,
WM.　C O B B E T T.

NOTES

[1] Catholic Emancipation had been during the 1820s second in importance, and in the space Cobbett gave it in his *Political Register*, only to Parliamentary Reform itself. Advocates of emancipation (chief among them Daniel O'Connell and the Catholic Association) wished to keep it separate from the more inflammable issue of reform. Cobbett, along with Hunt and most English radicals, opposed this tactic. Even after the passage of the Relief Bills in 1829, Cobbett continued to assert that by 'emancipating' the Catholic landowners, lawyers and aristocrats in Ireland at the expense of the now disenfranchised 'Forty-Shilling' freeholders, the measure had in fact been shown to be more harmful than useful to the main body of the Irish people. (See n.17, p.77.)

[2] *Tithes*: 'I want to see the whole taken away: the tithes, the church-lands, and all other property held by the clergy in virtue of their clerical functions and offices', Cobbett made plain in his *Letter to the Labourers of England* (26 December 1830.) At this time he contended that the 'entire Protestant Hierarchy' in England as well as Ireland, should be 'repealed' by a reformed Parliament, 'unestablishing by law that church which has been by law established.' But this view, derived from his experience in the United States, he knew to be unrealistic in England where the Protestant religion inside the Anglican Church was upheld by the monarch and constitution.

[3] Before the Relief Acts, Catholics and Dissenters generally in Ireland had been obliged to pay church-rates on top of tithes towards the upkeep of the Church of Ireland.

[4] In the event, Cobbett did not keep his promise to the letter. On arrival, he was a guest for three days of General Cockburn, at his country mansion at Shangana, near Bray. At the end of his journeys, he stayed there again. Cobbett was also entertained at public dinners in Dublin and Cork.

[5] Cobbett's *History of the Protestant Reformation in England and Ireland; Showing How That Event Has Impoverished and Degraded the Main Body of the People in those Countries*. (London, Vol.1, 1824-6; Vol.2, 1827), saw enormous sales in Europe and America, in numerous editions and translations. 'I have published a book that has exceeded all others in circulation, the Bible only excepted,' boasted Cobbett.

[6] Cobbett left Normandy Farm for Ireland early on the morning of Tuesday 9 September, five weeks after the Parliamentary adjournment.

[7] Cobbett had said in May, 'My cough is gone, and, though a great weakness remains, I have begun to rise early in the morning.' He maintained that no man could feel really well unless the wind was in the west, and while in Ireland regained much of his old vigour. For a man of seventy-one he 'has yet much of the hale and stout appearance for which he has been so remarkable through life ... his step is wonderfully firm, and his voice is clear', in the view of a Dubliner.

[8] The electors of Oldham.

[9] Dean had been Cobbett's farm-manager since the years at Botley, where he had taken a farm in 1805.

[10] Almost certainly a reference to Mrs Mary Anne Clark, ex-mistress of the Duke of York. She had been an engagingly frank witness in court in 1809,

when the Duke was charged with selling army commissions.

[11] The farm was made up of 160 acres of poor land, much of it rough pasture and coppice, with some arable. Cobbett had acquired a long lease in 1832, at the rent of £1 an acre. The farmhouse at Normandy is no longer standing.

[12] Cobbett was now publishing his *Register* and his books from 11, Bolt Court, off Fleet Street. He often said that his office-rooms (now in Johnson's Court) had once been the apartments of Samuel Johnson: the 'Dr Dread-Devil, who wrote in the same room that I write in, when I am at Bolt-Court'. In fact, Johnson's rooms, in the renamed Johnson's Court, have been shown not to be identical.

[13] What Cobbett considered to be 'female infatuation' was at this time much on his mind. His recently acquired secretary, James Gutsell, was having a love-affair with Mary Kenner the dairymaid, wife of one of the Normandy farm-workers.

[14] The English adventurer and home-colonizer in Illinois.

[15] Arthur Young (1741-1820) had contributed articles to the *Political Register*, including a defence of the land-enclosures. An opponent of the revolution in France and of radicalism in England, he was nevertheless a strong advocate of allotments for the dispossessed cottagers, and in 1800 became an opponent of the enclosures everywhere dispossessing them.

[16] Bourne Mill stands about a mile from Farnham, at an inflow to the River Wey. The sandhill nearby was Cobbett's childhood playground: 'It is impossible to say how much I owe to that sandhill!' said the grown man.

[17] George, 'the man who minds the cattle', was Mary Kenner's husband.

[18] This farm-boy – as G.D.H. & Margaret Cole point out – appears sometimes in Cobbett's text as Deadman, Dedman, and Dodman.

[19] Another farm-labourer's boy.

[20] Dick was one of the eight Marshall children.

[21] The Turvill family lived nearby, at Ash.

[22] Cobbett could be surprisingly careless in his spelling of proper names. Mrs Kenning must be Mrs Kenner, the milkmaid.

[23] Cobbett's reference is to the original Elizabethan Poor Law; or 'Old Betsy's Poor Law' as he often called it.

CHAPTER 2

Political Register, 27 September 1834.

To Daniel O'Connell

Dublin, 23 September, 1834.
My dear Daniel,
 I have received your letter of WELCOME by the hands of Mr Edward Dwyer; and also your kind letter of invitation to your house at Derrynane.[1]
 With regard to the first, I will not pretend to believe that I am altogether unworthy of the character you have given me, while as far as good intentions and zealous endeavours go, no one can over-rate me there. If I do not (as I certainly do not) deserve *all* the praise that you can bestow on me, I have, in the commendations thus bestowed on me by you, and in the honourable reception that I have found in Ireland, a powerful motive, in addition to all those which before urged me on to action, to endeavour to deserve *all* your praise, great as it is.
 I did not set my foot on Irish ground without bearing in mind the fact, that I had resolved never to come hither, while the unmitigated 'COERCION BILL' should remain in force; and, without bearing in mind this other fact, namely, that it was YOU, and you ALONE, who had prevented it so remaining.[2] Never shall I, as long as I live, forget your attitude, your manner, your agitation, your anxious and impassioned tone, when you asked, *whether it was intended to renew the Coercion Bill*; nor shall I ever forget the indignant declaration of your resolution to oppose it. It was your conduct, in that five minutes, which produced all that followed; it was your conduct

in that five minutes that brought me here; your country's gratitude you know you have; and I here, with the greatest respect, beg you to accept of mine.

With regard to the second matter; your invitation to Derrynane. I could, by going thither, not possibly add, in the view of either your countrymen, or mine, one particle to the proof of that respect and admiration which I bear towards you: if the visit could do this, nothing should prevent me from making it. But, while it could be of no use in this respect, I find, upon full and minute inquiry and calculation, that it would retard me ten or twelve days in that progress which I am performing, not for pleasure, nor to gratify curiosity, but from a sense of duty; from a desire to acquire that knowledge which I did not before possess, and the possession of which is necessary to enable me duly to discharge that duty which my excellent constituents have a right to expect at my hands. For these reasons, and because the loss of ten days would be injurious to my object, I beg you to excuse (as I know you will) my not visiting you now, receiving my assurance, that, if alive and well next year I will go from my home to your house for the express and sole purpose of showing my respect towards you and your family. And with this assurance I remain,

Your faithful,
and most obedient servant,
WM. COBBETT.

First sitting of the reformed House of Commons, 1833, showing Daniel O'Connell, leaning forward, and William Cobbett, to his right

Political Register, 27 September 1834.

Speech by Mr Finn, Member for Kilkenny, and Address by Mr Nevin Welcoming William Cobbett to Ireland, With William Cobbett's Reply

Mr Finn came forward and said:

Fellow-countrymen, let me introduce to you William Cobbett (long-continued cheers); a man who rose from the ranks by his own merits, and has always adhered to the interests of his 'order'. (Cheers.) At Edinburgh they have been celebrating the arrival of Earl Grey. (Loud groans and hisses.) They have been entertaining Earl Grey and the Ministers, and those who have any thing to give. Here we have assembled to congratulate upon his arrival amongst us the able statesman, the man of powerful mind and of great honesty. (Cheers.) I feel myself honoured in doing honour to him. (Cheers.) I feel myself honoured in joining with my fellow-countrymen to pay my respects to a man who has done so much for the poor of his own and the poor of this country. (Cheers.) I say this, and I would feel for ever degraded if I adopted the sycophantic course of going out of my way to pay respects to the mere Minister of the hour. (Hear, hear, and cheers.) I shall now merely say this: When Cromwell, from the top of Slievenamann, viewed the rich valleys that surrounded him, and looked upon ten or fifteen Irish counties, he turned to his soldiers and said, 'Is this not a country worth fighting for?' I say to you, and say to Mr Cobbett, 'Is this not a country that we are ready to fight for if required?' (Hear, hear, and continued cheering.) Half of the men who fought at Waterloo under Wellington were Irish soldiers. We fear neither death nor danger, and they must learn to govern us for our own interests, and not for a corrupt oligarchy. (Cheers.) They must do us justice, or they shall do it. [sic]* (Hear, hear, and continued cheering.) Conscious of our strength we do not forget the might that slumbers in the peasant's arm. We are told that they

* '... they shall do it.' Mr Finn probably said, 'they shall rue it.' Or, 'they' should read 'we'. -Ed.

will save us all trouble upon this point, and will govern us well: I say, 'God send us a safe deliverance.' I entertain but slight hopes from them. If they are not true to the people they must be false to themselves; and no Tory Government was ever hurled from power with more contempt and execration than the Whigs shortly will be, unless they are determined to do justice to the people of this country. (Hear, and long continued cheers.)

Mr Nevin then came forward, as chairman of the meeting at the Exchange, and read the following Address:

TO WILLIAM COBBETT, ESQ., M.P.

Sir, It has frequently been the lot of Irishmen to go forth to welcome to their shores strangers of rank and station who visited them clothed with power and authority. The iron rule to which we have been submitted, and the extreme and uniform misery of our condition, have made us always too prone to hope for good in any change, and to recognize in every new face the lineaments of a benefactor. And hence, as the feelings of expectation have poured themselves out in the language of anticipated acknowledgements, and premature thanks for benefits always hoped for but never conferred, the expressions of a too credulous confidence have given to simple sincerity and good feeling the semblance of self-abasing adulation.

But in expressing to you, sir, on your safe arrival into Ireland, congratulations springing from the bottom of our hearts, we address a man who has no rank but that which public fame gives to exalted public virtue, and no power save that which has been acquired by a lifelong devotion of those rich gifts with which it has pleased God to endow you, to the cause of truth and justice. Even then, if it were possible to express in terms beyond your deserts, the thanks which we owe to you, and to you alone of the public men of England, for the benevolent sympathy which you have manifested for our wrongs, for the unstinted justice with which you have demanded on our behalf the whole of our rights; for the generous magnanimity with which you, a Protestant, put to hazard your popularity with the Protestants of England, by your liberal, enlightened, and manly vindication of that religion, the cherished hate of which was the ground of the mis-government of Ireland, it is impossible for envy itself to taint with suspicion the motives with which we offer you the tribute of our deep and lasting gratitude.

We know, sir, that you are not one of those who profess to have been endowed with all knowledge, and never in any instance to have been incapable of falling into error – we know that you have exposed yourself to the charge of inconsistency from the wise in their own conceit, because you did not refuse to gather wisdom from experience, and had the candour to confess, and the justice to atone for, an error, when you found that you had in any case committed one. We know that you have sometimes been mistaken in your estimate of Irishmen, whom we justly hold in honour; but we also know that your constant motive has been that love of justice, and that hatred of oppression, by which you are eminently distinguished; and that from the first hour in which the condition of Ireland attracted your observation, your language has been the language of attention to our complaints, of indignant reprobation of our wrongs – in a word, the language of a man who, founding his love of freedom on principle, was willing to extend to all the full measure of justice which he demanded on his own behalf.

But, sir, if you had no claims to the peculiar acknowledgements of Ireland for peculiar services already rendered to us – if you were not now induced to visit our shores by the desire of becoming better acquainted with our grievances, in order to qualify yourself the more effectually to urge the redress of them – if you visited us only as the vindicator of English freedom, as the inveterate enemy and powerful assailant of the corrupt, squandering and sanguinary system of misrule which long overbore the rights of your country as well as ours, and with no other claim to our respect than the title which the suffrages of your countrymen have conferred on you, of the *poor man's friend*, it would be due to our own character, as men worthy of freedom, and sincerely determined to attain it, to show that we have a sympathy for the champions of freedom wherever they are to be found, and that where tyranny acknowledges a foe, there we are proud to recognize a brother and a friend.

It would become us to recollect the glorious example you

have set of an unbending integrity, of an uncompromising assertion of public right, and of an untiring war against public corruption. It would become us to recollect the sound political information which you have diffused, the public pure morality which you have inculcated, the spirit of independence which you have kept alive among your countrymen. It would become us to recollect your sufferings, as well as your exertions; the fine and imprisonment which you suffered in 1810, for maintaining that English soldiers ought not to be lashed in England by German mercenaries; the exile in which you were obliged to seek safety in 1817, for the crime of having maintained that the people of England and Ireland were entitled to that reform which is yet but half accomplished, and which perfidy would make a merit of conceding when it could no longer be possibly withheld. It would become us to recollect that persecution and oppression only added new force to your patriotism, new fire to your zeal, new vigour to your exertions; that in prison, in banishment, with a patience never to be irritated, with a perseverance never to be subdued, you pursued that reform, the partial accomplishment of which now presents you to us in the honourable position of the representative of a constituency instructed by your lessons, animated by your example, and indebted in a great measure to your exertions for the freedom of which they, at least, among Englishmen, have made a wise and honourable use.

That it may please God to give you health and strength to attain the goal to which your honourable life has tended, and to receive the reward of your exertions and your sacrifices, in witnessing the full and peaceful restoration of freedom, independence, and happiness, to both countries, is the earnest desire and fervent prayer of those who, in the ardent language of their country, but in language not more ardent than their feeling, bid you a hundred thousand welcomes to the shores of Ireland.

Mr Cobbett's Reply and Address:

GENTLEMEN, Looking upon this address as coming from you all, the answer I shall read to you shall be the answer to you all. (Hear, and cheers.) Gentlemen, you are all, of course, aware that I must have seen this address; it would be affectation to say that I had not seen it before. It is not becoming to play the hypocrite, nor to pretend to be all-seeing persons; and it would be particularly unbecoming to pretend that one had not seen an address, an address to which he came prepared with an answer – which I shall now read to you! Let me now say that I witness in you no rare instance of that fault which I have always seen in Irishmen – whatever service might be done for you, whether great or small, your gratitude was always tenfold too much for the service rendered. (Cheers.) Gentlemen, the reception you have given me is far beyond any merits of mine. (Cheers, and cries of 'No, no'). Now, gentlemen, I shall read to you the answer to that very elegant address, which, though it certainly exaggerates my merit, still I will not say that it is altogether unjust. (Loud cheers.)

Gentlemen,
　　A great many years have rolled over my head; but, if age had so benumbed my feelings as to make me insensible to this Address from you, I should, I hope, have fortitude enough left to cease to wish to live.
　　I will not affect to believe, that I am wholly unworthy of the commendations which you so generously bestow upon me; but, that love of justice which you ascribe to me, and which, I trust, has always marked my conduct in all the relationships of life, bids me avail myself of this occasion of assuring you, that, though I have been, perhaps, more conspicuous than most other English and Scotch members of Parliament in expressing my sentiments relative to the treatment of Ireland, I am, in entertaining sympathy for her sufferings, very far, even amongst them, from standing *alone*; while, with regard to the *people* of England, and Scotland, be assured, that, with very rare exceptions, they feel every wrong done to Ireland as a wrong done to themselves. Truth and sincerity and duty also bid me declare to you further, that I believe, that the present Ministers are sincerely disposed to better the lot of Ireland. Nature, reason, their own fame, their own interest, now, at last, dictate this to them in tone so commanding, that it is impossible that these should not prevail over those prejudices and passions, which, for so many dismal ages, have been

tearing this fine country to pieces, and making strife, beggary and misery to reign, when all ought to have been peace, plenty, and happiness.

It is not, be you assured, Gentlemen, *want of feeling* for Ireland; but *want of knowledge* of the nature, the extent and the real causes of her sufferings, which has hitherto prevented the application of remedies to an evil so great, so notorious throughout the world, and so dishonourable to the very name of England. It is, more especially, *this want of knowledge* in the *people* of England, who, in the end, always have decided, and always will decide, every great public question. Boundless is the gratitude which Ireland owes to her mighty and devoted advocate for her emancipation from a slavery of three centuries duration; but, even all the terrors, with which his matchless talents and zeal unparalleled were able to fill the breast of obdurate and insolent oppression, would not have prevailed, had not the deep-seated prejudices been first rooted out of the minds of the people of England; had they still been under the sway of that unnatural antipathy to the religion of their fathers, which, for so many ages, had been sedulously and systematically implanted in those minds.

Believing that I have some influence with a large part of this people; knowing, that, for them to pursue the path of justice, it is only necessary, that they clearly see that path, and I have deemed it my duty to come and to see with my own eyes, the real state of their and my fellow-subjects, the suffering people of Ireland; to make known to them the results of my observations; and, at the same time, to communicate to the people of Ireland themselves my opinions with regard to remedies, called for by evils, the existence of which no man living has the hardihood to deny, and no man fit to live the callousness not to deplore. From a very early age I entertained the desire, that my country might always be renowned as the greatest, the free-est and most happy in the world: this desire clings to my heart more closely as the years advance upon me; and, it is my perfect conviction, that she must cease to be that great, free and happy country, unless full and complete justice be speedily done to the people of Ireland.

Gentlemen, you have enumerated some of the wrongs, which I, during my public life, have had to endure: they have indeed been many; they have been cruel; they have been injurious; but, had they been still more numerous, more cruel, more injurious, this Address from you, this kind and cordial welcome to the shores of Ireland, would have been more than a tenfold compensation for them all.

The reading of this address has pretty nearly tired me; and you are all, I suppose, pretty tired by this. I shall not detain you longer. I shall only observe that I have struggled for the liberties of Ireland with peculiar pleasure. (Cheers.) Being sent to Parliament by the good people of Oldham, I must say that I would have been of no use if I were not supported by the Irish members of Parliament. But for them I should have been all alone; and though it would be somewhat difficult to do it, I should, I suppose, have been hooted out of the place, if it were not for the honest support of the Irish members, amongst whom I may mention the honourable gentleman who stands on my left. (Hear, hear, and cheers.) You have nothing to do but go on perseveringly and sedulously, supporting your members, for your members can do nothing without your support. (Cheers.) A member with a petition in his hand is something, but without it he is nothing, and what he states is simply his own word and his own opinion. With a million of men at his back he is listened to with a degree of attention which would not otherwise exist; and he would not be heard at all, if he had nobody at his back. (Cheers.) Support your members; never be afraid of tiring them with petitions, or of wearying them; they have nothing else to do, but to listen to your complaints, and attend to your wrongs. (Hear.) Pursue this course, and I shall live to see Ireland, as I always wished her to be, happy and prosperous. (Long continued cheers for several minutes.)

(Mr Cobbett, upon stepping from the balcony into the drawing room, laughingly observed, 'I am as young a man as ever I was.' For the ladies who were present, and the gentlemen of the deputation, Mr Dodd had prepared a very elegant déjeuné.)

Political Register, 4 October 1834.

To Charles Marshall, Labourer, Letter No.II

Of Normandy Tithing, Ash, Farnham, Surrey.

Dublin, 27 September 1834.
MARSHALL,
    After I wrote to you, the other day, about the MENDICITY, I went again at the dinner time. You know, I saw the breakfast! that is the *ground oats* and *butter-milk* or *water*, or *skim-milk*, (sometimes one and sometimes the other), boiling in great coppers for the breakfast; and now I went to see the *dinner*; and the gentlemen, who have the management of the place, showed me all about it. There are about *three thousand* persons fed here, and, if they were not thus fed, they must either *die*, or *thieve* or *rob*; or more properly *take by force*; for, in such a case, the words *theft* or *robbery* do not, according to the just laws of England, apply to the act; though they do apply, and, I hope, always will apply, in England.
    I saw this 'dinner'. In one long room, there were about 500 women, each with some potatoes in a bowl, mashed, as you mash them to mix with meal, for your hogs. These people go to one end of the room, and, one at a time, get their mess. There are persons to put the potatoes into the bowl, which they do by taking the potatoes out of a tub, with a tin measure, holding about a quart, and putting the thing full into the bowl, which is then carried away by the person who is to eat it; and all these persons are, as they eat, *standing up* in the room, as thick as they can stand. Each, as soon as the mess is eaten, goes away; and, as there is room made, others come in; and there were about three hundred then waiting in the yard to take their turn.
    There were about a hundred little girls in a *school*, and about as many boys in another; neither had shoes or stockings, and the boys had *no shirts*. Their faces were pale, the whole hundred not having so much red as your little round-faced chap that

was set to keep the birds away from the cabbage seed in Dodman's field. Yes, Marshall, that little chap, with his satchel full of bread and cheese or bacon; he was at the *proper school*![3] He and Tom Deadman and little Barratt will make strong and able men like their fathers; will live well, and be well clothed; and will be respected like their fathers; and be happy in that state of life in which it has pleased God to place them; and will not, I hope, listen to any fanatical man, who would persuade them, that to starve in rags, in this world, has a tendency to give them a crown of glory in the next.

In another place I saw a great crowd of women sitting and doing nothing, each with a baby in her arms. They were sitting in rows, waiting, I believe, for the messes. Some of them were young and naturally handsome; but made ugly by starvation, rags, and dirt. It was one mass of rags; not rags such as you see on the beggars or gipsies that go to hopping at Farnham; but far worse than any that you ever saw tied round a stake to frighten the birds from our wheat and our peas; far worse than the Kentish people and South Hampshire people put on a scare-crow to keep the birds from their cherries. And this is the condition, Marshall, in which the Scotch *feelosofer* vagabonds wish to persuade the Parliament to reduce the wives and the daughters of the working people of England![4] while they talk of *educating* you all, at the same time! Ah! Marshall, these vagabonds want to give you *books*, and to take away the *bread* and *meat* for themselves.

In another place I saw the most painful sight of all: *women*, with heavy hammers, *cracking stones* into very small pieces, to *make walks in gentlemen's gardens*! These women were as ragged as the rest; and the sight of them and their work, and the thoughts accompanying these, would have sunk the heart in your body, as they did mine. and are the women and girls of England to be brought to this state?[5] Would not every man in Normandy suffer every drop of blood to be let out of his body rather than see your sisters and daughters and mothers and wives brought to this state? If I were not *sure* that Tom Farr would perish himself rather than see his sister brought to this, he should not live under my roof a moment longer. And what, then, of his good and industrious and kind and tender mother! The bare thought would drive him mad! Yet, Marshall, it is my duty to tell you, that the half-drunk and half-mad and greedy and crawling Scotch vagabonds, whose counsels have beggared the Scotch working people, are endeavouring to persuade the Parliament to bring your wives, mothers, sisters, and daughters into this very state! Be on your guard, therefore; be ready to perform *your duty* to prevent the success of these crawling villains, who hope to get rewarded for their schemes for making you work for 6d. a day, and for putting your wages into the pockets of the landlords. When I get back we will have a meeting at Guildford to petition the king and Parliament on the subject; to this meeting you must all come; for, though the law does not give you the right of *voting*, it always gives you the right of *petitioning*; and as I shall hereafter show you, it gives you a *right* to *parish relief* in case you are *unable* to *earn* a sufficiency to keep you in a proper manner. This is as much your *birth-right* as is the lord of the manor's right to his estate; and of this we will convince the crawling and greedy vagabonds before we have done. It is our duty, too, to exert this right to endeavour to better the lot of our suffering fellow-subjects in Ireland. Mr Dean will tell you, that I have always set my face against the ill-treatment of Irish people who go to get work in England. Their own food is sent away from them to England, for the benefit of their landlords; we receive the food, and it is monstrous injustice in us to frown upon them, if they come and offer their labour in exchange for a part of that very food which they themselves have raised.

I hear that discontents are arising again in England, on account of the *lowering of wages*. Mr Dean will not lower the wages of anybody. He knows that I never gave a *full* working man *less* than 15s a week, though found a good house and garden and plenty of fuel. And I know that a man, with a wife and only three small children, cannot live, as he ought to live, on less, though flour were cheaper than it is now, as I hope it will be. But, Marshall, let us be just; let us do as we would be done by: many of the *farmers* are not able, in the present state of things, with all these taxes and monopolies arising out of them, to give the wages that I give, without being *ruined themselves*; theirs is, in many cases, a life of greater hardship than that of the labourer: they are compelled to give 8s 6d for MALT, which, if there were *no tax*, they would have at this moment for about 3s 6d. They would give their men beer, they would keep the young people in their houses, as I do; but they are *unable* to do it without being ruined and becoming labourers themselves. Then the landlords: why should their *rents* not be paid? Not to get their rents is to lose their estates; and why should they have their estates taken away? those estates are as much *their right* as good living in exchange for your labour, and as parish aid in case of inability, are *your rights*. So that I hope that you will duly consider these things; and not conclude that, though others may not give the wages that I give, they would not do it if they could.

It is my opinion that, if flour were only 5s a bushel, 15s a week is not *too much* for a really *able*, *sober*, and *trustworthy* labouring man, who has a wife and only three small children. And I never did, and never will, make any distinction between a *married* man and a *single* man. Why should I? What have I to do with the man, more than to pay him duly the worth of his labour? and how is the single man ever to be in a fit condition to marry, and to lead a happy life and to rear a family, unless he has, from his earnings while single, the means of starting well in his new state of life? The old saying, that 'when poverty comes in at the door, love flies out at the window', is perfectly true. And how is poverty to be kept *out*, if there is nothing of any worth to begin with?

I have not time to write any thing more to you now. I will, in future letters, tell you the *causes* of all this misery, and you will want nothing more to make you all resolve to use all the lawful means in your power to prevent it from falling on yourselves.

Two things, I hope, you will all attend to in my absence: first, cheerful obedience to Mr Dean, in all things, 27 years of experience having convinced me that he will require from you nothing but that which is proper, and that nothing will induce him to do any thing towards anybody that is unjust, or *hard*. The other thing is, my hope that none of you will go to *any drinking place* on any account. You have no need to do it; when you have not good beer at the farm-house, I give you the means of having it at home with your wives and children; and therefore, if any of you should disobey me in this respect, and should set at nought the example which you have in Mr Dean, as well as the precept that you have thus received from me, Mr Dean has my full authority to act towards you accordingly.

With giving you this important precept, and in the hope that all of you and all belonging to you are well,
I am,
Your master and friend,
WM. COBBETT.

Political Register, 4 October 1834.

To Mr SMITH,
At the Printing-Office,
Bolt-Court.

Dublin, 27 September 1834.
Dear Sir,
   You will please to cause 500 copies of each of these Letters to MARSHALL to be struck off, in the manner described in my last letter. Put them up in a coach-parcel, and send them by the Farnham coach, directed to Mr Dean at Normandy, Ash, Farnham, Surrey. This is not giving you *trouble*, but *pleasure*; and therefore I offer you no apology. I hope that all the *unstamped* will send these letters about.[6]

I am,
Your faithful
And most obedient servant,
WM. COBBETT.

P.S. Put an ounce weight of each of them under cover, and direct it to our county member, John Leech, Esq., Lea, Godalming.[7]

Political Register, 4 October 1834.

To the Members of the Meath Club

Dublin, 28 September 1834.

Gentlemen, – I thank you for the great honour you have done me, in presenting to me this elegantly written address; which, however, honourable as it is to me, I chiefly value on account of the effect which it is likely to have in England, at this critical time, when desperate, and half-mad and half-drunken and inordinately greedy Scotchmen are bent on an attempt to prevail on the Parliament to adopt measures for reducing the people of England to the state of those of Scotland, who are now robbed of those Christian laws which their fathers established three hundred years ago; an attempt, which, if it were to succeed, must render the lot of Ireland worse than it is now.

These Scotch monsters of the school of the Parson MALTHUS,[8] it is, at present, my great object to combat, by explaining fully to the people of England the means which these monsters are employing, and the object they have in view; and my business to Ireland is to see, and tell the people of England, what is the state of Ireland, what is the extent of her sufferings, what are the causes of these, and what they ought to do, not only to prevent similar sufferings from being inflicted on themselves, but what they ought to do, to rescue Ireland from her sufferings: and, gentlemen, in the performing of this my duty, this address from you must and will give me great support.

Besides these considerations, gentlemen, I have particular pleasure in receiving this address from the county of Meath, whose sensible and spirited conduct has greatly contributed to produce the taking of the first steps towards the deliverance of Ireland from her worse than Egyptian bondage.

WM. COBBETT.

Political Register, 4 October 1834.

To Mr John Dean

Dear Sir,
I suppose that the parcels of printed letters will get to Farnham every Tuesday night. And you must get them over to Normandy. Send about 200 of each Number, by one of the boys or men, to Mr Whitlaw, at Compton, who I hope will get them to Godalming, Bramley, Elstead, *Frencham*, Seale, Hazlemere, etc. and all about that side of the Hog's-back. You will take care to get all the rest sent to Farnham, Guildford, Chertsey, Egham, Bagshot, and to all the parishes round about us, especially Purbright and Chobham. Be very diligent about this. Any of the men will carry them on a Sunday, or in the evening, to such a place as Purbright or Aldershot. You will observe, that I have this matter *greatly at heart*; and therefore, I beg you to act accordingly. My native county shall not be unjust towards Ireland for want of knowing her treatment, and for want of knowing the miseries so unjustly inflicted upon her; nor shall the people of that county be steeped in similar misery by the schemes of the renegado Scotch villains, or by any body else, without seeing what these schemes are, and to what consequences they lead. Do not mind a little *expense* in giving effect to my wishes as to this matter. If there be nobody *in other counties* to do their duty to the working people, no man shall ever have to say that that duty was neglected by

Your faithful friend,
WM. COBBETT

P.S. I have, three successive nights, to numerous assemblies, (consisting chiefly of gentlemen or persons of property) in this city, urged the *justice* and *necessity* of POOR-LAWS for Ireland; and, not only poor-laws, but *our poor-laws*; the act of Queen Elizabeth, ALL the act, and NOTHING BUT the act. I have maintained the RIGHTS of the poor, by an appeal to the *laws of God*, and the *laws of England*; and, I have the pleasure to tell you, that I was heard with the greatest possible attention, indulgence, and kindness; and this kindness has, indeed, marked the conduct of every one in Ireland towards me. – Get all my people together, in the evening, or on Sunday, and read these letters to them; and remember me to farmers West and Fagotten and Barry, and Horne who, like the primitive teachers of Christianity, *preaches* on the Sunday, and most laudably *mows his barley* on the Monday, that I hope that his cows, which I forgave so often, will not, during my absence, give way to their luxurious, inordinate, and most ungodly appetites, so far as still to covet my corn, when they have pasture of their own, and while my humble-minded and frugal heifers are content with the pickings of the common.[9]

Political Register, 4 October 1834.

My Proceedings in Dublin

Mr Cobbett's Lectures

Our space does not admit of our giving this week more than one of the important lectures delivered by Mr Cobbett, on the evenings of Wednesday, Thursday, and Friday, at the Fishamble-street Theatre. We give the first, that of Wednesday.[10]

Mr Cobbett made his appearance on the stage at seven o'clock precisely. He was greeted with the most enthusiastic cheers which were continued for several minutes. Having taken his seat at a table in the centre of the stage, he rose in a few seconds afterwards, and thus addressed the assembly:

Gentlemen, I begin as I ought to do, by expressing to you the pride and gratitude which I feel for the manner in which I have been received in Ireland. (Cheers). Gentlemen, my satisfaction is the greater on this account, because I know the effect which the manner I have been received in will produce amongst my countrymen in England, and which it is my most anxious wish to produce; that is, a most favourable impression in regard to this country; being perfectly satisfied that by no other exertions but theirs will Ireland ever be delivered from the state she is in now.[11]

Gentlemen, when we were boys we read in 'the Seven Wonders of the World'; but of all the wonders of the world Ireland is the greatest, for here we see a country teeming with food; we see that food sent in to other nations, in many parts of the globe, and we see at home the people starving and in rags, and without ever partaking of that food which their country produces. I have for a long while been desirous to ascertain the causes of this state of things, and to try if this greatest of wonders could be unravelled.

I have returned to the spot, near as I possibly could, where I was born.[12] With whatever station I have, or ambition, and whatever literary fame there is about me, I have returned to that plough from which I started when I was fourteen years of age. (Hear, hear, and enthusiastic cheers for several minutes). I live now within six miles of the place where lie the graves of my father and mother, and it is my vanity to return and spend my time amongst those whose fathers or grandfathers were my playmates. I have returned, as nearly as I could, to the point from which I started, and I every day see the faces of those who know my humble origin, and can show the lowly grave stones of my parents.[13] I am sure then I shall get the credit of not being actuated by any very ambitious or selfish motives. (Cheers). Remember also, gentlemen, that I am not here pleading the cause of clients who can fee me. I plead the cause of the poor, the needy, and the oppressed — those who cannot possibly give me a reward — I plead their cause (hear, hear) — I plead the cause of those who cannot express their thanks to me; and, I will tell you more, of those who will never hear of my interference on their behalf, nor of my name.

Let us look to the wonders I was speaking of with steady eyes, if we can; I am sure that no man who sees them can look on with a dry eye. (Hear). Let us look at them with this view particularly, to try if we can repair in part the evils that are in existence. (Hear). I have been part of my life, for eight years, in the colony of North America.[14] I saw that colony settled after the rebel war; I was there in an English regiment myself; I saw the colony increase very fast; I saw the whole of the people for four years; I saw 260,000 persons who would have expired of hunger if it were not for the bread, if it were not for the meat, if it were not for the butter that came out of this island. Two hundred and sixty thousand persons there were fed by this country. Not a soul of that 260,000 that was not living better than those by whom the food had been sent out! I have seen the Negroes in the West Indies, of whom so much has been said, and for whom there has been so much *tenderness* and *sympathy*, that I have 278,000 persons put their names to one petition calling upon Parliament to put an end to the *miseries* of the negroes; I have seen the food with which they were constantly fed for years; I have seen those negroes better fed than the people of Ireland; and I have seen that the food which they mostly received came from Ireland, from a people who had not as good food as was sent out to the negroes. I could never see the sense or justice of taxing the people of England,

Scotland, and Ireland, for the benefit of the owners of those negroes. I voted against every penny of that grant from beginning to end. But if it were just in England (and I do not admit that it was) to give £20,000,000 to assume a tax £800,000 a year for the negro owners, is it not most unjust to refuse a tax which would keep from starving the people of Ireland? If it were just, and I say it was not, to give so much for the negroes, is there a God in heaven and shall we dare to say in HIS face that it is just in those who did that, to refuse food to those who are in a state ten thousand times worse than those negroes? Nova Scotia, New Brunswick, all the colonies of North America, except Canada, are fed with this food of Ireland. Is this wrong? No. Supposing we are to keep colonies (a question I shall not now discuss), it is not wrong in Ireland to supply them with food; but it is wrong when those who raise the food and supply others, have not a sufficiency for themselves. (Hear). England herself, why she receives food from Ireland; it is a great blessing to her that Ireland can supply her. Not only London itself, but all round about it, is supplied by this country. Every country town in England has at this moment a supply of Irish flour, Irish meat, and Irish butter; and, curious enough, as it was only last spring I entered into possession of my present place, I had not time to make up my own bacon and pork, and my fellows are now eating Irish bacon. (Hear, hear, and loud cheers). There they are with their red cheeks, their fat round faces, their clean shirts, their Sunday clothes; they live well, and have their decent table-cloths laid before them every time they eat their victuals. While this is the mode of the husbandman and artisan living in England, what, I say, can be the cause that those who raise the food in this country, and who send it over to the English farmers to eat, have not a morsel of food to put into their mouths? I saw the day before yesterday a mother with her four little children lying upon some straw, with their bodies huddled close together to keep themselves warm. I have written over to one of my labourers (and desired the printer to circulate the letter round the parish), that if I find that George, the man who minds the cattle, should suffer them to have under them straw so broken and so dirty as that poor woman was lying upon, I would turn him out of the house as a lazy and a cruel fellow. (Cheers). Be assured that a statement like that cannot but be of service, and it ought not to be humiliating to you, because you do not govern yourselves. (Hear, hear, and loud cheers). I see I have touched upon a favourite strain.[15] (Hear). Be assured that a statement like that is much more likely to spread among the working people of England, from whom you will receive more redress than you can ever hope for from flummery promises. (Hear, hear).

Amongst the causes to which have been ascribed the present state of Ireland is this, that 'the people are lazy, careless, and are wanting in trustworthiness'. Another is, 'the existence of the Catholic religion'; another, 'the refusal of Catholic emancipation for a long time'; another 'tithes'; another 'the Union'; another 'absentees'; another 'agitation'. Now, gentlemen, as to 'the laziness of the Irish people', the 'laziness' and 'carelessness'; never before did it come to pass that food was sent out of that country to feed another, in which the people were lazy and careless. As much corn, flour, cows, sheep, pork, bacon, beef, butter, are produced in Ireland as cannot be matched by a like number of people in the whole world, England herself not excepted. These things cannot be created except by labour. It is impossible to produce them without labour, they are not spontaneous; and, therefore, the general answer at once to this charge is, that it is false. (Hear, and loud cheers). The people cannot, with justice, be accused either of laziness or carelessness. It has happened too, to me, to have seen some Irishmen out of their own country. I have been told by one Irish gentleman, 'Mr Cobbett, you do not think it, but really the Irish do not like meat.' (Hear, and laughter). 'They like to have their cabins without a chimney, and that the smoke if it will go out at all, should only escape through the roof.' (Laughter). I could not deny this, because it was said to be a fact; but then it is an unbelievable fact. My answer to him was this, I have seen the United States of America, and I have seen other colonies;[16] I have seen Irishmen in those places, and I never yet saw them that they loved other food better than meat and bread; they did not like dirty clothes, they did not like filthy rags, but they liked to be well dressed. They have laboured successfully, and if I should say more so than those of any other European nation in the United States, I should speak the truth. Besides, I have seen how they have risen to eminence in the United States, and to be persons of the first consequence there. A gentleman, recently from that country, who went over the names, assures me of this fact, that of that eminent body of men, the members of Congress, the one-third part are Irish, or men whose fathers were Irish, or the descendants of Irishmen. (Hear, hear, and loud cheers). It is then a false accusation to make against them to say that they are not industrious, and that they are wanting in trustworthiness. They are not, God knows, wanting in literary acquirements, or in oratory: for if you were to take the one hundred Irish members out of the House of Commons, I wonder what sort would be the remaining 558. There would not be an equal number of men of talent for the one hundred Irishmen I can assure you. (Hear). But then it is said that it is 'the Catholic religion that makes the Irish a lazy, slothful, and degraded people.' This statement is a sheer slander, for what was England before the reformation but Catholic? What was England at the time she conquered France but Catholic? Why, England was Catholic when she possessed herself of Calais and Boulogne. Every body knows that England was when Catholic a much greater country, comparing her with other countries, than she is now, though she drains Ireland to make her great. But why does not the Catholic religion make the Irish people lazy in America, unless this, that it is changed by crossing the Atlantic, and that the salt of that element takes all the vice out of it? (Laughter). There are sixty or seventy thousand Catholics in New York; the Catholics rule by their vote that great emporium of the United States; how comes it that these energies are so much increased there, if the Catholic religion itself makes people lazy here? It is the same always, and, however other religions may change, we know this of the Catholic, that it is the same in all countries. (Hear). How is it that it has not produced similar effects in America, that is given full scope to their physical and moral qualities, and they are exerted there as they would be here, if you had the same species of government. (Hear and cheers). Now, a favourite object with me is the farm that I spoke of; and, as with things in which there is less real value, we are more fond of them, so it is the case with me, and it happened that in looking out for a person in whom I could confide, who would, I know, do justice to the labourers, take care of my house, my neighbours, and superintend every thing as though I were there; the person that I got to do all these things for me is a

Roman Catholic. (Hear and cheers). In England I have got one that the Catholic religion did not spoil.

(Mr Cobbett next referred to the refusal for so long a time of Catholic Emancipation,[17] and which, although he admitted it was a glaring injustice, and tended to produce strife and heartburnings, was however not a sufficient cause for the present condition of the country. This indeed was proved by the simple fact, that emancipation was granted, and that still the grievances and complaints of the people of Ireland continued. As our space is limited we proceed to a more interesting topic).

Next, said Mr Cobbett, as to tithes.[18] I petitioned Parliament for a total repeal of the church in Ireland. I petitioned for its absolute removal. I wished that England should be taxed so as to give Ireland a chance for the removal of the heartburnings that oppress her, and that she might have quiet and security. That I considered my duty, and I therefore petitioned to have it wholly removed. I wished to have no pitch-patch work, and that there should be no misunderstanding about it. (Hear, hear, and cheers). But I must say, at the same time, that, removing religion out of the question, tithes laid on the land are no hardship; tithes are part of the expenses of the land. In England I pay £160 rent to the landlord, and I pay to the parson £45, or £55, I forget which, for tithes. Now, if I did not pay that to the parson, I should pay it to the landlord. There would be no difference in the sum, and it would be a benefit to me to pay it to the parson, if he lived in the parish, for he would employ somebody, and the people would have the benefit. When the people are of the same religion as the established church it is a folly to represent tithes as a hardship. In fact, the thing should be paid, and it was some benefit to have the little gentry beside so many great gentlemen. It is well to have to give it to the parson; for, if you gave it all to the squire, he would become too big, and would spend it all out of the parish, while the parson must spend some of it in it. This, however, does not apply to Ireland; for here the people are of one religion and the clergy of another, and, generally speaking, tithes create heartburnings, and lead to violence and crimes, and add to the misery already existing and arising from other causes. But let this be borne in mind, that supposing tithes and hierarchy were altogether abolished, still it would be short of having that accomplished which it is our duty to have done for the people.

Next, as to the Union.[19] I have certainly seen in the city of Dublin very great distress, such as could not exist if the country around it were prosperous. I only want the evidence I have on this point, to be convinced that the misery I see here is general throughout the country, and that it must extend for many miles from Dublin: for a man would not look at the distress around him, he would not remain here to suffer misery, if he could go out of it. And here let me observe, that the whole of this misery could not be removed by what you look for, a national Parliament; for the misery existed here before the Union. (Cries of no, no). The misery was not, perhaps, to such an extent then; but no man will say, that before the Union Ireland was as well off as England, or as she ought to be. (Hear). Ireland was badly off before the Union, and if a Parliament were restored to Dublin – and it is my opinion (I will not say that it ought to have very great weight, when you have members so well acquainted with the country) – but my opinion is, that the Parliament ought to be restored to Dublin. (Hear, and loud cheers). I repeat now what I said in my place in Parliament, and I say that it is impossible for any reasoning man to believe that eight millions of people will continue feeding another nation of ten or twelve millions; for you feed a great part of them, two millions at least, Yorkshire, Lancashire, and the West of Scotland; it is not possible to believe that there will be for a long time peace or tranquillity amongst the eight millions held as a colony by the ten or twelve millions. (Hear, and cheers). I shall not now enter into the subject of the Repeal of the Union, as enough of my opinions on that question are known to you;[20] but if the alternative be adopted, if the Union were repealed, if your Parliament were restored to you, even if you had an Irish king or queen, yet, it is my opinion, unless there was a still greater measure to benefit the working people of Ireland, I will not say that your misery would be so great, but that there would be nearly as great a state of misery as there is at this moment. (Hear).

The cause of the misery was, that those who work, and those were the majority of the people in every country, those who laboured had not what they ought to have, a due share of what they laboured for. (Hear). This should not be left to charity:

there were as charitable people in Ireland as there were in England, and if it were not for the law that no man should die of starvation, he believed the people would be in as bad a state in England as they were here. (Hear and cheers). He was satisfied the great source of the evils of Ireland was the misery of the people, and the cause of that misery was the want of a law to ensure to them the due share of what they laboured for. (Hear, hear, and cries of 'No poor-laws'). This, Mr Cobbett continued, was a large question, and one that should be rightly considered in all its bearings. He said that they should pass such a law, and if such a law as he spoke of did not pass for Ireland, great and terrible must be the ultimate consequences. People could not continue to endure hardships and injustice for ever. (Hear). This was his great object in visiting Ireland. He knew he could not succeed in that object until he had got the mass of the common people of England to support him; without this aid he knew he could do nothing, for the Government had never, in one instance, done a good thing that had not taken its spring from the common people of England.

(Mr Cobbett sat down amid loud and long-continued cheers from all parts of the theatre.)

Political Register, 4 October 1834.

To Correspondents

I beg, that until my return to England, no one will give himself the trouble to *write to me*, on any subject whatsoever. A man cannot do more than *one thing* well at *one time*. I have quite enough to do here; and I will never, till I am again in England, *open* any letter that shall come to me *from England*. Some inconvenience may arise from this, and possibly some injury; but, these I must submit to. At any rate, such is my determination.

NOTES

[1] This letter forms Appendix III, p.284.
[2] The Coercion Bill of April 1833, one of the first measures to be brought before the reformed Parliament; and one of a long series of bills enacted at Westminster designed to maintain the Union with Ireland. The Act of 1833 suspended yet again the Habeas Corpus Act, and made provision for trials under forms of martial law in place of judge and jury. The Act, as has become usual with such legislation, was passed for the period of one year. Less usually, when it came up for renewal, disagreements as to its general application throughout the kingdom broke out in Parliament. These led to the fall of Grey's ministry in July 1834. Cobbett had had many violent disagreements over O'Connell on Irish policies, but declared that it was O'Connell's impassioned opposition to any renewal of the Act, that impelled him to see Ireland for himself.
[3] The 'proper school' for a farm-labourer's child was, in Cobbett's view, that of useful and varied experience and leisure, alongside peers and elders, and without recourse to educational pedantry, mystery and religious tracts. Schools he looked upon as factories or barracks; and he opposed enforced school attendance, above all for the children of working people because he assumed that their educators would instil in them the ideas of the landlords, parsons and factory-owners, teaching them to be submissive and incapable.
[4] The 'Scotch feelosofer vagabonds': Cobbett's rogues' gallery (not all were Scotsmen) of 'gallon-loaf-men' derived from the original 'gallon-loaf-man', the Whig MP for Wiltshire, John Benett. It was he who in 1814 calculated that the price of a gallon loaf, and threepence over for clothing, would prove wage enough to keep a labourer alive for a week, with strength enough to work. Pre-eminent among the 'Scotch' of this band was 'Peter' McCulloch (in fact J R McCulloch, the economist,) among the most rigid of the expounders of the 'dismal science' of Malthusian sociology.

⁵ A reference to the Poor Law Amendment Bill, which after fierce opposition from Radicals in the Commons, had been passed by the Lords in July, and had received the Royal Assent on 4 August. 'If I have life, and health, I shall move for its repeal', Cobbett declared a few days later. (PR 16 August 1834) He kept his promise on his return from Ireland.

⁶ Cobbett probably meant, 'I hope these letters can get posted around the county and side-step the government surcharge of Four Pence on each newspaper', but didn't like to say so in so many words.

⁷ John Leech, Cobbett's local MP, was the member for West Surrey in the first reformed Parliament. Two of a kind, radical and hard-hitting farmers, they often spoke together at county meetings in Surrey, Sussex and Hampshire.

⁸ Thomas Malthus (1766-1834): the mild-mannered Surrey clergyman and perennially controversial author of *An Essay on the Principle of Population*, published anonymously in 1798 as an answer to Godwin's cloudy *Political Justice*. As far as Cobbett was concerned, Malthus' *Letter to Samuel Whitbread*, in 1807, was an eye-opener. Here the parson denounced as inexpedient a parish planning-application to build houses for the village poor, on the grounds that this would encourage the married couples to produce children. It was for Cobbett a chilling illustration of the practice of the 'miserable science' of the 'merciless Malthus'. 'I have, during my life, detested many men, but never any one so much as you!' were the frank opening words of a fiery letter Cobbett sent Malthus from America in 1819.

⁹ Farmer Horne, who preached on Sundays, lived at Ash. Of the other neighbours we have no information.

¹⁰ These *Three Lectures on the Political State of Ireland* were published by P. Byrne in Dublin before the end of 1834, but have never been reprinted.

¹¹ Cobbett's homespun view that the task of liberating Ireland could be accomplished only by the people of England, can be compared with Marx's assessment 35 years later, in a letter to Engels: '... For a long time I believed that it would be possible to overthrow the Irish regime by English working-class ascendancy. I always expressed this point of view in the *New York Tribune*. Deeper study has now convinced me of the opposite. The English working class will *never accomplish anything* [Marx's emphasis] before it has got rid of Ireland. The lever must be applied in Ireland. That is why the Irish question is so important for the social movement in general.' Karl Marx and Frederick Engels, *Ireland and the Irish question* Lawrence & Wishart 1978, p.387.

¹² Billy Cobbett, third of four boys, was born at Farnham, on (despite his own and some succeeding estimates) 9 March 1763.

¹³ Cobbett's grandfather George 'was a day-labourer, and I have heard my father say,' wrote Cobbett 'that he worked for one farmer from the day of his marriage to that of his death, upwards of forty years.' His grandmother he remembered well: 'She used to give us milk and bread for breakfast, an apple pudding for our dinner, and a piece of bread and cheese for supper. Her fire was made of turf from the neighbouring heath and her evening light was a rush dipped in grease.' Cobbett's father, also George, had started work as a plough-boy, but learned to read and write, taught himself some geometry and was in local demand as a land- surveyor, then settled down as landlord

of the 'Jolly Farmer' at Farnham. In the American revolutionary struggle, 'my father was a partisan of the Americans'. Of his mother, a shadowy but warm picture emerges. George Spater, *William Cobbett: The Poor Man's Friend*, Cambridge 1982, quotes her son as remembering of her, 'that when I and my brothers were little children, and used to run about the house, tearing at our mother's gown or apron in order to worry her into giving us apples or something or other, she used, when we had tired out her most exemplary patience, to exclaim, "Be quiet, you plagues of Egypt, do!" '

[14] In March 1785, 22 year-old Corporal Cobbett of the 54th Regiment of Foot (the West Norfolks) sailed from Chatham to join the main body of his regiment at Halifax, Nova Scotia. Within weeks, the regiment found itself sailing for the then 'village' of Saint John, on the Bay of Fundy, famed for its perilous tides. Disembarking here Corporal Cobbett lost overboard in his army box his boyhood copy of Swift's *Tale of a Tub*, his most precious possession. From Saint John the regiment moved up the 'reversing falls' and river to Fort Howe, at Fredericton, the new capital of New Brunswick. Six years later Sergeant-Major Cobbett arrived back in Portsmouth, engaged to marry Nancy Reid, whom he had first seen scrubbing out a wash-tub (emptying out a tea-pot, according to Nancy) in the married quarters at Saint John. This time he was carrying as a precious but dangerous possession, a box of secretly transcribed papers with which he intended to indict four commissioned officers of his regiment on charges of peculation and corruption that included selling the men's rations and firewood.

[15] That of Irish independence.

[16] William and Anne Cobbett lived in the United States from October 1792 until their return to England in June 1800. Driven back to North America again after the suspension of the Habeas Corpus Act in March 1817, the Cobbetts sailed for Liverpool two months after Peterloo. This time Cobbett carried with him the bones of Tom Paine, the revolutionary Republican.

[17] The question of Catholic Emancipation was first raised within the government by Pitt. George III refused even to consider it, and Pitt resigned in 1801. In that year and the next, Cobbett wrote against Emancipation in the *Register*. From 1807 onwards Cobbett gave ready support to the principle, but considered it a diversion from the social struggle. The emancipation movement gathered pace and in 1823 Daniel O'Connell formed the Catholic Association. In the following year Cobbett published the first volume of his stormy *History of the Protestant Reformation* which the English establishment received with a stunned, then horrified silence. The Protestant 'reformation', as Cobbett penned it, had little to do with religion, a great deal to do with the destruction by the new lords of private wealth, of a whole social web of popular rights and communally-held property. Partly, too, it was written to further the cause of Emancipation, which had come by this time to be identified with the cause of Ireland. In 1825 Burdett's Emancipation Bill for the Irish Catholics was carried in the Commons, but thrown out by their more intolerant Lordships. In 1829, on 5 February, the King's speech in Wellington's new ministry recommended a 'review of the laws which impose civil disabilities on his Majesty's Roman Catholic subjects.' The way was cleared for the Bill for Catholic Emancipation, brought in by Peel, to become law on 13 April 1829.

[18] In 1819, while in America, Cobbett bombarded the Reverend Baker, his parson at Botley with: 'Oh, no! *Tithes* do not mean *religion*. Religion means a *reverence for God*. And what has this to do with tithes? Why cannot you reverence God, without Baker and his wife and children eating up a tenth part of the corn and milk and eggs and lambs and pigs and calves that are produced in Botley parish! The parsons in this country, are supported by those who choose to employ them.' But by and large Cobbett gave some support to tithes in England. He implied that a Protestant people employing a Protestant church should not cavil at paying its ministers from a 'charge on the land' to be borne by the landowners. Cobbett had long recognised that Ireland presented a different scene. Rather than see Irish Catholics coerced into providing for an English and Protestant clergy, Cobbett argued not merely for the abolition of the tithes, but for what he called the 'repeal' of the entire Protestant hierarchy in Ireland and in England. He favoured what he thought of as the relaxed American pattern, with the Episcopalian Church set free to compete as best it might for voluntary support. The issue was a momentous, material and bloody one. Even as Cobbett was speaking in the theatre, three years of tithe war were still flickering in the south and west. Skirmishes swift to become legendary battles, such as were fought at Newtownbarry, Mullinahone, and Wallscourt and Thomastown in County Tipperary, were being balladed across the country. The girl Catherine Foley, killed by the police in County Cork, spoke for the courage of the much-subjected peasant women. Only in May, the army had left nineteen peasants dead or dying at Rathcormack, in resistance to a tithe-enforcement of 40 shillings in arrears, owed by a widow.

[19] The rebirth of republican and nationalist activity in Ireland, blazing out in the great rebellion of the United Irishmen in 1798, induced Pitt to make hasty arrangements for an Act of Union. The intention, barely concealed, was to place Ireland politically and then economically at the disposal of the British state. Apart from the threat posed by an independent and republican Ireland at the very time when the European monarchs were falling before the revolutionary armies of France, the growing strength and independence of the Irish economy was matter for concern. Limitless cheap food from Ireland, necessary to keep workers' wages depressed in England, was to be kept flowing by turning over more arable into grazing land, and the whole island into an agricultural colony. Acts of Union were secured separately at Westminster and Dublin (where the compliance of the land-lordly majority in Parliament proved only too easy to purchase); and the joint and fateful Act of Union took place in London on 1 January 1801. England and Ireland were now deemed to be a political entity, with Westminster its sole seat of Parliament.

[20] For Cobbett's views on a Repeal of the Union see his article in *Political Register* 17 May 1834, reproduced in Appendix II. See also his Dublin lecture of 8 November 1834 in Chapter 7.

CHAPTER 3

Political Register, 11 October 1834.

To the Citizens of Kilkenny

City of Kilkenny, 30 September 1834.
Gentlemen,
   In answer to your kind and generous commendations on me I have, first, to offer you my most profound and sincere thanks; and then, on your Address, so pregnant with important matter, to observe
   1. That if by *increased intelligence* of my countrymen you mean the increase in their quantity of *reading and* writing, the facts are these: that during the last thirty years of that prodigious increase the quantity of *crime* in England has increased tenfold! And that, as to comfort, the decrease has been in an exact proportion to the increase of that which is *most falsely* called 'EDUCATION', which is not education, but a scheme for making the people quiet under all the sufferings of hunger and cold.[1]
   2. That with regard to your loss of manufactures and trade, it is in the nature of our fiscal and paper-money system to create monopolies and to draw all property into great masses; and, as Caligula wished that the people of Rome had *but one neck*, that he might decapitate them all at a single blow, so our Government, from ignorance rather than from evil design, seems to aim, in all its measures, at getting all wealth into great heaps, and as near to itself as possible, that the wealth may be, with the least possible trouble, available for its fiscal purposes; while landowners, acting upon the same principle, have been moulding twenty farms into one, driving the small holders into the ranks of wretchedness, rendering that estate a wilderness

which before contained a happy community, and by the misery which they have thus created challenging an inquiry into their own rights of possession.

3. That with regard to a legal provision for the destitute, to deny the justice and necessity of such provision is to set at nought the dictates of reason, the laws of England, and the laws of God. As a matter of policy, *here*, gentlemen, is the only effectual remedy for non-residence, for monopoly of land, and for the evils arising from drawing manufactures into great masses. The landowners, compelled to feed and clothe, or to employ, the millions whom they ruin by their grasping and short-sighted policy, will THEN, for their own interest, put an end to the evils that they have created.

Gentlemen, I am sure that your wishes for my happiness come from your hearts, and I assure you, that few things would contribute more to that happiness than being able to assist in restoring perfect freedom and happiness in Ireland, and in rendering its peace and harmony perpetual.

WM. COBBETT.

Political Register, 11 October 1834.

To Charles Marshall, Labourer, Letter No.III

*Normandy Tithing, Parish of Ash,
Farnham, Surrey.*

City of Kilkenny, 1 October 1834.
MARSHALL,
    From Dublin to this city is about 70 English miles. Very fine lands all the way except in very few places, and there the land is better than the greater part of the enclosed land in our part of Surrey; and as to our *commons*, these people could not be made to believe, that there is any land so poor in the world; and yet I shall have to tell you presently, that those who do the work on this fine land, are in a state of poverty the most complete. When I get home, I will put INTO A LITTLE BOOK a full account of all that I see here. I can only tell you in these letters, of such things as will enable you to judge of the real state of the working people in this fine country; such things as will serve to show you what the Scotch, crawling vagabonds are endeavouring to persuade the Parliament to make you and your children submit to; giving you to understand, at the same time, that the Scotch nation, who are as good people as any in the world, detest and abhor these vagabonds as much as I do.
    In coming from Dublin I came through a horse-fair in a little town. I should think there were two thousand or so horses here, none of them what we would call *large* horses; but, there was not a *poor* one amongst them all; and I have not seen a *poor* horse, colt, cow, ox, steer, heifer, sheep, hog, pig, goose or turkey, or fowl, since I came into the country; *man* and *woman*, and *working* man and woman, are the only animals that suffer here from hunger and cold.
    In this city of Kilkenny (which is the capital of a county of the same name), which is beautifully situated on a fine river, and which contains more than twenty thousand people, there are two societies for *assisting the poor*, one called the *charitable*, the other the *benevolent*. These societies make collections of money

to relieve the poor; but, so great is the number of these poor, so low the wages, so great and horrible the want, that these societies have been obliged to refuse all assistance to such as are *able to beg*; and also, to all persons who are *able to get one meal in 24 hours, of the very worst sort of potatoes, which they call 'LUMPERS'*. And, mind, Marshall, I have the proof of these facts under the assurance of gentlemen of the city, and under the hands of the managers of these very societies. And, Marshall, I beg you all to mind what I say, this is the state to which, it is my firm belief, all of you and your children will come, if you do not do your duty by petitioning the Parliament to protect you. If the poor-laws of England be put down, this is the state to which you must come; and about that great matter I will tell you another time; so that you and all of you may understand what to do.

I told you, in my first letter, that I saw fine *Swedish Turnips* and *Mangel-Wurzel*. They belonged to a rich gentleman, who got some of my seed. I have not seen another piece of either in the country! Having seen the people in the cities, I went, yesterday, to see them in the country; and I saw the state of both labourers and farmers. There was one village with about as many houses as there are in the village of Ash, about 70 or 80 perhaps, the scattered ones and all. The places, which I *call* houses, were in general from ten to twelve feet square; the walls made of rough stone and mud, whited over, and about nine feet high; no ceiling; rough rafters covered over with rotten black thatch; in some a glass window the size of your hat, in two or four little panes; in others no window at all; but a hole or two holes in the wall; about a foot long, and four or five inches wide; the floor nothing but the bare earth; no chimney, but, a hole at one end of the roof to let out the smoke, arising from a fire made against the wall of that end of this miserable shed; this hole is sometimes surrounded by a few stones put on that end of the roof a foot or two high; generally it is not, and in cold weather the poor, ragged, half-naked creatures *stop up the hole to keep in the smoke to keep them from perishing with cold*! The fuel is *peat*, just such as that dug out of our moors, and never a stick of wood; and the people get the big *dead weeds* to light their fires and to boil their potatoes. One of these places costs the landowner about *four pounds to build it, and the poor creatures pay from thirty shillings* to *two pounds* a year rent for them, without any garden, without an inch of land, without any place for even *a privy*; WOMEN as well as men must go to the *dung-heap before the door*; and the former are exposed to that which your wife, or any woman of Normandy, would die at the thought of! And, Marshall, this is the state to which the crawling and greedy Scotch vagabonds would fain have the Parliament reduce you, in order to enrich the landowners, hoping to get from them rewards for their schemes. But, will our member of Parliament, Mr Leech, listen to such damnable advice? No; and it is our bounden duty to support him in his opposition to all such hard-hearted schemes.

As to the *goods* in the hole, there are, an *iron pot*, a *rough table*, or a *board laid across two piles of stones*, seats of stones, or of boards laid from one stone to another; and that is all the stock of goods, except a *dish*, of which I shall speak presently. Every hole has a pig; the pig eats with the family, and generally sleeps in the same place. The potatoes are taken up and turned out into a great *dish*, which dish is a shallow basket made of oziers with the bark on. The family squat round this basket and take out the potatoes with their hands; the pig stands and is helped by some one, and sometimes he eats out of the pot. He goes in and out and about the hole, like one of the family; the family sleep, huddled up together, on dead weeds or a little straw in one corner of the hole, and the pig, on a similar bed, in another corner. The pig is the person of most consequence; he is sold to *pay the rent*: if he fail, the family are turned out into the naked air to perish, which has been the case in many thousands of instances, there being *no poor-law* here to save their lives.

I must speak to you about *the farmers* in my next letter. In the meanwhile pay great attention to what I have said here; and all of you make up your minds to be brought into this state: or *resolve* to do your duty in the manner that I have before described. Men are brought into this state by *little* and *little*, until at last they cannot help themselves. Mind this! And attend, all of you, to the advice of

Your master and friend,
WM. COBBETT.

Political Register, 11 October 1834.

To Lord Althorp[2]

Waterford, 4 October 1834.
My Lord,
   Though rambling about in Ireland, I see a little of the goings on amongst your *enfans chéris*, the blacks! Your lordship remembers the stentorian and *sensible* cheers which stunned us when Fowel Buxton presented, with the assistance of the two door-keepers (who seemed to me to blush at the delusion which they were mechanically assisting to keep up), the petition of his *two hundred and seventy-eight thousand* ENGLISH FEMALES, in behalf of the *fat* and *muscular* black fellows, and not one of whose tender bosoms ever heaved a sigh for the millions of real sufferers of their own sex in Ireland,[3] who raise a large part of the food that Buxton's tender-hearted and crack-skulled and canting petitioners eat, and who would be glad of the offal left by the blacks: your lordship must remember those cheers; and you may remember that I voted against giving one single farthing of that TWENTY MILLIONS, which would have bought all the incumbencies and all the advowsons in Ireland, and would have removed one great cause of the troubles of a country and a people that ought to be as dear to us as our own country and countrymen: and you ought to remember also your telling us that 'all Europe was filled with *admiration* at our *generous humanity.*' I thought that if this were so, '*all Europe*' was a fool, or was imposed on by the Yorkshire cant.
   First and last, that measure must ruin the sugar colonies; and, according to appearances, the ruin is already coming. However, it is merely a *question of time*: that the ruin will come is certain; and then we shall hear what you have to say. I do not care a straw about the *colonies*; it is the *money*, the £800,000 a year, that I care for. Why pay this money; why *tax us* to get the means of revolutionizing the colonies? this will be a memorable instance of the just punishment of CANT. A canting conventicle is bad enough; but a canting government is a despicable thing indeed.

Hoping, that at any rate, the blacks will not *cost* us any thing more; hoping that you will ask for no more of any constituents' *money* for them,

I am,
Your lordship's
Most humble and obedient servant,
WM. COBBETT.

Political Register, 11 October 1834.

To the Kilkenny Weavers

Gentlemen,

With great pride and gratitude I receive this Address from you, whose occupation and whose good sense and public spirit call my mind back to the same occupation, and the same qualities in my excellent constituents of Oldham. In answer to the address, be pleased to receive from me the following observations, accompanied with my sincere thanks:

1. That with regard to the strange assertions ascribed to Mr Spring Rice,[4] as my constituents have placed me in a situation to say TO HIS FACE any thing which I shall deem it my duty to say in disapprobation of his conduct, I abstain, in this case, from saying more of that conduct, than that I lament that his statements should have been so very contrary to the facts, and that I would fain hope, that those statements must have arisen from misinformation or from error in judgment, rather than from a deliberate and premeditated design to deceive and mislead the House of Commons and the people of England.

2. that with regard to the Union and its effects on the condition of the people of Ireland, while it is impossible to recollect the means by which it was effected, and to believe that the end *can ever be good*;[5] while it is notorious that the lot of the Irish people has been growing worse from the day of the Union to this day, while common sense tells us that the Union must of necessity produce absenteeship, and draw away a considerable part of the means of employment of industry in all its various branches; and, in short, while it is too much for insanity itself to adopt the belief, that eight millions and a half of people can, for any length of time, continue in a state of *colonial relationship* to twelve millions, about two or three millions of whom they supply with food; while all this presents itself to the mind of every really sane person in the whole kingdom, still there is another cause, besides the Union, which cause we must not leave out of our consideration, if we would arrive at a correct conclusion, and suggest an effectual and peaceable remedy.

3. That this cause is the *drawing of all property*, and especially manufacturing property, *into great heaps*; that the Statute Book tells us, that, five hundred years ago, there was a Cloth Hall, regulated by law, in each of 32 out of the 40 counties of England; that within the period of my life, every labourer's house in the eastern, southern, and western counties of England, contained a manufacturer; that *now*, the *then* dispersed and happy millions are huddled together in dense masses, and condemned to toil for swollen-up masters who rival lords in wealth, and who surpass them in arrogance and haughtiness and cruelty. In the first happy period the existence of a soldier in time of peace had never been heard of; in the second place the army amounted to an average of less than ten thousand men, and there were only three barracks in England; now there are in time of peace more than a hundred thousand standing soldiers, and more than a hundred barracks; while the miserable operatives, whom these are intended to keep in order, have frequently for their Sunday clothes the cast-off habiliments of these very soldiers, and who have not each a third part of the food of one of these soldiers.

4. That the *accursed instruments* by which this desolating and enslaving change has been affected, is that paper-money, which made its first appearance a hundred and forty years ago, which has, by slow degrees, brought us into our present state without any set of our rulers ever seeming to have perceived the danger, which has gone on making the rich man more rich, and the poor man more poor; which has, at last, divided society into two classes, distinct in interest, and hostile in feeling; in which state of society, justice, reason, and human nature herself say there must *be a change*; and that that change may be peaceable and equitable, is the ardent prayer of

Your grateful,
And obedient servant,
WM. COBBETT.

Political Register, 11 October 1834.

To The Citizens of Waterford

Gentlemen,

Without stopping to lament that any language that I have at my command must be placed in the shade, when used in answer to an address such as that which you have done me the honour to present to me, I will at once proceed to observe,

1. That there are a great many Englishmen whose feelings for the sufferings of Ireland are by no means inferior to my own, but who have not the same means as those which I have long had, of giving any considerable effect to those feelings. In them silence regarding your wrongs, or want of zeal in your defence, might be excusable, while either would be most base and criminal in me.

2. That with regard to your *religion*, it was for a thousand years the religion of my own forefathers as well as of yours. It was to the wisdom, the integrity, the valour, the industry of Roman Catholics, that England owed all her famed institutions, all her glory, all her solid power, all her noble edifices, all the riches and beauty of her fields and her woods. I knowing this and being myself emancipated from the ignorance with which greedy craft had shackled my mind, seeing my countrymen still under the influence of that ignorance, seeing that ignorance made use of for the purpose of oppressing you, and having at my command a pen and a press; if I had neglected to use the, to me, easy means of removing that ignorance, I should have been the very basest, the most unjust, and cruel of all mankind.

3. That my present situation in society, considering not the mere station, but taking into view the rare political integrity, the not less rare discernment, the distinguished public spirit of those who placed me in it, is certainly most honourable; and it is also certain that I have not obtained it by means such as those employed by the Roses, the Jenkinsons, the Huskissons, the Cannings, the Addingtons, the Vansittarts, the Wilberforces, the Broughams, and many other men of origin so obscure as almost to tempt us, in spite of their printed

pedigrees, to adopt a belief in the theory of equivocal generation.[6] But, gentlemen, let us be just: the disinterested exertions of the man whose body is satisfied with dining on a crust and skim milk, and sleeping on a plank, are not to be raised to a level with those of a man whose carcass craves a bed of down, and is, even there, agitated by dreams of venison and claret; the proofs of public spirit shown by the man, the greatest delight to whose vulgar eyes is the sight of a well-tilled field, whose sweetest music is the ploughman's whistle and the jingle of the traces, and the utmost of whose ambition is the possession of a well-fed and gaily-harnessed team, are by no means to be put upon a level with those of the man to whom museums and galleries and harmonious bands (at the people's expense) are necessaries of life; who must have a ribbon at least, though associated with chains, and who reckons his soul well sold if it bring him a coronet. With an abatement made on this principle, gentlemen, I receive your encomiums as justly my due, and as such worthy of you and me.

4. That, great as is the value which I set, for my own sake, on this generous conduct on your part, I value it a thousand times more on account of the great good effect which I know it will have on the minds of my countrymen, who, for the far greater and more efficient part, will consider every mark of friendship shown to me as shown to themselves. It has for many years, and for purposes too well known to need stating to you, been the constant endeavour of the most unjust, most cruel, most greedy, most perfidious of all mankind, to make the people of the two countries view each other with jealousy and suspicion, and to fill their hearts with mutual hostility. It has been, for a like number of years, my constant endeavour to counteract this truly hellish series of efforts; and, gentlemen, I am now, at last, cheered with the hope, that, by our joint exertions, our endeavours will be crowned with success.

WM. COBBETT.

NOTES

[1] At Botley, Cobbett had said: 'If the farmer ... if the labourer be expert at ploughing, sowing, reaping, mowing, making of ricks and fences, loading the wagon, threshing and winnowing the corn ... though neither of them can write or read, I call neither an *ignorant* man. The education of these men is a finished one, though neither may ever have looked into a book.' And some years later: 'It is not the *mere capability* of reading that can raise a man in the scale of nature. It is the enlightening of his mind.' We have already noted Cobbett's distrust of a state and church education which took care that the children of the working people were doled out the ideology of the rich, to impress on them the 'natural' order of things.

[2] Althorp was leader of the House in the reformed Parliament. He had recently described Cobbett as 'an enemy of the education of the people', after Cobbett had opposed a grant to the British Museum, to be funded from a levy on common foodstuffs. Cobbett had objected to ordinary Londoners shouldering a tax-burden which the cultured wealthy, judges and others, would scarcely notice.

[3] 'The daughters of the Irish peasantry have been the cheapest slaves in existence – slaves to their own family, who were, in turn, slaves to all social parasites of a landlord and gombeen-ridden community,' wrote James Connolly, *Reconquest of Ireland*, Dublin, 1915. See also 'Woman' in *Selected Writings*, Harmondsworth, 1973.

[4] Thomas Spring-Rice, of Mount Trenchard, County Limerick, a wealthy Anglo-Irish landowner and MP for Limerick, threw in his lot with the English Whigs. He was Secretary to the Treasury in Grey's administration between 1830 and June 1834, when Cobbett was delighted to see him dismissed. Spring-Rice had introduced the Bill providing for the two much-ruffled wings of emancipation: the disenfranchisement of the forty-shilling freeholders, and the payment of Catholic clergy from state funds.

[5] Among the 'means' Cobbett here refers to were the emoluments discreetly handed out to the Catholic aristocrats, hierarchy and large landowners for their compliance with an Act which they were in any event disposed to support.

[6] Cobbett lumped these together as being all in one way or another '*low* and *little* men', who had begun as Pitt's protégés, and then moved on to become scholarly advocates of the wide 'THING' of sinecure and corruption, resting on the paper-money and funding system. Of George Rose, Pitt's Secretary of the Treasury and jovial doyen of the swarm of sinecurists, Cobbett said his savage piece in *A New Year's Gift to Old George Rose* (*PR*, 4 January 1817). Of the reforming Huskisson and eloquent Canning, Cobbett said, quoting Swift, that the climbing of the tree of preferment had naturally been performed 'in the attitude of crawling'. William Huskisson had in 1809 been silent at the flogging of English militiamen at the hands of the King's Hanoverian mercenaries. The young men had refused to march further without the 'marching guinea' they were entitled to by Act of Parliament. 'I do not blame you (Cobbett said witheringly to Huskisson) for changing your opinions: I blame you for

changing them from good to bad ... in accordance with your interest.' Henry Addington ('The Doctor', to Cobbett) had with fatherly consideration bestowed on his 12 year-old child a sinecure worth £3,000 a year. In his capacity as Home Secretary, Sidmouth, 'The Doctor', had bloodily repressed the riots of 1812; and five years later drew up the 'gagging-acts'. Henry Brougham, an increasingly moderate reformer, had in 1820 condoned the use of government provocateurs and spies. Years later, as Lord Chancellor, Brougham was the prime mover of the Poor Law Amendment Bill, for which final coat-turning Cobbett indicts him in *Legacy to Labourers*. But, with the possible exception of Malthus, Cobbett detested none of this crew more heartily than the obsequious William Wilberforce, Member for the rotten borough of Bramber. In face of the poverty and oppression of the working people, of one million official paupers in England alone, Wilberforce preached to the English workers Christian patience and submission, to be taken 'with cheap soup'. Nor did Cobbett ever forget Wilberforce's part in persuading Pitt to press forward with the Combination Act of 1799, nor his ready approval of Sidmouth's 'gagging-bills' and spy-system in 1817. As to Wilberforce's role in the Government's unilateral abandonment of black slavery, Cobbett looked on it as mere sanctimony and hypocrisy masking a cold heart. 'No Wilberforces!' Cobbett had shouted joyfully as he fled England for safe haven in America. 'Think of that! No Wilberforces!'

CHAPTER 4

Political Register, 18 October 1834.

To Charles Marshall, Labourer, Letter No.IV

*Normandy Tithing, Parish of Ash,
Farnham, Surrey.*

Waterford, 6 October 1834.
MARSHALL,
    I broke off my last letter in telling you, that I would tell you about the *farms* another time. There are *some* large farmers, and these have *barns* and thrashing-machines; but the greater number have from 5 acres of land to 40 perhaps. *Our acre* is about three-quarters of an *Irish* acre; but I speak of *our acre*. Where there are barns, they are of *stone*. The ground of all this kingdom seems to be upon beds of stone, and great part *lime-stone*; so that all buildings are of these, stone and mortar; and the *fences*, where there are any, are of stone. The farmers, in general, have *no barns*. They put their sheaves into little cocks and seldom thatch them; and they do the same with the hay. They beat out the corn (wheat, etc.) in *their miserable houses*, and winnow it by the wind, on cloths, having no vans to do it with. They then put it into bags holding about six of our bushels, which are lifted on a *car* (a sort of *bed* of a cart without head or tail or sides, which, when wanted to carry potatoes or apples, are made of oziers), and carry it and sell it to the corn-dealers, who send almost all of it to England. The farmer and his family are all in half nakedness or rags; their lot is little better than the mere labourers. They raise wheat and barley and oats and

butter and pork in great abundance; but never do they *taste* any of either, except, perchance, a small part of the meal of the *oats*. Potatoes are their sole food. I wish the farmers of our parish could see one that I saw in the fine county of KILKENNY. His dress was a mere bundle of rags, tied round his body with a band of straw; his legs and feet bare, no shirt, and his head covered with a rag, such as you would rip out of the inside of an old cart-saddle. The landlord generally lets his great estate to some *one man*, who lets it out in littles; and this *one man* takes *all* from the wretched farmer. Some of the farmers in England grumble at the poor-rates. Well, there are *no poor-rates here!* Let them come here then, and lead the life of these farmers! They will soon find that there is something worse than poor-rates! And if the Scotch vagabonds, of whom I have spoken so often, should succeed in their schemes, you may tell the farmers of our parish, that they will be *in this very state*; that their wives will have no hats, bonnets, or caps; but must, in wet weather, *have a wad of straw tied upon their heads*! Mrs West, and Mrs Fagotten and Mrs Heathorn would look so nice, naked up to the knees, some rags tied round their middle, no smock, and their heads covered with a wad of straw! And this will be their lot, if ever the poor-rates be abolished in England; as the Scotch villains (who have *beggared the industrious people of their own country*) are endeavouring to prevail on the Parliament to abolish them in England.

Marshall, I have now been over about 180 miles in Ireland, in the several counties of Dublin, Wicklow, Kildare, Carlow, Kilkenny, and Waterford. I have, in former years, been in every county of England, and across every county more than one way. I have been through the finest part of Scotland;[1] I have lived in the finest parts of the United States of America. And here I am to declare to all the world, that I never passed over any 50 miles, in my life, any 50 *unbroken miles*, of land so good on an average during the whole way, as these 180 miles. Perhaps there are parts, *patches*, of England better than this land; but take England, one with the other, it is nothing like so good as this; and yet here are these starving people! And this is only because they have *no law* to give them their due share of the fruits of their labour!

In coming from Kilkenny to Waterford I and my friend (Mr O'Higgins), in a post-chaise, came through a little town called

MULLINAVAT, where there was a fair for cattle and fat hogs and apples.[2] There might be 4,000 people; there were about 7 acres of ground covered with cattle (mostly fat), and all over the streets of the town there were about THREE THOUSAND BEAUTIFUL FAT HOGS, lying all over the road and the streets; and our chaise was *actually stopped and blocked up by fat hogs*; and we were obliged to stop till the civil and kind people could get them out of our way! There was a sight to be seen by me, who had never seen thirty such hogs together in the course of my life, these hogs weighing from *ten* to *thirty* score each! Ah! but there arose out of this fine sight reflections that made my blood boil; that the far greater part of those who had bred and fatted these hogs were never to taste one morsel of them, no not even the offal, and had lived *worse* than the hogs, not daring to taste any part of the *meal* used in the fatting of the hogs! the hogs are to be killed, dried or tubbed, and sent out of the country to be sold for money to be *paid to the landowners*, who spend it in London, Bath, Paris, Rome, or some other place of pleasure, while these poor creatures are raising all this food from the land, and are starving themselves. And this is what we shall come to *in England*, unless we call upon our member, Mr Leech, to protect us.

I will tell you more about these *landowners* another time; but I will now, before I conclude this letter, give you *one fact* which will enable you to judge of what would be the lot of the working-men in England, if there were to be no *poor-rates*. There are here, as there are in England, several sorts of potatoes: some are called *minions*, others *apple-potatoes*; these are the best. Others are called *lumpers*; and these are the *worst*. When men or women are employed, at six-pence a day and their board, to dig *minions* or *apple-potatoes*, they are not suffered to *taste them*, but are sent to another field to dig *lumpers* to eat; and this is called *boarding* them! That fact is enough: it is enough for you to know that THAT is what the Scotch vagabonds mean when they propose to bring you to 'COARSER food': it is enough for you to know THAT to *rouse you all to a sense of your danger*, and to urge you to come to a *county-meeting* and to do your duty like men, true to your country and true to the King and to the laws of England.

I hope that all of you are well; and that not a man of you will ever again suffer a potato to grow in your gardens, or be brought into your houses; and if any one bring a potato into my house, except to *stuff a fat goose*, or a *fat suckling pig*, Mr Dean has my order to *discharge that person directly*. You have peas and beans of all sorts for summer; carrots, parsnips, beets for winter; white cabbages *all the year through*; the best of bread, bacon, and puddings always; and if you still hanker after that accursed root without which Ireland could not have been brought to its present state, and which has *banished bread* from the labourer's house here;[3] if you still hanker after this 'COARSER food', you shall go elsewhere to get it; for you shall not have it in the service (in house or out of house) of

Your master and friend
WM. COBBETT.

Political Register, 18 October 1834.

To The President of The United States of America[4]

Kilkenny, 8 October 1834.
SIR,
   Here I am, in the country which has the honour to be the birth-place of your father and mother, and which was very near to having the greater honour of being the birth-place of yourself. The accounts, which you get from England, will show you the *good*, the *glorious good*, which your wise and just measures are producing there. They have brought down prices *one-third* in that country, and have filled CORRUPTION with a degree of alarm, that makes her knees knock together. Here, WHITE LAMMAS WHEAT sells (highest price) at 18 shillings the barrel of 280 pounds; that is, at 33 shillings THE ENGLISH QUARTER; so that the 30 millions a year to be paid to the fund-holders now demands about *three times and a half* as much wheat as it demanded before Peel's Bill was passed!
   What wise men we have to manage our affairs! If your countrymen support you in your measures for giving to your country a currency of HARD-MONEY; if they do their duty, as all the world knows that you will do yours, you and they will establish for ever, the security, the power, the glory of the United States, and make your country, for ages, that which it now is, the refuge and the avenger of the oppressed of all other nations. There are persons *here*, who are sending away to you thousands upon thousands of men, with *gold in their pockets*: no, not *to you*, to CANADA: convenient *filtering-stone*! For, there all the feeble remain, while the stout and useful cross the line, and join their well-fed and well-clad countrymen in the United States, to add to her wealth and her power. But, we have *so much gold*! and *so many able men*! It would be to be niggardly not to send you *some* of both!
   When it pleased God to permit a portion of the creation to be imbued with *malignity of the most hellish character*, He, in mercy to mankind, took care that that malignity should be

accompanied with *imbecility*, which, in the end, must counteract and punish the malignity. Without troubling you with a description of the particular instance by which this doctrine is so amply illustrated and verified, and which instance will, indeed, instantly suggest itself to your mind; it is with inexpressible pleasure and gratitude that I behold in you, sir, the greatest and most efficient instrument in His hands, in accomplishing this work of counteracting and of punishing.

Sir, I should fail, if I were to try my best, to do a tenth part of justice to the admiration and the honour with which your name is pronounced by the millions of men of sense and of virtue in this kingdom; and I have only to hope, that you will do me justice to believe, that, in this respect, no one of all the millions surpasses him who has the honour to be,

Your most humble
And most obedient servant,
WM. COBBETT.

Political Register, 18 October 1834.

To Lord Radnor[5]

*On his reported speech, in the House of Lords,
on the 21 of July, 1834,
on the New Poor-Law Scheme.*

Evergreen Lodge, Cork, 12 October 1834.
MY LORD,
   I am now about to speak to you on the subject of that 'LAW OF NATURE', to which your grave and sober and sensible Scotch Mentor[6] *appealed* (in justification of this project) *from* the *law of the land* and the revealed law of God. The 'LAW OF NATURE' is, in fact, no law at all. It means a state of things, in which every man has a right to make and use that which he can get into his possession, if he have need of that thing. Nature; man's nature, teaches him (unless his nature be perverted and vicious) not to kill other people; not to cut them, or bite them, or be in any way cruel to them; it forbids him to eat that which others have earned, unless he cannot sustain life without it; but, it supposes no restraint at all on any man, other than those restraints which are imposed by the dictates of nature herself. It is a very curious affair, that this '*law of nature*' is cooked up by the barbarous and nasty MALTHUS, and by his disciples; it is pleaded in bar of the express law of God, and the express law of the land, for this savage purpose; but is held in abhorrence; is held to be even legally seditious, when pleaded by poor men, in bar of the rights of property. Poor SPENCE[7] was imprisoned two years; and EVANS[8] was tried for high treason, for no other offence than that of asserting, *that all the lands belonged to all the people at large, and that the people ought to take them into their possession*; and, whether your lordship recollects the fact or not, it is the fact, that one of the express grounds for passing the gagging and the dungeoning bill of 1817, was, that the 'PRETENDED REFORMERS' (which was a lie, however); that the '*pretended reformers asserted, that* the land was the people's farm'; and this is to be seen in the report of the committee of the Lords, who

proposed the passing of the power of imprisonment, the gagging, and the dungeoning bills; the bills that enabled SIDMOUTH and CASTLEREAGH to cram the dungeons with men that had committed no crime; the bills that drove me across the Atlantic, whence, with my long arm, I so belaboured the greedy and savage borough-mongers.

Yet suppose the charge against the reformers to have been true, instead of being a scoundrelly lie; suppose the allegation to have been true, what more did it amount to than that we pleaded the LAW OF NATURE against the law of the land; that we pleaded, 'that the land was the people's farm'; that we denied proprietorship in the land to all men: supposing this to have been true, instead of being, as it was, a scoundrelly lie; what did we do more than your steady, sober-minded, and humane Scotch guide now does? He pleads the 'law of nature' (and we shall presently see with what object he pleads it) against the law of the land; and, what, I say, did we do more, even if the lying allegation against us had been true?

The charge was, that we said, in so many words, '*that the land was the people's farm*'; and, my lord, is your park, or are your farms, yours, any more than they are ours? Did NATURE give them to you? Is your BODY part and parcel of them? Have the ELEMENTS combined to say, that no one shall share in them but yourself? Oh, no! Your estate is no more yours than it is that of the poorest man that toils upon it; by NATURE it is no more yours than it is his; there is no express law of God to give it to you; and you have not a shadow of right to the possession of it, if you appeal to the LAW OF NATURE against the law of the land.

You have no strength to secure the exclusive possession of it; *nature* has given you no means of compelling any one to give you a farthing for any part of it: you live at your ease, and without toil: you live sumptuously, in consequence of being able to draw from the estate that which is earned upon it by others: you do not make a single ear of wheat to come, nor a blade of grass: were there no law of the land; were there no constable, justice of the peace, jailer, judge, and hangman, you would have no more of the produce of that estate, than that which came out of it by your bodily labour; and that is all that you would be entitled to. It is very right; and, if it were necessary, I could show, that it is very useful and beneficial to a people at large, that there should be a certain portion of the kingdom parcelled out in large estates; and that there should be constables, jailers, judges, and hangmen, to keep the owners of estates in quiet possession of them: but, then, they must cast aside appeals to the 'law of nature', and take away the argument of your Scotch guide; his *best* argument for the passing of this bill.

His assertion was this; that all legal relief to the necessitous was wrong, was an evil; and that even all that which was called *charity*; benevolence, as it was called; that even these were evils; because they either tended to make the parties receiving relief, idle, negligent, improvident; or, in case of the parties being really objects of deep compassion, they prevented the *parents and kindred of the poor and indigent from obeying* THE LAW OF NATURE, *and giving the relief that was wanted*. He is reported to have said, that, 'when he came to the third species of charity, that which went to support the aged and infirm, he would say, *that it was against* all sound principles'. CHADWICK, *who is to be the Secretary to this Board*, and whom *you applaud to the skies*, by implication at least, speaks thus of a proper officer, to manage the poor;[9] he says, that this proper officer must be 'a man of remarkable intelligence, remarkable activity, remarkable firmness, and of remarkable disinterestedness, ready to sacrifice himself to the performance of his duty; a man of great penetration, of great firmness, that will refuse *to relieve the real indigent*, regardless of popularity; ready in the performance of a thankless duty to incur the curses of the profligate, the censures of the sentimental, and the enmity of the powerful, he must be a man not of *narrow sympathies*, governed by *the appearances of misery before him*, whether those appearances *be real* or *assumed*.'

Now, this is the doctrine upon which your lordship has supported this bill, according to the report given of your speech. It would be insincerity of which you are not capable; and it would be the excess of foolishness besides, to pretend that you supported the bill after the hatcher and mover of it had laid down these principles as having guided him in the framing of the bill. You are incapable of attempting to shuffle; but the most shuffling and tricky fellow that ever sponged a living out of the taxes would not get out of this conclusion. Well, then, these principles that you make *your own*: the words were spoken by BROUGHAM, and written by CHADWICK, the penny-a-line reporter; but they become *your words*, if the report of your speech be correct; and you are for *an appeal to the law of nature*, and for putting the poor under the hard-hearted wretch described by CHADWICK.

It is NATURE'S law that parents and children and brethren and kindred should take care of one another and relieve one another's distresses; share with one another the last farthing and the last bit of bread. This is NATURE'S law, and God's law too; and your lordship remembers well what the apostle says, that 'he that neglects his own kindred is worse than a heathen.' In accordance with this law of nature and law of God has been the law of the land, until the day on which you passed this Poor-law Bill. The law of ELIZABETH, in making a legal and certain provision for the destitute, took care to provide that the fathers, the mothers, the grandfathers, and the grandmothers, should relieve the necessities of the children and the grandchildren, if *able to do it*; and that the children and grandchildren, if able to do it, should relieve the necessities of their fathers, mothers, grandfathers, and grandmothers. But do you not know? Yes, you know it well; whatever plea of ignorance the Scotch projectors may have, you have no plea of ignorance on this score, my lord: you know well that it every day occurs that persons are found in a state of the utmost destitution, having neither parent nor child, nor any relation in the whole world, able to afford them the smallest degree of relief; and you know besides, that the working people, aye, and many tradesmen and farmers too, have been brought into this state, not by any offences, or negligences, or bad conduct of their own; but by having their earnings taken from them by taxes laid on by the two Houses of Parliament; and which taxes, as far as they operate upon the working people, were kept on to the last penny, at the time when you were passing this bill.

But, my lord, is shame completely banished from this world? Is there no such thing left appertaining to human nature? My lord, I have no pleasure in ripping up these things. I have no desire to stir up the boiling rage of the working people, but hearing *you*: I would not have minded what was said by BROUGHAM or GREY, nor by any such people: but when I hear *you* support and praise a project, founded upon an assertion that the industrious classes of this country disregard the precepts of nature and the commands of God, by leaving their kindred to starve; when I hear you saying this; when I see a reported speech of yours sanctioning this horrible libel on this good and kind and just working people, I cannot refrain from asking your lordship to look at the conduct of those; to look at the conduct of the *aristocracy*, and see how *they* act as to this matter; to look at the millions; I deliberately say millions, which they swallow up every year, in pensions, in sinecures, in allowances, in grants; to look at the fifteen hundred thousand pounds given to the poorer clergy during the Regency of George the Fourth; given to *relieve the poor clergy*, while the rich clergy took away the endowments which the poor clergy ought to have had. And do the *relations of your lordship* receive nothing in this way? Yet you are of ability to relieve them. The 'law of nature', and the command of God, bid you relieve them. How many peers are there, and how many members of the other House, who, by themselves or by their relations, do not receive *relief* of some sort or other, out of the taxes paid, and in great part paid by the labouring people? What becomes of BROUGHAM'S LAW OF NATURE here? The *'law of nature'* bids me provide, if I be able, for my own kindred; but the *'law of nature'* does not bid me provide for the *relations of the nobility*; and as to the commands of God, they forbid me to keep silence, while I see the relations of the rich pampered up and kept in luxury out of the fruit of the labour of the poor.

I never yet heard anything worthy of the name of an apology for taxing the food and the drink of the working people, for the purpose of collecting the means of feeding and clothing, and keeping in the style of gentlefolks, the brothers and sisters, and uncles and aunts, and cousins, *of lords*, or other men of great estate. I never heard anything worthy of the name of an apology for this; and I should be glad to hear some one attempt it; at any rate apologised for, and justified too, it speedily must be; or we must hear the open declaration, that you will continue to do it BECAUSE YOU HAVE THE POWER! And indeed we are little short of hearing this declaration now; but we must have it out, plain and entire: this Poor-law Bill gives the people *the challenge*, and stirs up all rights and all claims to their foundation.[10]

You charge the industrious classes with an abandonment of

the Christian duty; the duty imposed by the law of nature also. Stop here while I think of it. Did the 'law of nature' give to the nasty and greedy parson MALTHUS his P E N S I O N ? He told us, that a law ought to be passed to refuse relief to all poor persons whatsoever who should marry after a certain day, to them and their children. He told us that for such persons 'there was no seat at nature's board.' Monster! did nature bid him, then, have a pension of a hundred pounds a year for doing nothing; and that pension, too, wrung from the sweat of the labouring people? God is just, but if there were not punishment to fall upon the heads of those who have the blasphemy to hold principles like these, God would not be just; but he is just, and justice he will inflict upon these persons; these audacious contemners of his law, these profligate blasphemers. The nasty MALTHUS says, that a man who shall marry and be in want, after notice given him, *'has no claim upon society for the smallest portion of relief.'* Impudent parson! What claim had *he*? And what claim have *the swarms* who are upon the pension list, upon the sinecure list, and upon the dead-weight list; and all the lists that swallow up the earnings of the working people? And is impudence to prevail *for ever*? Is it *always* to be thus? Are we *always* to be told that Englishmen were born to be slaves; and that their food is not C O A R S E enough yet? No, it is not *always* to be thus; a day of justice must come, and will come; a day of judgment it will be, to those who plead the law of nature for giving pensions to the rich, and for not giving relief to the poor.

When I stopped at the beginning of the last paragraph I was about to notice the audacity of charging the industrious classes of this country with an abandonment of the duty of relieving their own kindred, as imposed by the law of nature and the law of God. And this is a foul charge, a base charge, an audaciously lying charge. It frequently happens amongst the industrious classes, that parents and grandparents have children and grandchildren in a state of great indigence requiring relief: it as frequently happens, that children and grandchildren possess the means of relieving parents and grandparents who are in a state of indigence. The law of ELIZABETH requires that these persons of substance shall perform these duties, and that the indigent persons shall not be thrown upon the parish. There is not, perhaps, one single parish in the whole kingdom which does not contain certain persons who must either die or be relieved by the parish, if they were not relieved by their kindred; and yet how few, my God! how few are the instances in which it is found necessary for parish officers to resort to the law on this score! It is a thing that we hardly ever hear of amongst all the thousands of the parishes, and all the millions of the industrious classes; and mind, it is a thing which the parish officers *never neglect*; and which they never neglect, nor the magistrates either, to perform in *the strictest possible manner*. Indeed they sometimes perform it in a manner so strict as to stand in no need of the example of Parson LOWE, or the precepts of CHADWICK, as I now shall show by an instance which I shall lay before your lordship.

At TICEHURST, in Sussex, lives an old man, upwards of eighty, I believe, who had had a son, who died and left behind him three children, two boys and a girl. The mother was dead, too, I believe; but the children stood in need of employment or of parish relief. The boys, and I think the girl too, were constantly employed by the farmers of the parish, but not earning a sufficiency, or rather, not receiving a sufficiency in *the shape of wages* to maintain them, they were got into the *poorbook*; and after a good while, the parish officers brought in a bill to the grandfather of all the disbursements that they had given out of the poor-book to the children; and he, refusing to pay, was summoned before the magistrates, who decided that he should pay. This poor man, who had had nothing but his labour to depend upon all his life, and who had been so industrious, so sober, and so frugal, as to have brought up ten children without going to the parish for assistance in any way whatever, when he told the magistrates that all that he possessed in the world were two miserable tenements, worth fifteen pounds a year, was told that he might *sell those tenements*! and thus be left, between eighty and ninety, to come to the workhouse at last. Things were in this state when the man made his complaint to me. How it ended I do not know, but the case, as far as I have knowledge of it, is enough: and, my lord, when a lord, or a squire, or a dignified parson, comes to cram his relations into the pension-list, why is he not summoned before the magistrates, to show cause why he should not maintain them out of his substance, by sale of his estate if he be otherwise destitute of means? And, again I say, shall we *never* see a day of justice; and while men of great estate are thus swallowing up the earnings of the poor in order to give relief to their relations, shall the poor be thus compelled to maintain their own relations out of the fruit of their own earnings? It is useless to talk about the matter any more; this Poor-law Bill has laid all bare; has ripped up every thing, and has given us but this one choice: JUSTICE to the industrious classes by one means or another.

The law of primogeniture has long been detested by a large part of the people of this country. My constituents proposed to make it a point with me that I should endeavour to cause the abolition of that law, to which proposition I did not assent; because while an abolition of that law would set at nought the succession to the crown, I could see, as I told my constituents, no harm that this law could DO THEM, *if the House of Commons did its duty*. Their opinion was, that it was this law, giving all the estate to one child, and leaving the rest with nothing, which threw that rest, with hungry jaws and naked backs, to be fed and clothed out of the labour of the people; that it tended to create unnecessary offices; military and naval academies; that it gave us two hundred and fifty admirals, and four hundred and fifty generals, when a dozen of each would be more than enough; that it ruined the colonies by heaping on them the sons and the dependants of the great; that it heaped livings in the church on the nobility and their relations, while it left the working clergy to starve, as in the case of your lordship's brother, that I mentioned before in my last letter, who has a great living and a prebend, while there are thousands of parsons, even incumbents, who have not each a hundred pounds a year, and while taxes are sweated out of the people to be given to these poor incumbents. And, in short, that the country was devoured in consequence of the nobility, gentry, and higher clergy, causing their endless litters to be kept in food and raiment, purchased by the earnings of the people.

This was all very true; and my answer was, that if the law of primogeniture could not exist unaccompanied with these things, I would call in the devil to assist me to destroy it, if I could not destroy it without his assistance; but that this was not the fact: the law of primogeniture could exist, and has existed for centuries, without these monstrous encroachments and swallowings existing at the same time. An instance or two in proof will be sufficient. We have now to pay £212,000 a year, as pensions to the widows of officers and their families; but in the year 1792, after the tremendous and bloody American war, when we had to fight with France, Spain, and Holland, at the same time, we had to pay only £9,381 a year. Monstrous difference! Yet the law of primogeniture existed in 1792, as well as it does now. Oh, no! It is not the ancient law of primogeniture that does us the harm; but it is the want of a House of Commons with a resolution that the people shall not have the money taken from them to be given to the aristocracy and their relations; and there must come such a House of Commons, or there *must come something that I will not attempt to describe*!

Thus, my lord, this Scotch *feelosofical* poor-law project sets us to work to rake up every thing; it makes us sift and analyse every claim, every acknowledged right, every title, and as Mr OASTLER[11] says, in a pithy little pamphlet, entitled, '*A Letter to the Editor of the Argus and Demagogue, on the validity of Sir John Ramsden's title to the sums of money he claims for Canal Dues; now, that the game is begun we must inquire into the validity of all property.*' I wish your lordship would read this little pamphlet of Mr OASTLER. I would insert it here, for it should be read by every man in the kingdom; and while I acknowledge myself not bold enough to do this, I beg Mr OASTLER to accept of my best thanks for his most meritorious little pamphlet: he has laid the matter bare; he has shown that it is our right and our duty *now* to *inquire into the nature and origin of property*: *now* to discuss the right to *rent*, as well as the right to *rates*. After expressing his hope, that *correct lists* will be published of those who reprobated the Poor-law Bill, he exclaims, 'What a glorious sight it would have been for England, if, when the Commons sent up to them the Poor-law Bill, the Lords had risen *en masse*, and said, "WE WILL THAT THE LAW OF ENGLAND BE NOT CHANGED"; then would the people of England have hailed them as their fathers and protectors: but, alas!' ... and then he goes on to say, that which I do not choose to repeat, but that which I believe to be true. I myself looked upon it almost as a matter of course, that the Lords would do this; and, therefore, I, seeing the bill had passed the Commons, exclaimed, 'THANK GOD THAT WE HAVE A

HOUSE OF LORDS!' I never could believe that the Lords would give their sanction to this bill. There was every reason in the world against the belief, and no one for it. What! There were the GREY newspapers suggesting the justice and necessity of *reforming the House of Lords*. Unequivocally asserting that an hereditary assembly ought to be allowed no longer to exist. There were others in abundance calling for the ousting of the Bishops from Parliament: there were publications coming forth every day, putting forth what proved to every man of sense, that your order was closely besieged by the money-monster, and that it must rely for protection, if protection it finally had, upon the millions of industrious and unambitious people; and this is the moment you choose, not only for agreeing to this bill in eager haste, but for improving it in point of harshness.

Very much, indeed, are you deceived, my lord, if you imagine, that none but mere labourers; none but what is called 'the poor', feel any interest in this matter. Faith! all men who are not landowners, perceive that they, if they be farmers, tradesmen, mechanics, they all perceive that the bill is not intended to do *them* good. They all know what the bill is intended to do; they all know what they are within the reach of possible poverty and possible want. In vain does your lordship talk about sparing the purses of *those who pay the rates*. Those who pay the rates pay the *rents*. Very kind of you, to be sure, to take the expending of the rates out of the hands of those who pay them *into your own hands*, or into the hands of *commissioners appointed by you*, and removeable at your pleasure; those commissioners having CHADWICK for their secretary too; CHADWICK, who was a runner under the Bishop of London and STURGES BOURNE, and who is now manifestly intended to be the soul of the commissioners.[12] Very kind of you, too, TO GIVE YOURSELVES THE VOTES AT THE VESTRIES, and in case of your absence, enabling you to vote by PROXY! My lord, and do you really imagine, that the farmers and the tradesmen, and all the industrious part of the people, who, in reality, pay all the taxes; do you believe that none but landowners and titled persons can see to the bottom of a scheme like this? If you do believe it, you are the most deceived of all mankind.

I suppose that BROUGHAM will call this bill the 'LAW

OF NATURE'; and I should not wonder if some half-mad, half-drunken, devil, were to step forward and assert, that, the *law of nature* gave you the right to the votes in the vestry, and the voting by proxy. If this be so, I trust in God we shall repeal the 'law of nature', as soon as we meet. Such NATURE as this we have never heard any thing of before.

All this while, it is the poor that are to be *bettered*, by the workhouse dresses, by the big workhouse, fifty miles off, by being left to starve, or submit to degradation, heretofore unheard of. They are to be *bettered* by the system of Parson LOWE!

This is the most shameful pretence of all: the most unblushing of all the instances of impudence on the part of the supporters of this bill: impudent enough to pretend that the *tenants* will be *benefited* by the landlords having the *votes* in the vestries, and voting by proxy! Impudent enough in affecting to believe that it will be a benefit to morals, and tend to promote chastity, to let loose the policemen, the soldiers, the squires' and lords' sons, the whiskered bands of the sister-services, the swarms of footmen, grooms, and coachmen, fed out of the taxes; impudent and profligate enough to pretend that the taking of all these from the prostitutes, and turning them loose with the security of impunity, upon the yet unprostituted part of the young women; quite impudent enough to pretend that this would have a tendency to promote chastity and to correct dissolute morals; but the impudence of all impudence is, to support this bill under the pretence that it would make the lives of the working people *more happy*, when there lie the instructions to the barrister who drew the bill, stating, 'THAT IT IS DESIRABLE TO BRING THE WORKING PEOPLE TO LIVE UPON COARSER FOOD THAN THEY NOW LIVE UPON.' Of all the impudence that the world ever witnessed, the impudence of supporting the bill upon the ground that it will make the working people *better off*, is the greatest.

Perhaps I do the supporters of this bill a wrong, after all. It may be, that they are actuated by motives of *piety*. They know that holy men have asserted, and have proved, that to keep the flesh in a tame state, is necessary sometimes to preserve the purity of the soul, and to ensure its salvation. Hence the fasts and the vigils so sternly exacted by priests of extraordinary piety; and these supporters may possibly think that taking away the bacon and the bread, and by supplying their place by potatoes and sea-weed, will have a tendency to ensure the salvation of the souls; and this motive may possibly have been powerful with the Bishop of London, and with his brothers, the bull-frog farmers of Norfolk, one of whom I saw at NEW YORK, preparing, as I understood, to be *citizenized*, being in search of '*profitable employment for capital*', emigration here being strictly associated with accumulation.

Ah, my lord! Nobody is deceived *now*! The bill was hurried along: there was too much of it for men to understand in so short a space of time: the House of Commons is less to blame than people generally think: the members had no time to read the reports, and no time at all to reflect on them. Not one member out of ten saw the drift of the scheme. Now, every one sees it; and every one sees that, unless it bring down *living* and *wages* to something like the Irish standard, it will fail in producing the effect intended by its projectors, and by a great part of its supporters. What have you to say, my lord, in answer to my positive assertion about the 'C O A R S E R   F O O D'? You must either say, that you believe me to tell a lie; and a wilful lie; and that I told this lie to the face of Lord ALTHORP, who could have contradicted me, and who did not do it: you must believe that this is a lie; you must believe that the instructions to the barrister contained no such words; or you must believe, that it is the intention of the Government to make their commissioners adopt regulations to force this C O A R S E R   F O O D upon the people. You must believe one of these two; the former you *cannot* believe; or, at least, if you can, no man living will *believe that you can*: you must, therefore, believe the latter; that is to say, you must believe, that it is the intention of the Government to make the commissions adopt regulations which shall induce the people of England to live on a C O A R S E R food; it being, of course, agreeable to the 'LAW OF NATURE', that those whose labour causes the victuals, the clothing, the houses, and the drink, to come, should live upon potatoes and sea-weed, while the lazy part of the community have the meat and the drink, and all the good things of this world. You must believe this; and yet you profess that you support the bill because you believe that it will make the working people B E T T E R O F F!

And, now, I have two things to ask of your lordship: first, *in what way are the people to be induced to live upon* C O A R S E R F O O D *than they live upon at present?* and, second, *why it should be desired* to make them live upon coarser food, than they live upon at present? And now, my lord, these are two *little pithy and most interesting questions*: they take us right away into the very heart of the scheme: they show us that the big workhouses, the ugly workhouse dresses, that the separating of man from wife, and both from children; that the vestry *votes* of the *proxies* of the landlords, are by no means mere idle fancies; by no means whims and caprices, not at all theoretical illusions; but that they have *real practical substantial* objects in view, bottomed upon the most solid of all foundations; namely, that of *pounds, shillings*, and *pence*; and of this I am now about to leave no doubt in the mind of any sane man living.

My first question is, in *what way* are the people to be induced to live upon *coarser food?* Be pleased to mind, my lord, that you must believe this to be intended by the bill; because I state to you, that this intention was expressed in the instructions to the barrister who drew the bill; because, I assert this; because, you can see the instructions whenever you please; because, you can contradict me, if you will; because, it was tacitly acknowledged to be true by the Minister in the House of Commons; and, because, neither PIS-ALLER PARKES,[13] nor any of the rest of them, have dared to contradict it, even in that worn-out battered old jade, the old *Morning Chronny*.

Very well, then, you believe it; and now, *how is it to be done?* By *preaching*, my lord? Will your brother quit his venison, hanging up and mortifying ready for his lips in the Close at SALISBURY; and, full of good meat and drink, tell the people at PEWSEY, that, if they have a mind not to go to hell, potatoes and sea-weed are the protection? This will never answer. The people at PEWSEY know all about his eatings and drinkings as well as he does; and they will say, that, if potatoes and sea-weed be so effectual with regard to their souls, he must be a madman to stuff in turkeys and wine and venison himself; or he must be a reprobate, having no sort of regard for his own soul. In short, they will ask, as poor ROBERT MASON[14] did the parson of BULLINGTON [sic], 'What God sent the corn and the meat for'; or why they should live upon potatoes and sea-weed, while he took away all the wheat and the meat of PEWSEY? They will ask, whether the *'law of nature'* formed his mouth for the wheat and the meat, and theirs for the potatoes and sea-weed; and, perhaps, the rubric would have compelled him to read to them just before, a lesson from the Bible, promising to the good and the virtuous, plenty and fatness. He might have read to them how ISAAC blessed his son, not by promising him potatoes and sea-weed; but in these words: 'God give thee of the dew of heaven, and the fatness of the earth, and plenty of corn and wine.' If he happened to read the 28. of PROVERBS to them, he would have told them that God has promised, that, 'he that tilleth the land shall have plenty of bread.' Any of the hundred chapters would answer the same end. He might have read to them that maxim of the apostle, 'That he that will not work, neither shall he eat.' Any of these would do; and what must they, after hearing their priest say, that good living was to be the reward of virtue; what must they think after this, at hearing their priest inculcate the necessity of potatoes and salt, in order to make them favourites with God!

Then this will not do. The Bishop of London might try his hand, and there would be an answer very soon for him. In short, it is so directly against nature, so monstrous a thing, to persuade people that it is for their good to live badly; that it is not to be accomplished except by *compulsion*. The terrors of hell and the hopes of heaven, may produce temporary, volunteer, poor living; but even these terrors and these hopes must fail, if practised for any length of time: that hunger which will 'break through stone walls', is not to be silenced by arguments. It must be *force*, then, of some sort or another; and there is but one species of force that could succeed; and that is, *the keeping of the good food away from the people*; the making of it impossible for them to get their good food into their possession. And *how* is this to be done? What are the means to be made use of to keep the good food out of their possession? Bayonets? No! tread-mills? No! It would require too many *muzzles* put upon their mouths, which the villainous Jews were forbidden to put upon the ox as he trod out the corn? No: for to muzzle one million would require four millions of unmuzzled ones at the least. It would be devilish work, indeed, before the lazy-bone dogs could muzzle the workers. Well, then, it must not be *direct bodily force*; it must be, not by withholding the food, but by WITHHOLDING THE MONEY WITH WHICH THE FOOD IS PURCHASED. Ah! how the light darts out when we just touch this point! How we begin to see all at once to the bottom of the whole thing! And what a strong hand it requires to hold us back from getting at the second question!

The second question is, W H Y ; W H Y is it desirable to induce the labourers to live on coarser food? Your lordship says it is to make them *better off*. Lord ALTHORP said it was *to relieve the farmer*. Your Scotch Mentor had, however, the discretion to tell you, *that it was to save your estates*. However, here we have it out from one and the other. Their *coarser food* is to come from the *lowering of their wages*; and that this is the intention, the main object, the grand purpose, the man that pretends not to believe, is at once the most stupid of creatures, and the lowest and *most cowardly of hypocrites*. Your Scotch Mentor is plain, he avows his object; the bill, he says, is *to save your estates*; and he says, that he himself may become a pauper if this bill do not succeed. Not questioning his steady and sober judgment, I take leave to dissent from his opinion, and to express my firm belief, so help me God! that T H E B I L L is much more likely T O M A K E H I M A P A U P E R , B E F O R E I T B E O V E R , than the want of the bill was likely to make him a pauper. My *wishes* upon the subject are nothing; but my *belief* is, that both your lordship and your Mentor are, beyond all measure, *more likely to become paupers*, W I T H the bill than W I T H O U T *the bill*; and so much for that.

My lord, LORD ALTHORP told us, that this bill would *relieve the farmer*. It seems strange to us if he could relieve the farmer by the bill; that is to say, to cause him to *pay less* in poor-rates, and yet *better the lot of the poor*! But he doubtless had in view *the wages*; and the wages are something. It is the wages which the advocates of coarser food have all along had in view; envying the happy state of the *landlords of Ireland* and the *heritors of Scotland*. Here we come to the ticklish part of the thing. Rents, undeducted from by rates, and very little deducted from by wages. ' R E N T S , ' ' R E N T S , ' ' R E N T S , ' as Lord BYRON exclaims, when justly lashing the landlords of England. Higher rents! Sweeping away the poor-rates, if they could be all swept away at once, would do nothing in this way. Tithes, which would go in an hour, only they *belong to the aristocracy*, for the far greater part, and indeed wholly; so that, having gone the complete round with the rest of the community in abolishing the tithes, they would only be bilking themselves; but even they are nothing compared with the wages throughout the far greater part of England.

Let us look at this matter a litle in detail. Suppose a farm of a hundred acres, at a rent of one pound an acre.

	Annual Rate		£100 0 0
	Poor-rates		27 0 0
	Tithes at 5s an acre		25 0 0
W A G E S	Wheelwright	10 0 0	
	Blacksmith	14 0 0	
	Collar-maker	7 0 0	
	Carpenter	3 0 0	217 0 0
	Bricklayer	3 0 0	
	Labourers	180 0 0	
			369 0 0

There, my lord, that's about it; and you will please to observe, that the tradesmen are to be included amongst those receiving wages; and that their wages must inevitably come down along with the wages of the labourers. I have not included the county-rates, and the greater part of which are expended in prosecutions for the preservation of the game of the aristocracy; but you see what a trifling concern all the rest is compared with the amount of the wages; and so it ought to be, for it is the millions that have to be maintained by the wages, without the labour of whom the land would be worth nothing more than so much moonshine spread over the face of the country; and those who work upon your estate have as good a right to a living out of it as you have to a living out of it; and if I do not *prove it to be better*, it is not by any means, because I cannot produce such proof whenever I like.

Now, then, we see how it is, that the farmer cares so little about rates and tithes, and how much he cares about *rent*; because he knows that if you take off these twenty-seven pounds, and these twenty-five pounds, the landlord would make him pay *fifty-two pounds a year more in rent*; therefore the farmers are all against this bill; and ALTHORP does not make them understand how it will relieve them. They ask, too, (cunning rogues!), why the landlords *should want to have the votes in their vestries*, and to vote by *proxy*, too, when they cannot be present. They ask, with a stare of surprise, why the great gentlemen and all the lords, should want to have *votes* in vestries all at once, and to vote there by proxy!

FARMER. (who rents the above farm): Why should the gentlemen not let us have the *trouble*, as we always have had it?

COBBETT. It is not the *trouble* that they want, farmer, but the *money*.

FARMER. What money? Why we pay the money to the poor; and it is *our own money*.

COBBETT. Yes, just now it is; but they mean to have it by means of this bill.

FARMER. How are they to have it? They won't become paupers, will they?

COBBETT. Not in name, farmer, though many of their families are so in fact. What they mean is, that you should give them the amount of the rates, instead of giving them to the poor.

FARMER. But I shan't though: if I don't give it to the poor, my landlord shan't have it.

COBBETT. He will have it, farmer; for he knows that you now pay twenty-seven pounds a year in poor-rates, and he will clap that sum upon your present rent, or else he will turn you out of your farm.

FARMER. Oh, God d – !

COBBETT. Don't swear: at least, not yet, till you have heard what they propose about the *coarser food* for the labourers.

FARMER (in Surrey). Coarser! what do they want any thing coarser than bacon and bread?

COBBETT. Yes, farmer: what think you of *potatoes* and *sea-weed*?

FARMER. Why that's *Irish* work.

COBBETT. Precisely so; and that is what the Scotch *feelosofical* vagabonds mean. They mean that you should give your labourers sixpence a day instead of two shillings.

FARMER. Why, the labourers would …

COBBETT. Hush! We shall all get into jail if we talk so loud.

FARMER. But what *good* would that do to my landlord now? The men wouldn't work: we couldn't live in our houses: we must all run away out of the country; but if we could bring them to this pass, why we farmers should get the money, and it wouldn't be any good to the landlord.

COBBETT. Sad mistake! Your landlord would soon find that you paid sixpence a day instead of two shillings, and that you paid your tradesmen just about in the same proportion; that in short you saved a hundred and fifty pounds a year in this way, and he would make you pay *him rent three hundred and fifty-four pounds a year*, instead of one hundred pounds a year. You would be a great deal poorer than you are now; your wretched labourers would be without shoes or stockings; their bed would be straw, and nothing but straw; you would be a set of wretched beggarly slaves altogether; and your landlord would drive a coach and six, instead of going in a gig.

I beg leave to assure your lordship, *that the whole scheme is thus seen through all over the kingdom*; and that now, none but natural fools are deceived with regard to it. Lord ALTHORP told us that the scheme was to *relieve the farmer effectually*. It is possible that the above may be an exaggeration of the degree; but clear as daylight it is, that whatever is squeezed out of the belly or bones of the labourer, whether in rates, or in wages, must go into the pocket of the landlord, and not one single farthing of it into the pocket of the farmer. I am sure that it is impossible that your lordship should not now see this. I should be sorry to believe, that you saw it from the beginning; and yet how could you miss seeing it, at the time when you made your reported speech, you having then heard all about the 'coarser food'; you having then heard all the opinions of parson LOWE and COWELL and CHADWICK and the rest of the gang; and you having heard the Lord Chancellor say, that the object of the bill was, *to save your estates*. I am loath to say that I believe that your lordship knew the tendency and object of this bill; yet, as I know you to be a man of sound understanding and clear perception, how am I to come to the conclusion, that you did not perceive its objects and tendency?

But, as to the execution of this project; as to the compelling the labourers of England to live upon potatoes and salt; or sea-weed; as to compelling them to go bare-footed, or bare legged, and to wear dirty shirts, and to go with unwashed hands and faces, from month's end to month's end, my lord **ALTHORP**, with all his anxious desire to reduce the *south* to the manners and living of the *north*, will no more succeed in it than he would in moving the sun from the south to the north; and rather than see him succeed in it; rather than see him succeed in taking one single step in such a progress, I would see a great deal more take place than I shall take the trouble now to describe. He never will succeed in getting on one single step towards that object; and all that will have been accomplished at this long-meditated blow at the rights of the poor, will only have taught the least thinking part of the nation to *look into rights of all sorts*, and to *call in question the claims of property of every description.*

In the midst of all this agitation upon this point, comes the ticklish question of the currency. There must come a discussion, and a general discussion of the *rights of the fundholders*, compared with the rights of the *landowners*; and the Poor-law Bill will have given an appropriate shake to these latter rights, just as these latter are entering upon a contest with the former. For my part, I was always ready to take part with the land against the money-people. *I am no longer so*: I am for whatever I shall deem most likely to restore the working people to the enjoyment of their rights.[15] There has now been a *great change made in the constitution of our country*. The law of **ELIZABETH**, which Hale describes as interwoven with the very constitution of our Government, has now been abrogated in effect. The local governments of the country have been supplanted by one general all-absorbing board, sitting in London, composed of three men, removable at the pleasure of the Government. This is, then, no longer the Government under which I was born: it is a new thing; and my duty now is, to endeavour, by all the legal means in my power, to cause the former Government to be restored. To up-hold the money-people may possibly be the only means of effecting an object so desirable. At any rate, the rights of the poor were as sacred as those of the *land*; and if they can be thus dealt with, I see no reason why I am to give a preference to the rights of the land before the claims of the money-people.

One-pound notes and legal tender will co-operate most harmoniously with the Poor-law Commissioners. Paper-money flourishes exceedingly in a state of things, such as this Poor-law Bill will produce! If the thing had been contrived on purpose; if a set of the cleverest men that ever were born had sitten in council for a whole year to devise the means of making the difficulties of this Government so great, as not to leave it a chance of escape, they could not have contrived any thing to surpass this poor-law project, which in its very nature, *un-fixes the minds of all men with regard to the rights of property*; which rouses all the indignant, all the angry feelings of the millions of the community; and directs those feelings against those *orders which depend wholly on extraneous support*; which possess a showy power, but which have at bottom no power at all, if once it be disputed by the millions.

I am of opinion that commotions without end will inevitably be produced by this Bill.[16] I will not doubt that there is wisdom enough left in the two Houses of Parliament to repeal it as soon as possible. I am thoroughly convinced that that is the only safe course. 'Try it,' as your lordship said, *'for a short period.'* Short period! I know not what is meant by a *short period*, and about *trial*. How is it to be *tried*, until the big workhouses shall be built? In short, how is it to be *tried*, till it has done all the mischief? Repealed, I am sure, it will be; or, if it be not, I am sure, that that will happen, which, as I said before, I shall not attempt to describe.

I have one more letter to address to your lordship on this subject. In that letter I shall inquire of you, upon what is founded the right of the state to compel men to come out to serve *in the militia*; and shall ask BROUGHAM and Mother MARTINEAU,[17] whether the 'LAW OF NATURE' imposes this duty upon them for the protection of a land in which they are *now* asserted to have *no share*. And in conclusion, I shall endeavour to give a little sketch of the history of the progress of the aristocracy in their *encroachments on the rights of the industrial classes*, and in their measures for changing the fundamental laws of the country; and I do hope, that while I thus zealously and laboriously discharge MY duty, those who possess a friendship for the cause of the people, and for the principles which I am here maintaining, will do their utmost to *cause these letters to be circulated in every part of the kingdom*. Your lordship has acted *your* part. I look upon you as at *the head* of those who have caused this bill to be passed. I am sorry to have to say this; but I should be ashamed, not to say it, and not to declare my belief in the fact, and my determination to oppose you by all the lawful means in my power.

I am,
Your lordship's most obedient
And most humble servant,
WM. COBBETT.

NOTES

[1] Cobbett had visited Scotland two years earlier, publishing his observations in his *Tour in Scotland and in the Four Northern Counties of England*.

[2] Some eight miles north of Waterford.

[3] The 'accursed' and 'ever-damned' potato. Planted in the Irish cottager's tiny patch, the sum of all his food, the innocent potato was always a fateful and sometimes a death-bearing crop. Cobbett did occasionally recognize other uses for the 'base' root, in other conditions. On the way to Scotland he had explained: 'This root is raised in Northumberland and Durham, to be used merely as *garden-stuff*; and, used in that way, it is very good; the contrary of which I never thought, much less did I ever say it. It is the using of it as a *substitute* for bread and for meat, that I have deprecated; and, when the Irish poet, Dr Drennan, called it "the lazy root and the root of misery", he gave it its true character.'

[4] Andrew Jackson.

[5] It was said of the third Earl of Radnor that he was almost the only political friend with whom Cobbett never quarrelled; but they disagreed over the Poor Law Bill.

[6] Brougham.

[7] Thomas Spence: a leading English Jacobin, member of the London Corresponding Society, revolutionary republican and early defender of women's rights and sexual liberation, was imprisoned many times before his death in 1814. He had declared it necessary to overturn 'not only personal and hereditary lordship, but the cause of them which is private property'. After Waterloo, Spencean societies flourished for a time among the artisans and discharged soldiers.

[8] Like Spence, Thomas Evans was a republican and agrarian socialist, who had supported the United Irishmen and Volunteers before and during the 'Ninety-Eight'. Seeking refuge in France he was, as Paine had been, held in prison for his trouble. arrested under the Six Acts in 1817, he was imprisoned without trial for a year. Cobbett seems to have admired Evans' audacity in describing all land in England and Ireland as 'the people's common farm'.

[9] Edwin ('Penny-a-line') Chadwick, a zealous administrator of the new Poor Law Act, had calculated the minimum diet to keep a work-house inmate strong enough for work, and had circulated his calculations to all Boards of Guardians.

[10] It was during the writing of this letter that Cobbett seems to have

decided to write the *Legacy to Labourers*. He completed the book on his return visit to Dublin and at Cockburn's house at Shangana.

[11] Richard Oastler, leading campaigner against child-labour in the factories. In 1832, led the pilgrimage to York of the 'factory slaves'.

[12] Sturges Bourne: one of Cobbett's 'gallon-loaf' men, Benthamite and member of the Poor Law Commission of 1832. Two years earlier, as chairman of the Hampshire Quarter Sessions, had sentenced farm-workers to transportation during the crushing of the labourers' revolt.

[13] Parkes was an associate of Brougham, in the Society for the Diffusion of Useful Knowledge.

[14] Robert and Joseph Mason were brother farm-workers at Bullington, Hampshire; and readers of Cobbett's *Register*. Joseph, the elder, had once carried by hand a petition of Cobbett's composition to the king, at Brighton. On charges (almost certainly frame-ups in the panicky time of the fire-settings) of demanding shillings with menaces, they were sentenced in 1830 to transportation for life. Cobbett came to the aid of their distressed mother by planting with Cobbett's-corn enough ground for her to keep a pig every year. In 1832 he gave a grand dinner at Sutton Scotney in honour of her sons and other victims of such judges as Parke, Alderson and Vaughan.

[15] It is true that Cobbett had not previously thrown landowners into the same pen with bankers and industrialists as common enemies of the working people.

[16] The Chartist 1840s were to provide the first of such commotions.

[17] Harriet Martineau, historian, had favoured the Irish cause. Author of *The History of England During the Thirty Years Peace 1816-1848*, London 1849.

CHAPTER 5

Political Register, 25 October 1834.

To Charles Marshall, Labourer, Letter No.V

*Normandy Tithing, Parish of Ash,
Farnham, Surrey.*

Cork, 17 October 1834.
MARSHALL,

Since the date of my last letter I have been in the City of Kilkenny, and have, in a long speech, urged the justice and necessity of poor-laws, such as we have always had in England. In another letter, when I get more time, I will tell you how our poor-laws came to be, and I will prove to you, that, in case of need, you have *as clear a right to relief out of my farm, as I have to my cows or my corn*, or as Mr Woodruff has to the land or the timber. Our rights are very clear; but not more clear than *yours* are. At present I must speak to you of some little part of what I have recently seen and heard. When I get back to Normandy, I shall make a book, relating to every thing about this country.

From Kilkenny, I came to Clonmell, the capital of the county of Tipperary, which is deemed one of the finest in Ireland. The land, in this distance of about 35 English miles, is very fine, except in a few places. But, only four *turnip fields* all the way. The harvest was here *all* got in. But, the grass! The fine grass fields covered with herds of fine cattle; fine oxen; fine cows; fine sheep; all seemed fat; and to every miserable thing *called a house*, a fine hog, so white, clean, and fat, so unlike the poor souls who had reared it up and fatted it, and who were destined never to taste one morsel of it; no, not so much as the offal.

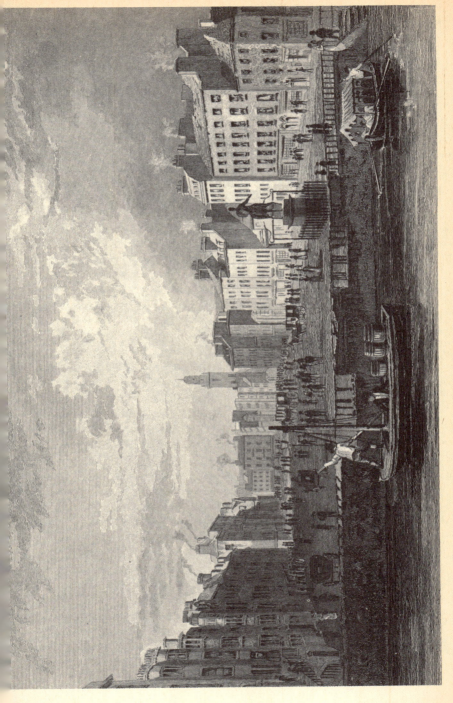

Grand Parade, Cork

At the town of CLONMELL, I went to see one of the places full where they kill every year for this purpose, about *sixty thousand hogs*, weighing from *eight score*, to *twenty score*. Every ounce of this meat is sent out of Ireland, while the poor half-naked creatures, who raise it with such care, are compelled to live on the *lumpers*, which are such bad potatoes, that the hogs will not thrive on them, and will not touch them, if they can get other potatoes. The *rooks*, which eat the good potatoes, will not eat these, though they be starving. And, yet, this is the stuff that the working people are fed on. There are about *eighty thousand firkins of butter*, and, perhaps, *a hundred thousand quarters of wheat*, and more of *oats*, sent away out of this one town; while those who raise it all by their labour, live upon *lumpers!* 'How,' you will ask, 'are the millions of working people made to submit to this?' I will tell you, when I get back to the Parliament House, or to a county meeting at Guildford. It will be better to say it *there*, than here!

From CLONMELL we came to FERMOY, on Saturday, the 11. instant. Fine land; a fine country; flocks of turkeys all along the way; cattle, sheep, hogs, as before; and the people, the working people, equally miserable as before. Here is a fine view, and beautiful meadows, compared to which the meadows at Farnham are not worth naming. From one side of this valley there rises up a long and most beautiful chain (miles in length) of gently sloping hills, and on those hills and on their sides, corn-fields and grass-fields are interspersed with woods and groves. But, standing on the bridge, and reviewing this scene, my *eyes were blasted* by the sight of three B A R R A C K S for *foot, horse*, and *artillery*; buildings surpassing in extent all the palaces that I ever saw; elegant and costly as palaces; buildings containing, they say, three thousand windows; and capable of lodging forty thousand men! 'Good God!' say you; 'what can all this B E F O R ?' I will tell you, MARSHALL, when I get to the county meeting at GUILDFORD, to•which you must all come. 'But,' you will say, 'do these *soldiers* live upon *lumpers* too?' MARSHALL, do not ask *me* any more questions about this matter. Ask Mr DEAN: he can tell you all about it.

But, now, MARSHALL, I am coming *nearer home*; and I beg you all to pay great attention to what I am going to say. You will think it strange, that all this food should be sent out of the country, and that the people should *get nothing back* for it. You will think, that we must send them *clothes* and *household goods* and *tea* and *sugar* and *soap* in return for the hogs and other things. To the *rich* we do; and to the *barracks*; but, the millions of working people have only rags for parts of their bodies, and they have neither goods nor tea nor sugar nor plate nor knife nor fork nor tea-kettle nor cup nor saucer.

The case is this: the owners of all the great estates *live in England or in France or in Italy*. The *rents are sent to them*; and, as there are *no poor-rates*, they get all the produce of the land from the miserable farmer, except just enough to keep him alive. They *spend these rents out of Ireland*; so that the working people here, who might eat meat three times a day, are compelled to live upon *lumpers*! And, be you assured, that this would be the lot of the English working people, if the Scotch vagabonds could succeed in their projects for sweeping away our poor-laws. If that were done, the English farmers would be a set of beggarly slaves, the landlords would take so much from them, that they would be able to give the labourers not more than 6d a day, and you would all be living in hovels without chimneys, and be eating with the pigs, that you would be rearing and fatting for somebody else to eat! I would rather see you all perish, and perish along with you!

But, MARSHALL, mind me well. You know, that, at PEPPERHARROW (only about four miles from your cottage) there lives L O R D M I D D L E T O N . You know that he was a long while Lord-Lieutenant of our county. Now, MARSHALL, H E is one of the G R E A T L A N D O W N E R S O F I R E L A N D . His real name is B R O D E R I C K . He is the owner of a *town*, called *Middleton*, half as big as Guildford. He is the owner of the lands for many miles round, and, it is supposed, that he draws, *yearly, from twenty-five to thirty thousand pounds from this estate*!

I came here to see things with my own eyes; and, I have, *to-day*, been to see this B R O D E R I C K ' S estate, which begins at about sixteen miles from this City of Cork; and the land of this sixteen miles, taking in two miles on each side of the road, the finest that you can possibly imagine. Ah! but, how did I find the *working people* upon the land of this BRODERICK? That is the question for you to ask, and for me to answer.

I went to a sort of HAMLET near to the town of Middleton.

It contained about 40 or 50 hovels. I went into several of them, and took down the names of the occupiers. They all consisted of mud-walls, with a covering of rafters and straw. None of them so good as the place where you keep your little horse. I took a particular account of the first that I went into. It was 21 feet long and 9 feet wide. The floor, the bare ground. No fire-place, no chimney, the fire (made of potato-haulm) made on one side against the wall, and the smoke going out of a hole in the roof. No table, no chair; I sat to write upon a block of wood. Some stones for seats. No goods but *a pot*, and a shallow tub, for the pig and the family both to eat out of. There was one window, 9 inches by 5, and the glass broken half out. There was a mud-wall about 4 feet high to separate off the end of the shed for the family to sleep, lest the hog should kill and eat the little children when the father and mother were both out, and when the hog was shut in; and it happened some time ago that a poor mother, being ill on her straw, unable to move, and having her baby dead beside her, *had its head eaten off by a hog before her own eyes*! No bed: no mattress: some large flat stones, to keep the bodies from the damp ground; some dirty straw and a bundle of rags were all the bedding. The man's name was OWEN GUMBLETON. *Five small children*; the mother, about thirty, naturally handsome, but worn into half-ugliness by hunger and filth; she had no shoes or stockings, no shift, a mere rag over her body and down to her knees. The man B U I L T T H I S P L A C E H I M S E L F, and yet he has to pay *a pound a year* for it with perhaps a rod of ground! Others, 25s a year. *All built their own hovels*, and yet have to pay their rent. All the hogs were in the hovels today, it being coldish and squally; and then, you know, hogs like cover. GUMBLETON's hog was lying in the room; and in another hovel there was a fine large hog that had taken his bed close by the fire. There is a nasty dunghill (no privy) to each hovel. The dung that the hog makes *in the hovel* is carefully put into a heap by itself, as being the most precious. This dung and the pig are the main things to raise the rent and to get fuel with. The poor creatures sometimes *keep the dung in the hovel*, when their hard-hearted tyrants will not suffer them to let it be at the door! So there they are, in a far worse state, MARSHALL, than any hog that you ever had in your life.

LORD MIDDLETON may say, that HE is not the *landlord* of

these wretched people. Ah! but his *tenant*, his *middleman*, is their landlord, and LORD MIDDLETON gets the *more rent from him*, by enabling him to let these holes in this manner. If I were to give Mr DEAN a shilling a week to squeeze you down to twelve shillings a week, who would you think was most to blame, me or Mr Dean?

Now, MARSHALL, pray remember, that this horrible state of things never could take place if the Irish people had those poor-laws, which the Scotch VAGABONDS would advise the Parliament to take from us. For then T H E L A W would compel those who have the estates to pay sufficiently those without whose labour the land is worth nothing at all.

And even *without poor-rates*, the people never could have been brought to this pass without the ever-damned *potatoes*! People C A N keep life in them by the means of this nasty, filthy, hog-feed; and the tyrants make them do it, and have thus reduced them to the state of hogs, and worse than that of hogs.

I repeat to you, therefore, that if any person bring a potato into my house, for any purpose whatever, Mr DEAN is hereby authorized and directed to discharge that person. And, MARSHALL, while I will give you, or any man, and all the men, *in the tithing*, the finest cabbage, carrot, parsnip, beet, and any other seed, and my corn to plant, I will *never again give constant employment to any man* in whose garden I shall see potatoes planted.[1] I have no right to dictate to you what you shall plant, but I have a right to employ my money as I please, and it is both my pleasure and my duty to discourage in every way that I can the cultivation of this damned root, being convinced that it has done more harm to mankind than the sword and the pestilence united.

I am very much pleased to hear from Mr DEAN that you are all sober and dutiful, and that you have made the farm so clean; and hoping that all of you and your wives, children and relations, are well, I am,

Your master and friend,
WM. COBBETT.

Political Register, 25 October 1834.

Mr Cobbett's Reply to the Industrious and Labouring Classes of the City of Cork

Gentlemen, – That any class of persons, in a city, so famed for good sense, public spirit, and political discernment; that any class of persons, in a city, which has chosen to represent it in Parliament that honourable Member who manfully took the lead amongst you on this occasion; that I should be honoured with an address of approbation from any class of persons in such a city; but, that such an address should come to me from the industrious and labouring classes of such a city, is an honour indeed.

Gentlemen, begging you to be assured, that I am fully sensible of the value of this mark of your approbation; participating with you in the very faint hope, that the men now in power may do something to rescue you from the state of ruin and dilapidation of trade, commerce, and manufactures, into which you have been plunged by their system of monopolizing and centralizing, which system, if unchecked, seems likely at last, to cause even law making to be carried on by machinery, moved by steam; trusting that your whole country will seek for redress of your wrongs, not in supplication to the wrong-doers, but in the wise and resolute exercise of the power which Ireland now has of choosing men to go to the Parliament, and there demand justice in her name, it being impossible for me to believe, that any wrong can remain existing, with a hundred able and resolute men to demand and insist upon redress;[2] having thus shortly, but most respectfully expressed to you my sentiments as to those matters, suffer me to beseech your particular attention to two of the topics alluded to in your highly valued address; namely, the presumptuous pretensions of the aristocracy, and the nature and effects of what is called the National Debt; with regard to which I beg leave to state:

That as to the presumptuous pretensions of the aristocracy, it will be my duty, in the proper time and place, to inquire fully and in due form, how they came, not by their ribbons and coronets, but by their power; and by the means of upholding that power; to inquire what portion of their immense possessions has had its source in services rendered to the state, and what portion has sprung from other sources; to inquire for what and in what degree they are entitled to the enjoyment of public power, and of respect and veneration from those who live under that power; to inquire in short, and to inquire legally and methodically, who they are, whence they sprung, what they have done for us, in order that we may duly estimate their value, and that we may, in obedience to the precepts of Holy Writ, cheerfully render honour to whom honour is due.

That, with regard to that prodigious and portentous phenomenon in the political region, curiously enough called the nation's debt, while everything purchased with money is called the King's, principles recently proclaimed, and measures recently adopted and pursued, clearly exonerate you and me, gentlemen, from all share in the duty of discharging that debt, and this will, I trust, clearly appear from these plain and undeniable propositions:-

1. That, as was held in the memorable petition of the county of Norfolk,[3] all unmerited pensions, sinecures, grants, allowances and public pay of every sort, ought to cease; and that the Crown Lands, and a large part of the public property, called church property, ought to be applied to public uses, before one farthing ought to be deducted from the interest of the debt.

2. That those unjust exactions having ceased, and that application having been made, an equitable adjustment ought to be adopted; that the interest of the debt ought to be justly reduced; and a just liquidation, or just payment of interest, ought to take place.

3. That the means of this liquidation, or payment of interest, ought to come out of the general taxes of the country, laid fairly upon all property, personal as well as real; upon the fruits of industry, as well as upon the land itself; because, though, the debt was evidently and avowedly contracted for the defence of the land; still, as the poor-laws gave the whole of the people a right, in case of need, to come to the land and demand a share of its produce, to defend the land was, in fact, to defend their right to that share; and, therefore, and only

therefore, they were, in conscience, and in accordance with the law of the land, bound to contribute from the fruit of their labour, towards the just liquidation, or towards the payment of just interest of the debt.

4. That now, however, all is changed! That an act has been passed, which abrogates the poor-laws; that the Lord High chancellor proposed this act upon the express ground, that the people have no share whatever to any share of the rent, or fruit of the land, though, to have relief therefrom, is necessary to save their lives; that, in many cases, the people have upon this principle, been driven off the land, as having no right to be upon it, though born upon it; and that in consequence of such driving off, 'vast numbers of them have perished in want'.

5. That, therefore, in a debt, contracted for the purpose of defending the land, the people, who own no land, can have no share; and that they ought not to be called upon to pay in any way whatsoever, out of the fruits of their labour, any portion of either the principal, or the interest of such debt.

6. That the fruits of the labour of the people, being thus wholly released from all contracts and obligations appertaining to the debt, the debt clearly becomes a mortgage, a real, a bona fide, a tangible mortgage on the estates of those, who borrowed, or who gave their assent to the borrowing of the money, including (with the nation's consent) those parcels of public property, called crown and church property; and that, as to the mode of satisfying this mortgage by making those estates legally available for a purpose so manifestly consonant with equity and honesty, the lenders, or stock-holders, may, I trust, safely rely on the sound sense and the justice of the people, and on the wisdom, the 'good faith' and the 'vigour' of a reformed Parliament.

Political Register, 25 October 1834.

To the Earl of Radnor

*On his reported speech in the House of Lords,
on the 21 July, on the Poor-law Scheme.*

Charleville, 18 October 1834.

MY LORD,

   I have this day seen a long train of most miserable though laborious, people, living worse than hogs, in places not so good as the pig-sties of our labourers; working hard *for 6d a day*, and many of them with a wife and five or six or more children to keep. This is what the P O O R - L A W   B I L L, 'amendment' bill, M U S T, if it be forced into execution, produce in England! Your lordship's speech tells us, that you wished to *relieve the rate-payers*, amongst whom you must have included *the farmers*. Now then, I have just got on the spot the *names of thirty-one farmers*, and farmers of *good land* too; amongst the whole of whose families (consisting of 227 persons) *six pigs* have been killed during the last year; and one of the six killed to save it from dying; and who have not tasted a morsel of meat of any other sort, and *not one morsel of bread* during the whole year! This is the sort of R E L I E F that you and Mother Martineau and Brougham and Chadwick and your favourite Parson Lowe would give to the *farmers of England*! This is the life of *farmers who know nothing of poor-rates*! This is the state to which the damnable Scotch quacks would reduce England. Ah! they are stopped! The half-drunk and half-mad wretches may be led about and palmed upon the people by half-silly and whole greedy fools of land-owners, but they will not succeed: they will become objects of public scorn greater than any of God's creatures, save and except their at once imbecile and greedy patrons. – So much as a sort of digression; and I now proceed to my *fifth letter*, with which I conclude a series of letters, by the means of which, and of which alone, Brougham and you and Mother Martineau will be remembered this day ten years ...

   MY LORD, – It is a curious thing that while all *rights* are denied to the poorer classes there is no want of disposition on the part of the aristocracy to exact *duties* from them. Amongst other duties is that of *military service*, and a submission to military law, and a liability to be *flogged* for disobedience of that law, and so liable in virtue of judgments pronounced, *not by a jury and judge*, but by persons set over them by the King, and by his sole authority, and dependent, even for their food, on his *royal* breath.

And now, my lord, according to what principle of our constitution, or of any constitution, is this a *duty* which the people owe to the State, or Government? On what ground is it that you call upon a working man, to whom you deny any claim of any sort upon the land; on what ground is it that you call on him, he being able-bodied; on what *ground* is it that you call on this able-bodied man to come forth and defend your estate, and your mansion, and all that you have belonging to you? Upon what *ground* is it that you call on him to quit his house; his aged, and perhaps helpless, parents and perhaps his wife and a troop of little helpless children?

The reasonable and legal ground is, that his services are absolutely necessary to the upholding of the laws against rebels in arms, or ready to take arms; or absolutely necessary to the defence of the country against foreign foes. And why should he thus be called upon to assume the ridiculous and hated military garb; to wield the bayonet instead of the spade or the reap-hook? Why should he be called upon thus, to be compelled to withdraw himself from the protection of the ordinary laws of his country, and to subject himself to the punishment of imprisonment, flogging, or to that of death itself, without trial by jury? On what ground is it that you thus call upon him? I wish to God that I could have your answer; that, however, I never shall have, either from your lordship or any other man of your order. You cannot answer without passing sentence on the principles of all those who have advocated this Poor-law Bill; or without asserting boldly at once, that the rest of the community were made by God *for the mere use of the aristocracy*. This is what you will not assert, though it would be the shortest and most satisfactory answer. Therefore, seeing that you will not answer at all I will make an answer for you.

Upon the supposition, for argument's sake, which I admit

only for the purpose of the argument, that men should be treated as they are now treated, when they are called out to serve in the militia; supposing this, merely for the sake of the argument, I allow that the law is just, which compels every able-bodied man to come forth in arms, if it be necessary, to aid and assist in upholding the laws against rebellious attacks; and in doing the same, to defend the country against foreign foes. I agree that this is right. And why is it right? Why should the working man, who owns neither house nor land, and who has nothing to eat, drink, or wear, but that which comes out of his labour, why should he, except in his quality of slave of the aristocracy, be compelled to quit his home, leave his parents, wife, and children; assume the military garb; take an oath which binds him to submit to be imprisoned, flogged, or put to death, without trial by jury; why should this be; why should he be compelled to do this, seeing that no rebellion, no invasion, no change of rulers, could possibly take from him that capacity to labour, which he possesses in his own body? The answer to this is, or rather *was*, that though he possessed neither house nor land, he in reality *possesses a share in both*. Before those spoliations by which the aristocracy took away his share in the tithes, his portion was like that which the working Israelite had in participating with the Levite; since that spoliation took place, his share has been awarded to him by the 43rd of ELIZABETH, which appoints not only the proportion of the share, but the manner in which he is to receive it: in short it provides for him a security for a subsistence, in case he cannot obtain that subsistence by his own strength. He has a share, then, in the houses and the land, compulsory contributions from which are to give him this security; he has an interest, and a deep interest, in upholding the laws, this provision for him being interwoven, as Judge Hale says, with our very constitution: he has an interest in upholding these laws and this government, against rebels, because those rebels might abolish this law, and take from him this security, take from him this his share of the houses and the land, which the law gives him. He has an interest in repelling an invader, in keeping out a conqueror, because a conquest of the country might make him worse off, seeing that the conqueror might abolish the law, which makes the land furnish him with protection against want.[4] For these reasons his interest, his safety, the safety of his parents, his family and his kindred, impel him to come forth and to serve in the militia. That being the mode of performing his duty, which the law has pointed out.

But, if the law of ELIZABETH be abrogated, in fact, though not in name: if MALTHUS tell him, that he has no claims upon society (that is to say, upon the houses and the land) for the smallest portion of relief, even in the time of his utmost need; if Malthus tell him this; if the Lord Chancellor tell him, that all the laws which provide for his security in case of want, are *bad laws*, and ought to be abolished; if the law be actually passed, framed upon instructions which say, 'that it is desirable that he should be induced to *live upon coarser food* than he now lives upon'; if your lordship support this bill upon these principles, and with these views, proclaiming your approbation of a system, which is to *make the obtaining of relief as irksome as possible*; which is to drag him, in case of hard necessities arriving, to a big distant work-house, there to have a workhouse dress put upon him; to be separated from his wife, and their children from both, and kept in that state of separation; to be kept at hard labour; to have his little goods taken from him; to be forbidden, even in case of sickness and death, to see parents, friends, or relations; if these be the terms on which you are to give him relief, it is clear that you deny that he has any rights at all to relief in any degree; and, indeed, this denial was flatly made by the Scotchman whose motion in favour of the bill you supported; and this being the case, what becomes of the grounds on which you call him out to serve in the militia to defend your estate? Does the '*law of nature*' furnish you with these grounds? Ah, my lord! first burn the Bible, then assert that they have no share whatsoever in the ownership of fruits of the land; then assert that you have the right to cause your estate to lie uncultivated and unpastured; then assert that you have a right to cause all the people of COLESHILL to die with hunger, or to perish with cold; then assert that God has given you a right; that it is agreeable to his laws, that you should, when you want them, compel them to come out, and leave their fathers and mothers and families, and to submit to be punished, in the most horrible manner, without trial by jury, and finally, to risk their lives in defence of your land at Coleshill: assert all this, and then find, if you can, that any thing so impudent and so insolent, and at the same time so consummately stupid, ever before proceeded from the lips of any human being quite drunk and quite mad, instead of half-drunk and half-mad!

Do I impute this impudence, insolence, and stupidity to you? By no means: none of these terms belong to conduct deliberately emanating from your own mind; but I do impute them to those on whose opinions and assertions, you have unfortunately been led to give your support to this measure. I am very sure, that your lordship has been grossly deceived: I am very sure that your view into the matter has only been skin deep: I am very sure of this, because the very first *'law of nature'*, SELF-PRESERVATION, would have prevented you from stirring up the question of *your rights* as a landowner. Do you perceive, my lord, the monstrous extent to which your denial of the rights of the poor would carry you, with regard to your own unquestioned professions? If your principles be sound, the landowners, a mere handful of men; who never do any work, have a right T O   C A U S E   T O   S T A R V E   A L L   T H E R E S T O F   T H E C O M M U N I T Y. Let us take yourself, for instance. Have you a right to cause the whole parish of Coleshill; I believe the whole parish belongs to yourself; and I know what a blessing it is to the poor people of that parish of which you are the possessor: have you a right, I say, to cause all the land in the parish of Coleshill to be uncultivated and unpastured, and to turn all the people out of the houses, and to knock the houses down? Let no one tell me, that it is not possible that you should not shudder at the thought of doing such a thing. I know that very well, but that has nothing to do with my question: my question is, have you a R I G H T to commit this abominable and tyrannical act? Using the word *RIGHT* in the sense in which BROUGHAM made use of it, and in which you adopted its use, you have a *right* to do it; for the law suffers you to do what you please with your houses and your land. But the same law says, or did two months ago, that you shall not play this odious and savage tyrant to the starvation and the perishing of the people of Coleshill, for the law compelled you, to furnish the people of Coleshill with houseroom, food, raiment, and fuel, fitting for them in their own native parish.

Take away this law (and it is now nearly taken away), and

then you have a right to starve, or cause to perish, the people of the parish of Coleshill! Nonsense to tell me that you *would not* do it; for I know that you would not if you could, and that you could not, if you would; what I say is, that the principles upon which you supported this bill are tantamount to the claim of right, on your part, to cause to starve and to perish the people of the parish of Coleshill; and of course, those same principles give the same right to every other landowner in the kingdom; and thus this vaunted constitution is at last come to this point, that a handful of men called *landowners*, have a right, if they be so minded, to cause all the millions of the community to die with hunger, or to perish with cold!

Monstrous principles! Worthy of the hungry Scotch place-hunters; worthy of prostituted writers and reporters; worthy of clerical hypocrites, who, while they utter these abominations, wheeze as if with the asthma, from the fat with which their carcasses are filled by the toil of those, to cause whom to starve, or to perish with cold, they insist upon the landowner's right. Monstrous principles, if advocated by any man: ten thousand times more monstrous when advocated by a man like you!

'I do not advocate such principles', your lordship will say. And I have just told you that you have been deceived, and that you have not seen the extent to which your principles would go. You do advocate these principles, in your support of this bill, after the speech of BROUGHAM, boldly proclaiming (he knew the company that he was in), that the poor had *no right to relief*: that they had no right whatever to a share in the produce of the land; and that the laws were bad, and ought to be done away with, that provided for relief even for the *aged and infirm*.

The principles which I have just illustrated in the supposed case of Coleshill, form the basis of this bill. You must assert that you have a right to do with Coleshill that which I have described: you must maintain, and boldly maintain, your right to starve and cause to perish, the people of Coleshill; or you must allow, that your right to your property is *limited*: that it is not *absolute*: that you have not created it: that you do not hold it in a grant directly from God: that you must allow further that, if the right be not absolute; that if you be not the sole and absolute owner, *some other party shares in the ownership*. This upsets the whole of your principles: it is not *yours* that the poor claim: it is *theirs*, and, they claim it in virtue of laws; in virtue of rights existing, ten centuries before the first of your recorded ancestors was born. To persons who held the principles, or whom he thought likely to act upon the principles, on which you have advocated this bill, ST AMBROSE (as quoted by Puffendorff) says, 'It is *the bread of the hungry* which you *detain*: it is the raiment of the naked which you lock up'; it is not *yours*, my lord, it is *theirs*; and our greatest lawyers tell us, that if you with-hold it, they have a right to take it.[5]

Nothing is so common as to hear, amongst the brutal bull-frogs; amongst the greedy fellows, who do not consider how much of their own safety they owe to the poor-law of ELIZABETH; nothing is so common, as to hear from such men, observations of this sort: 'Why am I to give my money to support people who do nothing for me? why am I to be taxed to keep other people's children from starving? what right have other people that call themselves poor, to take a part of my property from me?' And I heard these very remarks one day, and not very long ago, and in a place that I will not name at present, from a purse-proud fellow bursting with fat, who owes every penny that he possesses in the world; he owes the means of showing his head in the place where I saw him, wholly and solely *to the toil of hard-working men*, from whose sweat, from whose unrequited labour, he has drawn together all that he possesses, even to the shirt upon his fat back, and to the handkerchief that encircles his bull-like neck. What, my lord, is such a reptile, when he has bought out some lord, by money accumulated in this way, who has thus successfully practised the system of *accumulation, concentration*, and *centralization*; is such a wretch to look upon himself in the light of a *Creator* of the earth; or as a grantee from God, if he believes that there is any God? These notions are all false: the property that the poor take is *theirs*; it is *their share*; and there is less reason, and far less reason, to deny them their share, than to deny the rent-charger, or the mortgagee, his share; a great deal better claim have the poor, than either he who has a rent-charge or a mortgage; their right being prescriptive, and making a part of the constitution of the land; his right being founded on mere modern individual convention.

Yet, nothing so common as the notions which I have just described; notions that have gained ground only because they were supposed to be too monstrous to be produced as a foundation of legislative action. But, having now been pushed into practice; having now, by this bill, and especially by your having advocated it, been forced upon us as a subject for discussion; we give them a serious encounter: we show their monstrousness: we retaliate upon those who made them, and we shall make it happy for the landowners, if we induce them to *retract*, while yet there be time; to retrace their steps, before it be too late; to seek peace while it may yet be found; to repeal this Poor-law Bill; we shall make it happy for them, if we succeed in this, and put a stop to the inquiry, on the part of the millions, as to *who it is that has the best right to the land*, who are the parties to whom God and the law of the land have allotted the fruits of it, and what is the share which those sacred laws have allotted to each party? Alas! my lord! how often has it happened in this world; how often does it now every day happen, that greedy men, by endeavouring to with-hold unjustly a small part of their possessions from others, are repaid for their greediness by losing the whole; and how almost invariably has it happened, and does it happen, that when, by acts of injustice, long repeated and persevered in, the millions are goaded on to the righting of themselves, they *terminate their work by repaying injustice in kind*! It is useless to say, that one should deplore this; we may as well say that winter is deplorable, or that thunder and lightning are frightful: they are things over which we have no control; our *wishes* on such a subject are as vain as would be those of the dwarf who would wish to be six feet high.

It is surprising that your lordship, as well as all the other advocates of the bill, should have placed implicit reliance on the opinions of the poor-law fellows; the brace of bishops, Sturges Bourne, Senior, and the rest of the newspaper *reporters*; very strange that you should have relied upon their opinions, and pay no attention at all to the evidence which they collected; that evidence containing the opinions of gentlemen, noblemen, magistrates, clergy, experienced farmers, and parish officers, which opinions, taken as a mass, are directly in the teeth of the opinions and recommendations of the poor-law fellows. You yourself prefer the opinions of these hired fellows even *to your own opinions, as stated in your evidence*. That a man of such understanding and integrity should be thus quack-ridden by bawling hare-brained creatures; that a man of princely estate, and of interests so great, depending on the peace of the country, and the good-will of the working people, always so ready to be grateful, and so cheerfully obedient to their superiors in wealth and rank; that such a man should be quack-ridden to this extent, and by such creatures, too, would be absolutely incredible were the fact not, unhappily, put beyond the possibility of doubt. What! not think your own opinions better than those of these notoriously hired people; notorious adventurers, too, from the very top to the very bottom! Not prefer even your own opinion to theirs, when, too, you see your opinion backed by that of all the noblemen, gentlemen, magistrates, and sensible persons, to whom this impudent crew applied for information!

If your lordship had paid attention to the *evidence*, you would have found, that all those who had to pay the poor-rates, with very few exceptions, deemed them indispensable to the safety of their property. One of the witnesses, a great farmer, being asked by one of the poor-law runners, whether the poor, if the law were not altered, would not *swallow up the whole of his property*; whether he would not be ruined by the rates? 'Ruined by the rates,' said he, 'the rates take away all my property? *The rates are the security of my property*; for the poor people must have a living; and if they did not have it given them, *they must and they would take it*!' A parson magistrate of Bedfordshire, the Revd Henry Brook Mountain, rector of Blunham, being asked whether the poor-rates had made the farmers poorer, answered: 'The farmers are aware that the burden of the poor-rates does not at all affect *them*: I T I S A R E N T P A I D *to the parish instead of to the landlord.*' The Revd T.C. Fell of Sheepy Magna, in Leicestershire, says, 'The poor-laws affect the *rent*, and not the *farmer's capital.*' Sir Thomas Phillips, Bart., Stephen Savage, overseer, and two other gentlemen, at Broadway, in Worcestershire, tell the brace of bishops and their comrades this: 'Agricultural capital is diminishing; but *not on account of the poor-laws, which rather tend to* KEEP CAPITAL *in the parish*; but because the great landowners spend less in their parish, by carrying the great bulk of their income annually to London, where it accumulates in the hands of *usurers* and *stock-jobbers*, and consequently does not return to the parish with the same rapidity nor in the same proportion as it is drawn out of it.'

Your lordship said, in answer to these lords who wanted delay, in order to have time to consider this question, that 'there had been *plenty of time for consideration*'. Have you read this evidence? I would stake my life upon the question, that you have not. If you had, on what ground did you assert, that the payers of the rates were anxious to get the bill passed?

However, the whole scheme is clearly seen to the bottom. Lord Althorp's object with regard to the bill was, to *relieve the distresses of the farmers*; to lessen the burdens of *those who paid the rates*; 'to relieve the *industrious farmer and tradesman*' from the burden of maintaining the idle and profligate poor. Before the thing came to you, Brougham had boldly declared that the object was to *save the estates of the lords*. So that, after all the pretences of Lord ALTHORP, here were you urging forward this terrible bill under the pretence of the necessity of saving your estate from the jaws of the poor!

All men are now satisfied that the object is, to lower rates, and, more particularly, to lower *wages*; and *to put the difference into the pockets of the landlords*. There is not a man in his senses who does not believe that the main object is this, and, of course, to bring the English labourers down to live upon the base food, and to be clad in the miserable rags, which are the lot of the wretched people of Ireland, where a good and honest labourer, as good and as true as any in the world, works for sixpence a day, and sometimes for twopence. This is the object; and if not of you yourself, it must be the object of the inventors of the scheme, or they must have been both drunk and mad at the same time, and both in an excessive degree. What! and do the *House of Lords* pass this bill? Yes, they do; and the majority of that House, thinking of BROUGHAM as they think, and talking of him as they talk, and treating *all his other new projects as they treat them*, embrace him here! Reject, with disdain, all his other 'improvements', suggested by the 'march of intellect'; but when he proposes to give them, instead of their tenants, the votes at the vestries; and to give them a voting at those vestries by proxy; when he proposes the big workhouses; the workhouse dresses, and says that the poor have no right to relief, and ought to be no charge at all upon the land; and when he tells them, that his bill *will save their estates*; then they cheer him; then you cheer even this HENRY BROUGHAM;

then you pass his project almost by acclamation!

Well, but there is this much of good in this transaction, that we have now, at last, their unequivocal declaration of designs with regard to us. We now know, even the dullest of us, what relationship we stand in with regard to them. Until this bill was passed by them, men were divided in their opinions with regard to the aristocratical institutions: W E A R E A L L O F O N E M I N D N O W : we now all know our duty with regard to that aristocracy; and may every curse that God has in store for the base fall on me, and stick to me for the remainder of my life, if I neglect any part of this my sacred duty. You have done all that you can do; and I will now do all that I can do; and I have to thank God, who has given me health to make that all not a very little. It has given me great mortification to know it to be my duty to select you as the object of this angry address; but it was your pleasure to become the great patron and protector of this bill; and, as you deserve, so you will, I dare say, be rewarded for that patronage and that protection.

In conclusion of this series of letters, I wish your lordship joy of the feelings inspired by reflecting on the part which you have acted on this memorable occasion; and

I am
Your most obedient
And most humble servant,
WM. COBBETT.

P.S. It was my intention to have noticed, before I concluded the above address, the various encroachments of the aristocracy upon the rights and liberties of the people in general. But those encroachments are so numerous, they are so important, it is so necessary to state them *fully* when they are stated; it is so necessary to give them a formal and permanent existence on record; and for the purpose of making them ground of action for the people; and they relate to matters so various, that this is a task which I must defer; but it is a task necessary to be performed as soon as possible; in order that the people may know what this aristocracy is; what this aristocracy has done to them: *and what it is their duty to their King and their country to do with regard to this aristocracy.*

The Poor-law *Commission* having done its work, it is high

time to think of our establishing that '*Reckoning Commission*', which was proposed to me about two years ago.[6] '*The rights of the poor*' having been so amply discussed, and inquired into, to complete our collection of statistical and economical knowledge, it seems indispensably necessary to inquire into the *rights of the rich*. To send our circulars into the several counties and parishes, and to make the discoveries and obtain a statement of the facts necessary to the completion of this singularly useful branch of 'Useful Knowledge'.

Political Register, 25 October 1834.

To the People of Salisbury

Limerick, 19 October 1834.
MY FRIENDS,
 LORD RADNOR has, I see, been shoving BROUGHAM upon you. It seems to have been a most *low* and despicable affair. A '*Lord High* Chancellor' bawling from *a public-house window* to a Lord and his footmen and tradesmen! I see that this same bawling fellow has been at the little town of FAREHAM, in Hampshire, bawling out nonsense there! However, I have no time to say more to you now. Next week, I will address a letter *to you*, and you will send a parcel of it to Mr BARLING. You shall know all about the fellow whom Lord Radnor has brought down from London to bawl to you. I will not quit this bawling chap, till you know him to the back-bone.

I am your friend,
WM. COBBETT.

Political Register, 25 October 1834.

Burning of the Parliament House

City of Limerick, 20 October 1834.
Here am I, having been last evening received with acclamations of joy, by thirty thousand men, preceding my carriage with not less than thirty banners, and with my ears still humming with their cheers, when, in comes the London post, this morning, bringing, in my insipid old friend and neighbour, the MORNING HERALD, an account of the B U R N I N G of the Parliament House. As to the C A U S E, whether by fire and brimstone from Heaven, or by the less sublime agency of S W I N G, my friend, the Herald, does not tell me; though this is a very *interesting* portion of the event.[7]

At this distance, a good five hundred miles from the scene, all I can do, with regard to recording the facts, is to direct my printer* (which I hereby do), not to insert my fifth and last letter to LORD RADNOR about the Poor-law Amendment Bill (which letter I sent him last night); but, to take from the London *daily papers*, all the different accounts, and all *their different sets of wise observations*, relating to this matter. This is all I can do at present in the historical way.

But my friend, the HERALD, has made one observation upon which, distant as I am, and agitated as the reader will naturally suppose my mind to be, I cannot refrain from offering a remark or two. My insipid friend says, 'that the M O B' (meaning the people of London), 'when they *saw the progress of the* flames, raised a S A V A G E shout of E X U L T A T I O N.' Did they indeed! The *Herald* exclaims, ' O , U N R E F L E C T I N G people!' Now perhaps the 'M O B' exulted because the 'M O B' was really a *reflecting* 'mob'. When even a dog, or a horse, receives any treatment that it does not like, it always shuns *the place* where it got such treatment: shoot at and wound a hare from out of a hedge-row, she will always shun that spot: cut a stick out of a coppice, and beat a boy with it, and he will wish the coppice at

---

* The printer very much regrets that Mr Cobbett's letter arrived too late for his wishes to be complied with.

the devil: send a man, for writing notorious truth, out of the King's Bench to a jail, and there put him half to death, and he will not cry his eyes out if he happen to hear that court is no more. In short, there is always a connexion in our minds, between sufferings that we undergo and *the place* in which they are inflicted, or in which they originate. And this 'unreflecting mob' might in this case have reflected, that in the building which they then saw in flames, the following, amongst many other things, took place. They might have reflected that it was in this House,

That the act was passed for turning the Catholic priests, who shared the tithes with the poor, out of the parishes, and putting Protestant parsons in their place, who gave the poor no share at all of the tithes.

That this was the V E R Y F I R S T A C T that was passed after this building became the Parliament House!

That the all-devouring church of England was B O R N in this very House.

That, soon after the people became *compelled to beg* or starve, in this same House an act was passed to put an iron collar on a beggar's neck, and to make him a slave for life.

That, it was in this House, that the aristocracy (who had got the abbey lands and great tithes), solemnly *renounced the damnable errors of the Catholic religion*, in the reign of Edward the Sixth.

That, it was in this same House, that they solemnly recanted, and received pardon and absolution from the Pope, in the reign of Queen Mary, bargaining to keep the abbey lands and great tithes.

That, it was in this same House, that the same aristocracy chopped about again *when ELIZABETH came*, and again solemnly renounced the damnable idolatry of popery.

That, it was in this same House, that the act was passed for plundering the guilds and fraternities of their prescriptive property.

That, it was in this same House, that all the tyrannical and bloody penal laws were passed against those who faithfully adhered to the religion of our fathers.

That, it was in this same House, that the Riot Act and the Septennial Act were passed.

That, it was in this same House, that the sums were voted for carrying on a war to subjugate the Americans.

That, it was in this same House, that the new treason-laws, new game-laws, new trespass-laws, and new felony-laws were passed.

That it was in this same House that the million and half of money was voted ... to be given to the parsons of the church of England, over and above their tithes to enormous amount.

That, it was in this same House ...

But I must break off. The post is going. I will finish the list next week ...

WM. COBBETT.

NOTES

[1] Cobbett might have been hard put to it to reconcile this stern admonition with his earlier toleration of the root when 'used merely as garden-stuff.'

[2] George Spater, op. cit. p.471, writes that Daniel O'Connell eventually commanded 40 of the 100 Irish votes in the Commons.

[3] 1823.

[4] Cobbett's comparison of the still-remembered 'rebel, invader and conqueror' from Normandy, was with the new ruling committee of landlords and industrialists in the reformed Parliament, intent on cuts in welfare provision, and by means of the Poor Law Amendment Bill.

[5] Cobbett's claim that the labourers and village poor were entitled under common law to a share in the property of the landowners was a revolutionary yet traditional one. It led at least as far back as King Alfred.

[6] The notion of a 'Reckoning Commission' to inquire into all landed property had been first proposed in the *Register* early in 1833. Cobbett returns to it in his 'Dedication to Sir Robert Peel', in *Legacy to Labourers*.

[7] 'Captain Swing' was the phantom leader of the 'Swing Men': 'these thrashers, hedgers, ditchers, ploughmen, mowers and reapers', who in their despair had turned to smashing the wealthier farmers' threshing-machines and burning their corn-ricks. (*Political Register*, 13 July 1833). The best account is Eric Hobsbawm and George Rudé's *Captain Swing*, Lawrence & Wishart, 1969.

CHAPTER 6

Political Register, 1 November 1834.

Answer to the Parish Priest and Other Inhabitants of The City of Kilmallock

Gentlemen, Not being able to stop at your city without breaking my engagement with the people of the city of Limerick, I could not avail myself of your kind invitation; and was obliged to confine myself to a mere passing view of those extensive remains of ancient grandeur, so consonant with the surprising fertility and inexhaustible riches of the surrounding country; so clear an evidence of the political wisdom, as well as of the piety of our ancestors, who, by foundations like these, kept constantly alive 'honour to God in the Highest, and on earth peace and goodwill towards men'; who, in this best of all possible ways, caused the produce of the earth to be enjoyed on the spot, and created a happy yeomanry, held by the ties of gratitude and veneration, in willing and cheerful obedience to their landlords.[1] With this passing glance, and with these melancholy reflections, I was obliged to content myself; those reflections being succeeded, however, by the bitterest execrations, coming from the bottom of my heart, on the memory of the ruthless spoilers, whose ferocious greediness has, at last, instead of that yeomanry by whom the monks were surrounded, placed a swarm of rack-renters, whose only food is an insipid and spiritless root, whose bed is the rejected produce of the hog, whose place of abode is inferior in point of comfort to that of the lowest and filthiest of animals in other countries, and who are liable to be, and frequently are, tossed out of, even of these, to perish with hunger and cold. If you, gentlemen, and your fathers, had, like us Protestants, ever abused and vilified what are called '*monkish ignorance and superstition*', you might have been said to be the makers of your own miseries; but, having, with a constancy and self-sacrifice, wholly unparalleled in the history of the world, remained, even unto the death, faithful to the religion of your fathers, the magnificent ruins which press the recollection of those sacrifices and of that matchless fidelity, to the mind of the beholder, cannot fail to fill him with indignation against the spoilers, with anxious wishes for your deliverance from your present miseries, and with a resolution to neglect nothing within his power to effect that deliverance.

Gentlemen, your kind and highly valued address, for which I tender you my best thanks, introduces so many topics, and each of so much importance, that it would be impossible for me to treat of them here, without far too great an encroachment on your time; but, gentlemen, I must observe, that, if the unconstitutional doctrine of passive obedience and non-resistance be taught in the schools to which you allude, I abhor those schools from the bottom of my heart.[2] With regard to the matters, relative to which you do me the honour to request my aid in your behalf and in behalf of ill-treated Ireland, I beg you to be assured, first, that I regard it as my bounden duty to render such aid to the utmost of my power; and second, that having now with my own eyes had the fact of this ill-treatment, and of all its attendant miseries, confirmed, and my excellent constituents of Oldham, who feel most acutely for all your sufferings, having charged me with the performance of that duty, I should, if I were to neglect it, be amongst the basest and wickedest of all mankind.

WM. COBBETT
Limerick, 19 October, 1834.

Political Register, 1 November 1834.

To Charles Marshall, Labourer, Letter No.VI

*Normandy Tithing, Parish of Ash,
Farnham, Surrey.*

*Castle Comfort, Abington, Co. Limerick
25 October 1834.*
MARSHALL,

Since I wrote to you from CORK, I have been over a hundred miles more of this country. There is no *sandy* ground here, and no *chalk*. It is all *loam* and *rocky stone*, and great part of this stone is *limestone* of a very dark blue colour. In some parts the stone is near to the top of the ground, and in others, quite at the top, so that the ground cannot be ploughed. But, even here, the grass is very fine between the rocky stones, and as good for sheep as our *downs* are. There are few *hills*, compared with our part of England: some about as high as those that rise up in our neighbourhood; and these they call 'MOUNTAINS'; but, the greater part of those that I have seen are covered with *grass* to their very tops; and have hundreds of cattle fatting on their sides, and the very tips.

I came, yesterday, along a country about ten English miles long, all the richest land that can possibly be. On the two sides of this road, and on those of its continuation for ten miles farther, there are about a hundred and fifty thousand acres of land; a bed of rich loam from 6 to 8 feet deep, and without a single *water-furrow* being wanted in the whole of it; and yet, on the whole of this tract, which is worth more than all the land in the county of Surrey, there is not one field of turnips, mangel-wurzel, or cabbages. The land is not tilled a tenth part so well as it might be. If *we* had it, it would be all a garden; and it is not the fault of the farmers and working people; but, of the L A W S , which suffer the landlords to take away and send into other countries all the meat and the corn, and compel the miserable farmers and working people to live on potatoes. But, all this matter I shall make clear to you all, in a B O O K that I shall make when I get back to **NORMANDY**, or before.

In my last letter I told you about the poor souls on Lord **MIDDLETON**'s estate; and, I shall tell you, that his poor creatures are looked upon as being *the best treated* of any in the country. Well, then, MARSHALL, if that be the *best of it*, you may guess *what is the worst*! No; you cannot guess: and God forbid, that the Scotch or the English place-hunting and tax-eating miscreants should ever be able to persuade the Parliament to *attempt* to reduce the people of Surrey to such a state as to enable them *to guess* at horrors such as I have beheld since I last wrote to you.

I have been T O S E E the people on the estates of several great swaggering fellows, who are called 'noblemen', and who live in England and spend there, or in France or in Italy, the money that the Irish corn and meat sell for. I have seen a few hundred of Irish F A R M E R S, now, MARSHALL, and have taken down their names, and a correct account of all about them. Marshall, you cannot call yourself a *poor man*; and, with 8 children, only one of whom can constantly earn his living, you cannot be otherwise; but, I solemnly declare to you, that I have seen no *Irish farmer*, who lives in a manner any thing like equal to the manner in which you live. At the house of one (who pays as much rent as Farmer HORNE) there was a boy six years old (stabbling about on the dirt-floor, in the urine of the pig) naked all but a rag round his middle, and we judged, some of us, that this rag might weigh four ounces, and, others, that it might weigh 6 ounces. This was a '*farmer's son*'! But, this farmer *pays no poor-rates* as Farmer HORNE does! And this farmer pays a working man only *6d* a day, while Farmer HORNE is obliged to pay him 2s. Ah! but the L A N D L O R D here takes away from the Irish farmer rent, poor-rates, wages, and all, and thus reduces the whole to beggary. And this, Marshall, is precisely what a FAMOUS SCOTCH V A G A B O N D , of whom I will tell you more another time, is endeavouring to cause to take place in England. Look sharp, then, and especially the F A R M E R S look sharp; be prepared to use, and in good earnest, all the lawful means in your power, to uphold the laws of England, those just laws, which were obtained by the good sense and resolution and best blood of our virtuous and wise and just and resolute forefathers.

In one street in the outskirts of the city of Limerick, (which is made a *fine city* by the trade of sending away meat and butter and corn out of Ireland), I saw more misery than any man could have believed existed in the whole world. Men sleeping in the same wisp of dirty straw, or weeds, with their mothers, sisters, and aunts; and compelled to do this, or perish: two or three families in one room, that is to say, a miserable hole 10 feet by 8 or 9; and husbands, wives, sons, daughters, all huddled together, paying *6d* or *8d* or *10d* a week for *the room*; and the rent paid to a *'nobleman'* in England. Here I saw one woman with a baby in her arms, both nearly naked. The poor mother's body was naked from the middle of her thighs downwards; and to hide *her bosom*, she caught up a dirty piece of old sack; she hung down her face (naturally very pretty); when she lifted it up, the tears were streaming down her cheeks. Her husband, who had just got better after illness, was out of work. She had two other children quite naked, and covered up in some dirty hay, in one corner of the room! At a place in the country, I went to the dwelling of a widower, who is 60 years of age, and who has five children, all *very nearly stark naked*. The eldest girl, who is *fifteen years of age*, had on a sort of apron to hide the middle part of her body before; and that was all she had. She hid herself, as well as she could, behind, or at the end of, an old broken cupboard; and she held up her two arms and hands to hide her breasts! This man *pays 30s rent* for an acre of the poorest land! And, am I to live to see the working people of GUILDFORD and GODALMING, and of my native town of FARNHAM, brought to this state! Yet, MARSHALL, mind what I say: to this state they will be brought, if they do not do every thing that the law allows them to do to prevent it. Mind, Marshall, I have *witnesses* to the truth of all the horrid facts that I state; and, I am ready to bring *proof* of these facts before a committee of the House of Commons. I have the *names* of scores of F A R M E R S , and an account of thousands, who *never taste* either *meat* or *bread*! Yet, they *do not pay poor-rates*!

Marshall, you know that there is a great swaggering fellow, in Sussex, that they call 'the E A R L O F E G R E M O N T'. I will give you an account of his 'F A R M E R S' another time. Tell Farmer HORNE, that I say, he ought to read these letters to his congregation, and to read to them those parts of the

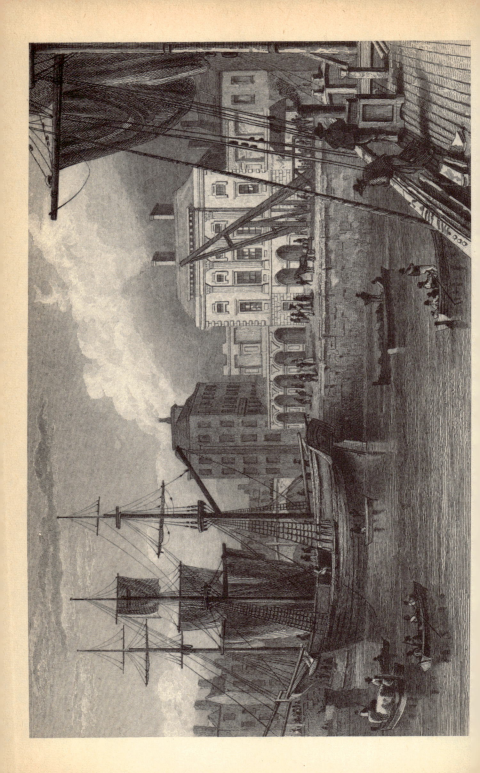

BIBLE which relate to the duties of the rich towards the poor. Be sure to get some of them to PURBRIGHT, and to all the parishes round about. Let them all see what the Scotch and English tax-eating vagabonds wish to persuade the Parliament to bring them to; and let them all be ready to come to a county meeting when I get back. Mr DEAN will read to you the account of the great kindness of the Irish people towards me. *'God bless you and your countrymen*!' I have heard from hundreds of thousands of voices, since I came to Ireland; and, if we do not do our best, in every legal way that we can act, to better the lot of their good and kind and most cruelly suffering people, we shall deserve to be reduced to their horrible state; our hard-heartedness, or cowardice, will merit sufferings even greater than those which they have to endure.

I begin to look towards NORMANDY again. I never see a 'farm-house' here, without thinking how happy one of these 'farmers' (who pay no *poor-rates*) would be, if he had a sleeping-place as good as that which you and TOM FARR made for our *bull*! You thought, that it would not be '*decent without paving*'! I declare to God that I have not seen a foot square of pavement in a farm-house in Ireland; and yet these farmers are not 'oppressed by poor-rates'! I once, thought of bringing SAM RIDDLE* with me. I wish I had, and then sent him down to his own home, in Sussex, to tell the farmers there what he had seen. He would have been able to tell them the consequence of getting *relieved* from poor-rates; and to relate to them *how* it was, that poor-rates prevented the land-lords from swallowing up poor-rates and wages along with the rents, and of reducing farmers as well as labourers to potatoes and salt.

Hoping that you all keep sober and very obedient to Mr DEAN, and that you will have every thing in nice order against my return, I remain in excellent health, and with sincere wishes for the health of you all,

Your master and friend,
WM COBBETT.

P.S. I shall, when I have ended my travels about Ireland, publish a *little book* with the following title:

*A farm worker at Normandy.

IRELAND'S WOES;
A
WARNING TO ENGLISHMEN.

And I will take care that you shall all have it to read, or to be read to you.

Political Register, 1 November 1834.

Burning of the Parliament House

Castle Comfort, Abington, Co. Limerick,
25 October 1834.
I began this subject, in a letter from Limerick, in my last *Register*. Want of time *cut me short*; and made me hastily put down only a few of the things done in the place now consumed by fire. I will, therefore, re-insert that broken-off article, and will continue it on to the present time, as well as I can, in the ABSENCE OF ALL BOOKS, which might serve to refresh my memory.

That, it was in this same H O U S E, that the Act of William and Mary was passed, providing for the contingent accession of the House of Hanover; that, in that act, which was entitled an Act for Preserving the Religion and Liberties of England, it was provided, that, in case of the accession of the family, no one having a *pension* from the crown, or holding any place of *trust* or *emolument* under it, *civil or military, should be capable of sitting in the House of Commons.*

That, it was in this same H O U S E, that this part of that act was R E P E A L E D; and that the House of Commons now contains great numbers of *pensioners*, and of persons living on public money, military as well as civil.

That, it was in this same H O U S E, that the P O W E R O F I M P R I S O N M E N T - B I L L, and the other bills of that sort, were brought in by Sidmouth and Castlereagh, and passed in 1817.

That, it was in this same H O U S E, that it was, in 1819, voted that the House would *not inquire* into the massacre at Manchester.[3]

That, it was in this same H O U S E, that Liverpool, in 1820, brought in the Bill of Pains and Penalties against the Queen of Geo. IV.

That it was, in this same H O U S E, that the members stood up, bare-headed, and with clapping of hands, received Castlereagh, when he returned from Paris after the *death of*

Marshal Ney,* and the breaking up of the *museums*.

That, it was in this same H O U S E, where Castlereagh brought in, and the House passed, the S I X   A C T S, in 1819.

That, it was in this same H O U S E, that were passed the laws for enabling the landowners to S E L L wild animals, called G A M E, and to enable the justices to T R A N S P O R T poor men, who should, by night, be found in pursuit of those animals.

That, it was in this same H O U S E, that the Bills establishing the Bourbon-like P O L I C E, were passed, and that the detected spy P O P A Y was suffered to go unpunished and his employers unreproved.[4]

That, it was in this same H O U S E, that botheration B R O U G H A M, in 1820, *defended the employment of spies* by government.

That, it was in this same H O U S E, where CASTLEREAGH was the *leader*, for many years, up to the 6 of August, 1822; and he C U T   H I S   O W N   T H R O A T, at North Cray, in Kent, on the 12 of that month, a Kentish coroner's jury pronouncing that he was I N S A N E, and had been so for *some weeks*; he being also Secretary of State for Foreign Affairs, and acting as such for the Home and Colonial Departments at the very time when he cut his throat.

That, it was in this same H O U S E, that *a million and a half of money* was, in the regency and reign of George IV, voted out of the taxes to be given to the clergy of the church of England, over and above their tithes and other enormous revenues.

That, it was in this same H O U S E, that about *three millions* of the people's money were voted for S E C R E T   S E R V I C E S, in the last two reigns, and in the present reign.

That, it was in this same H O U S E, that the reasonable and just proposition, made by me, to cause the great landowners to pay as heavy stamp-duties as the *little ones*, and to cause the *land* to pay as heavy duties as *personal property*, was rejected.

That, it was in this same H O U S E, that my motion for a repeal of the M A L T - T A X was rejected by the reformed Parliament.[5]

That, it was in this same H O U S E, that the I R I S H

---

*Executed under the authority of the Allied Powers in November 1815.

C O E R C I O N   B I L L was passed, amidst cheers to insult Mr O'Connell.[6]

That, it was in this same H O U S E, that a petition from the electors of SANDWICH, complaining that Sir Thomas TROUBRIDGE, one of their members, had obtained his commission in the navy by criminal means, was, *while the facts were not denied*, rejected by the *'reformed House of Commons'*.

That, it was in this same H O U S E, that my resolution against Sir R O B E R T P E E L was 'E X P U N G E D' upon a motion, put by Lord ALTHORP W I T H O U T N O T I C E, and amended by the Speaker without the leave of the House.

That, it was in this same H O U S E, that the sums were voted for the new palaces, and for the famous gate-way.

That, it was in this same H O U S E, that were passed the Cash-Payment-Suspension Act of 1797; P E E L's Act, in 1819; the Small-Note Bill of 1822; the Panic Act of 1826, which, at last, leaves the taxes unredeemed, while the wheat is brought down to forty shillings a quarter.

That, it was in this same H O U S E, that the BANK, the PAPER-MONEY, and the FUNDS were enacted.

That, it was in this same H O U S E, that L O A N S were voted, which, at last, have created a debt, the bare yearly interest of which amounts *to thirty million of sovereigns in gold*!

That, it was in this same H O U S E, that a vote to take off a *part* of the tax on the people's daily drink was rescinded.

That, it was in this same H O U S E, that STURGES BOURNE'S Bills were passed, giving *plurality* of votes, at vestries, to the R I C H, and authorizing the employment of H I R E D O V E R S E E R S.[7]

That, it was in this same H O U S E, that the petitions on behalf of the poor D O R S E T S H I R E M E N were unattended to.[8]

That, it was in this same H O U S E, that the *'Poor-law Amendment Bill'*, brought in by Lords A L T H O R P and B R O U G H A M, was passed, in 1834.

That, it was in this same H O U S E, now consumed by F I R E, that the vault (now let down by fire) resounded with P R A I S E S on 'the M A G N A N I M O U S Alexander', when he had *burnt to ashes* a city with three hundred thousand people in it; and, beyond all doubt, with not less than *a thousand women in child-birth*, to say nothing of the sick, the decrepit, the aged, and the infants![9]

Oh, God of mercy! Might not those, whom the insipid and time-serving wretch of the *Morning Herald* abuses; might not that people of London, whom the base crew of R E P O R T E R S, reeking with the heat of gin, and always eager to libel their own suffering country; might not the people of London, instead of being '*unreflecting*', have D U L Y R E F L E C T E D on the hundreds of things, of which I have, from the mere memory, mentioned only a *small part?* These things are always present to *my mind*. Why should they not be present to the minds of the people of London?

With regard to *what is to be done* in consequence of this fire; *how* the fire came to take place; what Mother Jordan's offspring[10] thought of the ruins and of the ashes, when they '*inspected*' them; as the base *reporters* tell us they did: these, and particularly *the latter*, are matters to be more fully dwelt on, when I possess more authentic information. But, I must say, that those who talk of this matter as of a *mere fire*, do not, may it please their *reporterships*, reflect. It is a G R E A T   E V E N T: come from what C A U S E it might, it is a *great event*. It astounds: it sets *thought* to work in the minds of millions: it awakens *recollections*: it rouses to remarks: it elicits a communication of feelings: it makes the tongue the loud herald of the heart: and it must in the nature of things ... it I S a great event! Say the base, stinking *reporters* what they will, it I S a great event!

I do not care one straw where the Parliament may meet: it may meet in a barn for aught I care. To be sure, it can, if it and our constituents, and the all-ruling governor of the world choose, do as it hitherto has done; but it cannot do the same things in the S A M E   P L A C E, at any rate. Mr SPRING RICE may again *lay upon the table* a bill for *altering the stamp-laws*, and never mention the matter again; but he cannot lay it upon the S A M E   T A B L E ! Another *bill of indemnity for stopping cash-payments* may be brought in; but it cannot be brought into the S A M E   P L A C E ! Aye, aye; say the stinking *reporters* (poh!) what they like, it is a *great event*!

WM. COBBETT.

Political Register, 8 November 1834.

To The Sensible and Just People of England

MY FRIENDS, – I have this day read an article in that paper which I have long called the 'bloody old *Times*',[11] relative to what is called 'THE O'CONNELL TRIBUTE', that is to say, a yearly contribution or subscription, which the people of Ireland voluntarily make, to be paid to Mr O'Connell, as compensation for his devoting his whole time, not only to serve them in Parliament, but to serve them with his pen, and by his personal interference on all occasions in their behalf, and by the unpaid-for application of his legal knowledge for their interests and their protection. This tribute amounts to about 13,000 or 14,000 pounds a year. You should be informed that Mr O'Connell is, without dispute, the greatest lawyer of his country; that he has four sons, three of whom are members of Parliament; that he has daughters; that, in short, he has a large family; and that probably the estate which he inherited might not exceed the reasonable wants of such a family in the most retired life. Circumstances placed him at the head of the cause of Ireland; his superior talents, joined to his zeal, his activity, his great sobriety, his astonishing industry, and, above all, his public virtue, and hatred of the oppressor of his country, made him be in a situation either to abandon the cause of his country, or to abandon his profession, with all the immense advantages which must have accrued from his pursuing that profession, not only to himself, but to every branch of his family. A long while he endeavoured to pursue his profession, and be the pleader of the cause of his country at the same time. To adhere to both was at last found to be impossible; he chose to adhere to the cause of his country; the people well knew that he could not do that with efficiency even for them, unless they gave him something like a compensation; they knew that he must be utterly unable to uphold an expenditure absolutely necessary to their interests, as well as to his own support, unless they came to his aid with pecuniary means.

The people of Ireland considered, too, not what he actually

lost by adhering to their cause, but *that which he might have gained by ceasing to devote himself to it*; and I beg you, my friends, to pay attention to this part of the subject. Not to suppose it possible; I say supposing it to have been *impossible*, that any earthly consideration could have induced him to have betrayed the interests of his country, to have done that which so many others have done, and who are called honourable, and noble too; to suppose that he could have abandoned the cause of Ireland, joined with her foes, become one of her grinding oppressors, one of the councillors for cruelty to be inflicted on her, and to have received, as his reward, an earldom perhaps, if nothing more, together with many thousands a year; to be, in short, one of those one hundred and thirteen privy councillors whom Sir James Graham showed to receive £650,000 amongst them;[12] to have had his sons rolling in wealth, if not ennobled too, as well as himself; and to have been drawing altogether out of your industry, as well as the industry of the people of Ireland and Scotland, probably £100,000 a year for himself and the branches of his family. Without supposing it possible for his nature to have permitted him to be capable of perfidy so atrociously ferocious as this, though precedents were so abundant before his eyes; without supposing this *possible*, still, far short of this, he might be quietly and by degrees sinking away from his exertions for the people, have jogged along, like a horse in a mill, and have placed all his sons in posts of emolument, with cool professions of love of Ireland still on his lips, and without him or any one of those sons doing any one thing on which a charge of perfidy or inconsistency could have been founded and brought home to them. He had, in short, the three things before him: perfidy to the people of Ireland, and rewards without measure; drawing off from their cause, honours of his profession, and riches greater than any family could need; casting aside every thing for the sake of Ireland, and relying on the justice of his countrymen for support. He, to his eternal honour, chose the latter; and the people of Ireland, to their great honour, and to the burning mortification of their foes, are doing him that justice which he expected at their hands.

Now, my friends, this is the case. Be pleased to pay attention to this statement of the case, and to bear it always in mind during the observations which I am about to address to you.

The sum collected is much about that which I have stated above; and I am assured, and I believe, that it is no more than sufficient, without any profusion on the part of any of his family – who, you will perceive, are all *proscribed*, through every department in life, where the influence of this powerful Government prevails – without any profusion on the part of himself, or any of his family, I am assured, and I believe, that this sum is no more than sufficient to defray the cost to him of his never-ceasing labours for his country.

You will easily suppose that it must be a prime object with the sons and daughters of corruption, with those who wish Ireland to be kept in the state which I have described to you in my letters to my labourer, Marshall; who wish that the great landowners of Ireland may continue to draw away all the fruits of this fine country while those who till the land are driven to live upon food worse than that of the hogs which they rear to be sent away; who wish even the farmers of Ireland to be a great swarm of beggars, not tasting meat nor bread from year's end to year's end, and the greater part of them clothed worse than the common beggars in England; who wish that the landowners of Ireland may still possess the power of driving the people off the land of their birth, and compelling them to perish with hunger, and with cold on the bare ground, or to go to foreign lands there to perish, or perish on board a crowded and filthy ship; who wish that the people of Ireland may still be compelled to render tithes to a church to which they do not belong, and which they hold in abhorrence. To all these, my friends, you must be satisfied that this tribute to Mr O'Connell is something that sears their very eye-balls, something that mortifies them to the very soul, a thing for which they would murder all the good and sound people of Ireland if they could, seeing, as they clearly must see, that it is an indication of the resolution of the people of Ireland to act upon the principles inculcated by the man to whom they pay the tribute. Not being able to poison or cut the throats of these people, and knowing that they are beyond the reach of their atrocious calumnies, they acting on the system of 'centralization', collect all the malignity into one phial, and pour it out upon the head of Mr O'Connell himself; not perceiving (for God has been pleased to put folly into the same animal where malignity has found its seat); not perceiving that this pouring out upon Mr O'Connell is the surest possible way of convincing the people of Ireland that they are acting wisely as well as justly. '*Love your* enemies', coupled with the conditions clearly implied, is a precept that ought always to be obeyed; but *'love those whom your enemies hate'*, is a precept full as wise and as just. It is an unerring guide, and one that we should always take care to have before us. If there be men who do not disguise their wishes to make you slaves and to plunder you, and if these men call upon you to suspect and to deride some other man, common sense tells you, without any other circumstance to assist it, that you ought to cling closely and firmly to that man. The fable tells us, that the WOLVES were engaged a long time in endeavours to DEVOUR THE SHEEP, one or two of whom they now and then got at and tore to pieces. But the DOGS so bravely defended the flock, that the wolves were compelled to desist from further hostility and further devourings. The latter, therefore, getting into a parley with the sheep, persuaded them that it was the dogs who had been the cause of all that had taken place before, and that if they would but get rid of the agitating dogs, the wolfish and sheepish nations might live in quiet for ever after. The silly sheep, agreeing to the proposal, bid the dogs go away, and these latter had hardly got out of sight, when all the noble family of wolves rushed down from the woods, tore the sheep to pieces, ewes, lambs, and all. My friends, we were taught when we were boys, to believe the Irish to be *wild*. *Wild* as they may be, they are not so silly and so ungrateful as the sheep were. The bloody old *Times* newspaper calls upon them to get rid of their dog; this base and boisterous herald of the merciless sons and daughters of corruption, this barker to that band of devouring wolves is howling to the people of Ireland to abandon, or to cripple, to muzzle, to knock the teeth out of the faithful guardian of this flock of oppressed people; but I can assure you that it howls in vain; that its howlings have no other effect here than that of making the people cling more closely to Mr O'Connell; that these howlings can do him harm only in your estimation; and it is my business to prevent them from doing even that, by the statement which I have already made, and by the remarks which I am about to subjoin, on the infamous article of which I have spoken.

In this article it said that Mr O'Connell is looked up to only by the wretched mob of Ireland; that the Irish people have no affection for him; that *'they give their mite from the fear of mortal violence from his hired ruffians'*, and *'from the dread of excommunication from their own priesthood'*; that 'it should be remembered that the miserable, houseless, ragged, hungry, perishing creatues, without potatoes to eat, or assets wherewith to buy a coffin, are *forced contributors*, and that in numberless cases, they are not only *importuned* for the tax with barbarous eagerness, but it is wrung from them with *outrageous* and *brutal* violence, even by the *cudgel*, while their babes are gasping for food; and that this man's heartless rapacity is as disgusting as his inhuman treachery.'

I will stop here to observe, that miscreant as this writer is, despised as he will be by you, without any inquiry at all into the facts, execrated as he will be by every Irishman who is not a villainous plunderer, it does not follow that, while there is law, or something called law, to punish those who indiscreetly defend Mr O'Connell when aspersed; it does not follow that Mr O'Connell is not for once in his life to appeal to an English jury, to say whether infamies like these are to be poured out with impunity. I will engage to bring a thousand witnesses from Ireland, that I myself have spoken to, who will swear to the falsehood of every fact that is here alleged. The libeller adds to the last words that I have quoted, these words: *'Towards Harding Tracey, who for him was sacrificed and his family starved'*; so that there is a direct and tangible charge of having sacrificed a man and his family by inhuman treachery. That the charge is most infamously false, I need tell no Englishman of common sense of justice, that the making of this charge is a crime, to be punished by the law, while there is any thing like law left in the land. Leaving this matter, as indeed I must leave it, to the decision of Mr O'Connell himself, I now proceed to make a few remarks on the passages that I have quoted.

And, first let me ask, what sort of readers those must be whom this man thinks likely to believe that *money* can be forced, even by the cudgel, from those who have not potatoes to eat? Those who can be made to believe that will set at nought the old maxim, 'that money is not to be got out of a flint stone.'

With regard to the rest of the assertions in this article, though not so *necessarily false as this*, they are really false. The money is contributed without the smallest degree of constraint of any sort; it is contributed by persons of some property, generally; a large part of it by persons who may be properly enough called gentlemen; and, so far from its being given by the dread of displeasure of the *priesthood*, and of the consequences of that displeasure, the priesthood have had nothing to do with the matter, any more than any other person in their rank of life. The Catholic chapels are the places for collection, as being the most convenient and less expensive. In some very few instances the priesthood deem this an improper use to make of the chapel; but they were induced to give way by the universal expression of the sentiments of their flocks. And it is a great mistake to suppose that the Catholics are the only contributors. A considerable portion of the sum is contributed by Protestants. There are instances in which Protestants are, by invitation, the collectors at the Catholic chapels. I myself was walking with a Catholic parish priest the day before the collection, that is to say, on the 25 of October, when he received a letter from a Protestant gentleman, which he opened in my presence, containing two pounds towards the 'tribute', the letter stating that the writer thought it the duty of every Irishman, who had the means, to do his part in making the contribution as large as possible.

So that the whole of this statement, made to you by this infamous newspaper, is atrociously false from the beginning to the end. This writer says, that the people of Ireland have 'no affection for him.' When we speak of affection, as applied to persons with whom we never come in immediate contact, we mean to say, very great regard, anxious wishes for the party's health and happiness; when a people entertain these feelings towards any man, we properly enough say they have an *affection* for him; and, taking this to be the true interpretation of the meaning of the word, if ever there were a people who had an affection for a man, this people have an affection for Mr O'Connell. In Dublin, after my entrance into it, I had 30, or 40,000 men standing before me. They applauded me; but they did not separate without making the street ring with their cheers for O'Connell. I was conducted into Cork by not less than 80,000 persons. They frequently cheered me; but as frequently gave 'Cheers for O'Connell'; and the last act, when they separated in the great street in Cork, was 'Three cheers for

O'Connell'. Just the same took place at Limerick, and at Kilkenny, at Waterford, at Clonmell, and even in all the smaller towns and in the villages wherever I have seen 20 persons assembled together, and have been an object of their attention myself, I have invariably heard their cheers for O'Connell. But it strikes me to mention that even out of Ireland there have been and constantly are marks of this affection. In London, a very considerable sum was subscribed to present him with a piece of plate. It cannot be said that he had any 'hired ruffians' there with 'cudgels' in their hands, to compel the Irish to subscribe. His cudgel-bearing ruffians will hardly be believed to be at New York; yet two hundred pounds were sent from that city to Mr Barrett, because he suffered imprisonment for an alleged libel attributed to Mr O'Connell.[13]

Now, my friends, if these be not proofs of *affection* towards Mr O'Connell, there are no such proofs to be found, and there is no such thing as national affection. Nor is this affection the effect of delusion, or the effect of what this beastly writer calls *infatuation*: it is founded in sense and in virtue; it is founded in a deep sense of the gratitude due to past services, and in a conviction that if the lot of Ireland be to be made better, Mr O'Connell is the man to effect that object, which, while it must be desired most anxiously by every humane person on the face of the earth, comes home so closely to the bosom of every Irishman, from the highest to the lowest. In short, and to conclude, if the Irish people were not to do the very thing which this prostituted English newspaper so calumniously condemns, they would deserve, not that which they now suffer; for no human beings can deserve that; but they would deserve to linger along without hope of amendment. This they do not deserve; and I have the very great pleasure in assuring you that the calumnies heaped upon their champion will, so far as they have any effect at all, tend to augment the amount of the 'tribute', rather than to diminish it.

I have not seen Mr O'Connell, nor any one of his family, since I came to Ireland, except his son-in-law, Mr Fitzsimon; but, never forgetting the support that I myself have received from him, were there no other consideration, I should have acted a very base part if I had not, the moment this vile libel reached my eyes, addressed you upon the subject in the manner that I have here done.

WM. COBBETT.

Political Register, 8 November 1834.

The O'Connell Tribute

To Mr Staunton, of the *Morning Register*.

Dublin, 29 October 1834.
DEAR SIR, – I have read in that corrupt and all-corrupting paper, the London *Times* of the 27 of this month of October, one of the most, if not the most, infamous of the publications that I ever read even in that paper, which I have known for thirty years to be engaged, with very little exception, in support of every species of corrupt government, and in advocating every measure of oppression and tyranny, always relying for its reward on the base, money-loving, monopolizing plunderers of the people in and about London. The article to which I allude relates to that which is now, with great propriety, called 'THE O'CONNELL TRIBUTE.' Under other circumstances, I might have been excused for contenting myself with a bare expression of my abhorrence of this instance of the villainy of this paper. But the circumstance in which I am now placed having given me a perfect knowledge of all the facts relating to this matter, it would be a shameful abandonment of my duty not to endeavour to remove from the minds of the people of England the impressions which the audacious falsehoods of the above-named paper are calculated to produce in those minds. This I shall now do; and the object of this letter to you is to request that you will be pleased to circulate my address to my countrymen through your paper, I having no other means of doing it in so speedy a manner.

I am, sir, your obedient,
And most humble servant,
WM. COBBETT.

Political Register, 8 November 1834.

To Mr Staunton, of The Morning Register

Dublin, 31 October 1834.
SIR,
I thank you for having inserted in your excellent paper of yesterday my address to my countrymen on the subject of the abominable slanders against Mr O'CONNELL and the Irish public, contained in the London *Times* newspaper of the 27th of October. It would have been very pleasing to me to have stopped here; to have confined myself merely to my thanks for this act of kindness on your part. But, sir, you published at the same time a short commentary; but short as it is you have done positive injustice to *my countrymen*, and not very clear justice to *myself*. This is what I think, and it has never been a practice with me to smother my thoughts in a case where I dared utter them. I do dare to utter them now; and, first quoting the commentary itself, I will make a few short observations upon it, which I trust you will have the goodness to lay before the public. The commentary is in the following words:

'MR COBBETT – THE O'CONNELL TRIBUTE.

'The people of Ireland will feel themselves bound to MR COBBETT in new ties of gratitude for the chastisement of E N G L I S H   F A L S E H O O D S and I N S O L E N C E contained in the present number of the *Morning Register*. Often has that S I N G U L A R writer excited our admiration by the vigour and readiness of his pen, but never, certainly, on any occasion more remarkably than the present.'

Now, sir, I have very seldom known any Englishman, especially when in another country, so base as to hear England attacked without an endeavour to defend her; and to me this accusation never could be applied; under all circumstances, whether at home or abroad; whether under the iron persecution of the Government or not; though exposed to all the evils of poverty; though tempted by all the allurements of certain prosperity; I have never failed to adhere, not only to my legal allegiance to my country, but have always made her character, her good or ill name inseparable from my own. I have always resented, as an attack upon myself, every species of attack made upon my countrymen in general; every attack upon the English name, as an attack upon the name of WILLIAM COBBETT; and, sir, in this I have found imitators, or co-operators more properly, in all my countrymen; and the poorer they have been, the more true I have found them to their country, though far away from her and doomed never to see her again. You, sir, have attacked the English character, and here am I to resent that attack, and to prove that my resentment is just.

You say, sir, that the vile article in the *Times* newspaper, chastisement of which by me, 'binds the Irish people in new ties of gratitude' to me; you say that this mass of calumny on MR O'CONNELL is 'E N G L I S H *falsehood* and *insolence*'. Now, sir, it is I R I S H *falsehood* and *insolence*, and not one particle of it *English*. The vile article itself, besides being the production of an Irish pen, is nothing more than an amplification of a letter from an *Irish correspondent dated in Dublin*, published in that very same number of the vile *Times* newspaper. I pray you, sir, look at that letter from Dublin. I pray you to observe that the whole is of Irish origin, and not the work of any of my countrymen; and then, I will not doubt that you will publicly retract your unjust accusation against them.

It is truly curious, that, in this very identical number of your paper, containing this charge relative to English falsehood and insolence, you should publish, from under the pen of MR O'CONNELL himself, that complete refutation of the infamous falsehoods relative to MR O'GORMAN MAHON, and to his pretended crouching to the Attorney-General. It is truly curious that you should have published this in this very same paper, and have sent through the world, from under the pen of MR O'CONNELL himself, the statement of the fact, that the mean and treacherous miscreant, who has hatched and promulgated the worst of lies against him, through the *Observer* newspaper, is a *renegade Irishman*! And this you send forth to the world in the very paper, in which you call the calumnies of MR O'CONNELL proceeding from *another Irish pen, English* falsehood and insolence.

It is a sorrowful truth, sir, but it is a truth; and if the promulgation of it, by the means of my pen, be disagreeable to you, I beg to observe, that you will have yourself to thank for it. It is a sorrowful truth that the worst enemies of Ireland have been and are Irishmen; and this remark applies particularly to the writers for the press. Not only the wretches who are writing in the *Observer*, and who are supplying the *Times* newspaper with the calumnies afore-mentioned, are Irish renegadoes; but the editor of the *Standard*, of the London *Morning Post*, of the London *Morning Advertiser*, commonly called the *tap-tub*, of that contemptible heap of filth called the *Globe*, all of them continually abusing MR O'CONNELL, and representing the Irish as a mad mob, whom it is necessary to coerce; *every one of these men are Irishmen*; the *John Bull* is under the sole direction of an Irishman: that same Irishman is the director and principal writer of the political part of the *Quarterly Review*. Now, here is the great body of literary stuff that is constantly at work against the character, the freedom, the rights, and the happiness of Ireland; and it is all Irish born and bred. On the other hand, there is the *Morning Herald*, there is myself, who, though little, tell for *something* at any rate, there is the *True Sun*, there are several weekly papers of immense circulation, there is the *Examiner*, a paper of long standing, and always of great talent, there are not less than two hundred provincial papers. Now, sir, of all these papers, not one out of twenty ever contains an article of foul attack upon MR O'CONNELL, or of inhuman assault upon the Irish people, except by chance such article may have been copied from the pens of the Irish hacks in London. The truth is, these papers are owned for the greater part by Englishmen, some few by Scotchmen; and none of them are so foolish and so bare, as to have in their employ renegadoes from Ireland. Besides which, as far as relates to the provincial papers, (some of which, such as the *Leeds Mercury*, the *Salisbury Journal*, and the *Sherborne Mercury*, have ten times the effect of any London paper), these papers are, in point of locality, unfitted for the debauched and hired renegadoes before-mentioned. This, then, is the *English* press; and not that part of it of which the *Times* and *Observer* are specimens, and which exist by corruption, and find, as their fittest tools, the renegadoes from Ireland.

Sir, I have always lamented these attacks, made upon my

countrymen by Irish writers; and I have frequently felt *deep resentment* on account of them. A little time to think has convinced me of the injustice of visiting upon already ill-treated Ireland the effects of resentment excited by these *indiscreet* (to use the mildest terms) defenders of their country. Let us look a little at facts, and see how they make out this charge of English *falsehood* and *insolence* and want of feeling for Ireland.

I am always ready to allow, and have been always eager to proclaim, the great gratitude due from Ireland to MR O'CONNELL for his exertions with regard to the emancipation bill. It suited the policy of the Duke of WELLINGTON and Sir ROBERT PEEL to ascribe that measure solely to those exertions. It was much better for them to do that rather than ascribe the measures to the resolute attitude and the petitions of the people of England; but, if the people of Englnd had come and placed themselves at the back of the opponents of the measure, that measure never would have been carried. It was Newcastle, Leeds, Manchester, Birmingham, Nottingham, and London, that carried that measure, co-operating with the astounding exertions of Mr O'CONNELL. And, sir, were there English *falsehood* and *insolence* at work, in the case of the Coercion Bill? Even the Irish renegadoes in the *Times* newspaper were *compelled* by the public voice of England to cry out against that measure. I carried it into the House, from Newcastle, from Shields, from Sutherland, from Stockton, from Bradford, from Oldham, and from other great towns, petitions signed by more than 150,000 persons, at least such is my best recollection of the number; but which is of still greater importance as to this matter, I carried in petitions against that bill, the most sensible, the most modest, and, at the same time, the most resolute, from a *great number of country parishes*, in the southern counties of England, particularly from Kent and Sussex; and, let it be recollected, that the very first petition that was received by any member of the House against that bill came from the little parish of Wingham, in East Kent, and the second from the little town of Battle, in Sussex; and yet you lump all Englishmen together; impute to them inherent and implacable hostility to Ireland, and brand them with a charge of falsehood and insolence. Leaving you and your readers, sir, to judge whether this be the likely way to obtain the cordial co-operation of your fellow-subjects in England, in obtaining a redress of these unspeakable grievances, which I, with mine own eyes, have now seen to exist, I will, in conclusion of this too long letter, respectfully offer you my opinion of the matter.

In the answer, which I gave to the kind and cordial address with which the citizens of Dublin were pleased to honour me, I took the liberty to observe to them that I believed that their grievances would never be redressed, *unless by the aid of their fellow-subjects in England*;[14] and I am now, after personal examination into the state of the country, and after attentive observation of men and things, fully confirmed in that opinion. In a *peaceable* manner, these grievances never will be redressed without such co-operation; and, though it is within the compass of possibility, that a change for the better might be effected by different means, the risk is too great for any lover of his country to attempt it, unless, at any rate, the whole race of those perfidious wretches, who are now renegadoes from their country, could be first extirpated, and swept from the face of the earth.

So much, sir, for what I deem your injustice to my countrymen. With regard to your injustice to myself: in the first place, I disclaim all praise coupled with an attack on England, or Englishmen; and, in the next place, I beg of you to have the goodness, if you should ever think it worth your while to mention me again, with an epithet prefixed to my name or character, not to make use of the epithet '*singular*,' but to cast aside, if you please, the phraseology of Lord BROUGHAM, the *Quarterly Reviewers*, and the like, and to make use of some word that shall be *definite*, as to the character which it describes; for instance, to call me good, bad, wise, foolish, or something that shall not be *equivocal*. This is after the English manner, to be sure; but, if you will condescend to observe it, in speaking of me in future you will very much oblige,

Sir,
Your most obedient
And most humble servant,
WM. COBBETT.

NOTES

[1] 'Their landords' – the bishops, abbots, abbesses, et cetera.

[2] Cobbett's advocacy of physical resistance to tyranny, though in accordance with the Church's teaching and the general practice of oppressed peoples, was more a gesture of goodwill towards the people of Kilmallock and Ireland than a realistic incitement to arms.

[3] Cobbett is referring to the Peterloo Massacre, August 1819.

[4] On behalf of the members of the National Political Union, Cobbett had presented a petition detailing Popay's conduct as government spy and provocateur.

[5] Cobbett had moved the repeal on 10 March. The tax on malt and hops was a matter very close to his heart. *Mr. Cobbett's Speech, and other Speeches, on his Motion for the Abolition of the Malt Tax* he published in pamphlet form earlier in the year.

[6] Between the Act of Union and 1846, no less than 18 separate Irish Coercion Bills were carried at Westminster, under various titles.

[7] Before 1818, rate-payers whether landlord or tenant, had enjoyed a single vote in the vestry. In that year Sturges Bourne's Act provided for multiple votes in accordance with the value of the rate. In 1831 and again in 1834 Parliament had legislated for even greater powers in the vestry to wealthier landlords, and allowed their votes to be handed in by proxy.

[8] The six Tolpuddle farm labourers were transported in 1834. Their sentences were remitted in 1836 after nation-wide pressure from the entire working class and radical movement. Cobbett, before his death was active in their defence in the columns of the *Political Register*.

[9] Cobbett is presumably thinking of Moscow, in 1812.

[10] Mrs Dorothea Jordan, mistress of the Duke of Clarence. One of her children was provided with a junior commission in a cavalry regiment at the tender age of 14; see Aspinall, *Mrs Jordan and her Family*, London 1951.

[11] The 'bloody old Times' was sometimes 'the Bourbon paper', 'Anna Brodie' (after John Walter's married daughter), or just 'the vile Times'.

[12] Graham was a great landowner and member of Grey's Whig cabinet in 1830, after Wellington's resignation.

[13] Richard Barrett was at this time in prison for advocating a repeal of the Union. In America, branches of the 'Friends of Ireland' (the parent society was in New York) were carrying resolutions of sympathy and collecting subscriptions on Mr Barrett's behalf. (See *Political Register*, 17 May 1834.)

[14] This may be compared with Marx's view: 'I have become more and more convinced – and the only question is to drive this conviction home to the English working class – that it can never do anything decisive here in England until it separates its policy with regard to Ireland most definitely from the policy of the ruling classes, until it not only makes common cause with the Irish but actually takes the initiative in dissolving the Union ...' (Letter to Kugelman, 29 November 1869, in Karl Marx and Frederich Engels, op.cit., p. 394.)

CHAPTER 7

Political Register, 8 November 1834.

To the People of Salisbury

Dublin, 3 November 1834.
MY FRIENDS,
    LORD RADNOR has thought proper to bring down amongst you a man of the name of BROUGHAM, who, if we are to believe his own assertion, was born in Scotland, but whose father lives at a little place in Westmoreland, called the 'BIRD'S NEST', and which this man calls 'BROUGHAM HALL'; a place altogether being not half as big as Lord RADNOR's stable and walled-in garden at Longford Castle. This man was a brawling lawyer for several years, and has now, for the Lord only knows what reason, been made a lord, and Lord High Chancellor. You must have been surprised to see this man brought down to Salisbury by Lord Radnor, and to see a Lord High Chancellor with his head out of a public-house window, making a speech to a parcel of men and women and idle boys and girls in the street, and calling them 'gentlemen', and Lord Radnor standing amongst them and huzzaing amongst the rest, especially after you found that the mayor would not let Lord Radnor and his friend into the council-house, which his father built, and in which he himself is the R E C O R D E R. All this must have surprised you moon-rakers! But it was this fellow's talking to you about his consistency which was the most impudent part of the farce. This man was the real author of the POOR-LAW BILL; in defending that bill, he said that *all poor-laws were bad*; that the

poor had *no right to relief*; and you know he had Lord Radnor's support in the passing of that bill. I will tell you more about this another time; but what I have to do with at present is that consistency of which he bragged, and of which I am going to give you a specimen.

This BROUGHAM, in order to get elected for WESTMINSTER, in the year 1814, gave it under his hand, that he was an advocate for *annual Parliaments*, and for *giving a vote to every man who paid taxes*; that is to say, *every man*, because every man who drinks beer pays taxes. In 1817 (three years afterwards) this same man, when the people were petitioning for annual Parliaments and this sort of suffrage, he abused them for it, called it madness, ridiculed annual Parliaments and universal suffrage. And he denied that he had ever been in favour of annual Parliaments and universal suffrage. Upon this denial Lord COCHRANE[1] brought into the House of Commons a paper written by his own hand; and then this BROUGHAM shuffled in the same shameful manner that I am now about to show you, by inserting an account of the whole transaction, as recorded in my *Register* of 22 February 1817.

I request you to read it all through with attention, and then to remember these three things:

1. That these two men have been fellow-labourers in the Poor-law Bill.
2. That Lord RADNOR was in the House of Commons, and heard pass all that I am about to relate to you.
3. That Lord RADNOR stood amongst the silly rabble, and cheered this fellow when he bragged of his consistency.

I am,
Your faithful friend,
And most obedient servant,
WM. COBBETT.

Political Register, 8 November 1834.

To Lord Althorp

Dublin, 3 November 1834.
MY LORD,
   I think the storm is gathering about you now: from every point of the compass the threatening clouds seem to be coming. It was impossible that it should not have been so from the natural operation of the funding and paper-money system, aided and abetted and rendered tenfold more mischievous by the effect of that monstrous bill of 1819,[2] my proposition to censure the principal author of which, you were resolved to prevent from remaining one moment on the records of the House, even at the expense of the inviolability of the orders of that House.
   But, my lord, completely dismissing from my mind every feeling of displeasure on account of that transaction, and expressing towards you that degree of respect which is due to your high station, and what I sincerely believe to be your good intentions, I cannot say that I see without pleasure the accumulation of embarrassments that now surround you; because I am convinced that there must be some tremendously powerful cause, some terrific peril, in order to produce that great change in the management of our national affairs which is necessary, and absolutely necessary, to the restoration of the happiness of the people, as well as the unequivocal power of the kingdom and the safety of his Majesty's throne; and if any efforts of mine have a manifest tendency to add to your embarrassments, let them, I beseech you, be ascribed, not to want of intention on my part to make such addition, but to a deliberate design to do it from a conviction that nothing but the last necessity will cause you to adopt those measures which experience has taught me are necessary for the deliverance of our country.
   I happen to know that your father has always taken and read my *Register*, and carefully preserved it from its very first publication. You must have read it too; and that being the case I need not tell you, that, so early as the year 1803, I not only

predicted, but gave good reasons for my prediction, that, sooner or later, the system of borrowing and of paper-money must bring the nation into a state in which (the constitution of England having been by degrees undermined) it should become a question whether the whole of the ancient laws, liberties, and institutions, should be swept away, and all the rights of property along with them; or whether, by one great effort, the Government (including the Parliament and the King of course, and having at their back the really patriotic and forgiving people) should snap in sunder all the trammels of every description invented for the purpose of upholding the system of funding and paper-money, and bring us back to something like the state in which our forefathers left us. If you have read the *Register*, you know that, in this series of one-and-thirty years, I have been constantly warning the Government of the danger of bringing us to this point; and I have all along been stating unanswerable arguments to show that to this point we must come. And this being the fact, is it being very presumptuous for me to entertain the hope and the expectation that you will be pleased to listen to me now?

Amongst your embarrassments there are some which you and a reformed Parliament could not have wholly avoided. You could not have avoided the monstrous weight of the debt. You found it created. It was difficult for you to know how to mitigate the evil. You found enormous, unnatural, anti-English, and most intolerably burdensome establishments; but their existence was inseparable from that of the debt. You found one half of the community living in idleness upon the labour and the penury and the half-starvation of the other half. You found the labourers of England become, in the course of fifty years, rack-renters of their cottages, instead of the owners of them. You found them stripped of the clocks, the feather beds, the Sunday clothes, the silver buckles, which were their common possession fifty years before. You found them just in proportion to the degree of their poverty, reckless, disobedient, listless, immoral, dissolute in their manners, disrespectful in their deportment, unskilful in their business, and every way deteriorated. You found the lands of England all worse cultivated than formerly; some of them not half cultivated; others not a third part; and some thrown up to lie fallow; and, which ought to have made you think that tranquillity and such a state of things were utterly incompatible, you found that this want of cultivation arose from the want of labour upon the land, while there was such a *surplus of labourers in the country* as to induce you yourself to bring into Parliament a bill (which was finally passed) to authorize the heads of parishes to raise money by compulsion upon the parishes for the purpose of defraying the expenses of sending able-bodied labourers out of England!

It is recorded of the first Lord Mansfield, that, hearing threatening howlings round the court-house, when he was giving his charge to a jury, he stopped and said, 'We must not mind this, gentlemen, as drunken men are stunned into sobriety, let us with resignation wait for the blow.' So say I in this case. If that which I have just mentioned, and the truth of which is well known to your lordship, be not a proof that we want something to stun us into sobriety; into sober thought on the perils that surround us, and into a resolution to do something to extricate ourselves from such peril, I know not what can afford such proof.

The difficulties which I have mentioned, and several others, were, at the time when you took possession of power, unavoidable. They might have been overcome, they may now be overcome; but *you* could not have prevented their existence. Not so with regard to others. You could not, indeed, have prevented the monstrous abuses in the established church in England as well as in Ireland; you could not have prevented that monstrous abuse which leaves between three and four thousand of the incumbents of the church of England each with an income far less than that of a journeyman tailor in London, while the revenue of the parishes of which they are incumbents would afford them on an average five hundred pounds a year, or thereabouts; these revenues being swallowed up by the superior clergy, being in general relations or dependants of the aristocracy. You could not have prevented the *existence* of this most crying abuse; but here was an abuse that you might have corrected in the very first session of the reformed Parliament; and now, owing to your not having done that, this great abuse remains one of your difficulties.

But there are other difficulties *created by yourselves*, of which I shall mention at present only two, both of which you owe entirely and solely to your having had the weakness to take

BROUGHAM for one of your colleagues. It has been the lot of that man to *swamp* whomsoever and whatsoever he has suffered to join with or to touch. Long before your ministry was formed, or the reformed Parliament made, I said, that if ever he obtained any considerable degree of power in the state, he would swamp first the Ministry to which he should belong; and next, any system which it should not be his object to uphold. Not, I allow, from any bad, or selfish, or mere grubbing design; but from his possession of great powers of talk; from his wild and innovating and perverse opinions; and from that restless ambition which I long ago saw was never to be gratified by anything short of his becoming the new modeller of the world.

The crack-skulled county of YORK, which WILBERFORCE used to call 'a little kingdom', and which is not, as a piece of dominion, worth nearly so much as the county of CORK, which has only six members to represent it, while the crack-skulls have thirty-seven; this crack-skulled county lifted him up, made him a personage before whom you and Lord GREY trembled, when you might, with all the safety in the world, have set him at defiance. Having clothed him with the highest honour you had to bestow; having made him a partner, and a head partner, in power; having given him the means of surrounding himself with greedy and gratified expectants; having, in short, placed yourselves at his mercy, you were compelled to become the foster-fathers of his schemes, or to brave his hostility, together with that of his indefatigable swarm of scribes and whisperers.

Here we have the source of the NEGRO SCHEME and of the POOR-LAW SCHEME. Can your lordship fail to perceive the terrible difficulties into which these have plunged you; and can you fail to remember the warnings given by me as to both these matters? With regard to the former, I told my constituents that, it being their desire, I would vote for the freeing of the negroes, out and out, at once; but not for the giving of one single farthing of the public money for the purpose of accomplishing that freeing;[3] and your lordship knows that I kept my word scrupulously. You also know that I warned you at the House of Commons, that the negroes would not work without compulsion; and that any attempt to make them work, without the means heretofore made use of, must be productive of confusion and bloodshed. I am of opinion that England derives no strength and no benefit from the raising of sugar and of coffee in any part of the world; I am of opinion that the benefit of possessing the West Indian colonies, merely as a military station, is very equivocal; an expansion of dominion tends to the weakness, rather than to the strength, of a kingdom. But, while these might be matters of dispute, it was little short of downright madness to entertain a hope of carrying on the colonies by a system of free labour, at whatever expense such a system might be attempted to be pursued.

It is possible that, after expending the twenty millions, after expending other millions, with a view of preserving something like order in these colonies, they may be held as dominions of his Majesty, and that bloodshed may in time become less frequent; but that these colonies can be held in future with any advantage to this kingdom, and without great cost and injury to her, is an opinion that can be entertained in no mind not insane by nature, or not rendered such by the application of laudanum and brandy.

The question of *humanity* is now pretty well settled; more misery has been caused, more blood has been shed already, than would have been shed in all probability in twenty years without the aid of this mad measure. But, did you not, my lord, in eulogizing that measure, only a few months ago; did you not perceive the effect which it must have in the United States of America, where there are about four slaves for every one that there was in our West India islands, and where slavery must be upheld unmitigated, or where the power and independence of the country must be abandoned?[4] I remarked on that passage in his Majesty's speech to us, in which you had advised him to express a hope that 'other nations' would follow our example. Most unwise was it to give that advice to his Majesty. It was sure to attract the quick sight of the Americans, who knew well that there was no other nation than their own to whom the remark could apply; who knew well that there exists nothing worthy of the name of slavery in the colonies of Spain, Portugal, or any other country; who knew well, in short, that they themselves were meant; and who would naturally conclude that that measure, which you wished to represent as one emanating from pure humanity, was, in fact, a measure of covert hostility against themselves.

Accordingly, they are proceeding with the usual good sense and resolution of that people, to counteract the effects of our measure. It has not required a word from the Government to produce this counteraction; facts, impressing themselves upon sound heads, have told the people what to do, and they have at once, and of their own accord, put to silence even the expression of opinions in favour of an imitation of our scheme. I think, at least I hope, that they overcharge the matter in accusing you and your colleagues of an intention to cause rebellion amongst the negroes in their country; but it will be very difficult to make any one of them participate in my opinion, or in my hopes, upon this subject; and we may be well assured, that this act, of which we boast as a wonderful act of humanity and generosity, will be treasured up in their minds as an additional proof of that implacable hatred of their institutions, their freedom, and their happiness, of which implacable hatred they had so many indubitable proofs in the reign of George the Fourth, which I have clearly shown in my history of that regency and reign. It is in the character of our Government to be resolved never to see or to hear anything that is disagreeable to it. Your lordship, doubtless, participates in this unfortunate taste; or I would send you an American publication, in which the question is gravely discussed, whether it be not as laudable to raise money in the United States for the purpose of *freeing white* persons in an *European island* that shall be nameless,[5] as it was to raise money to free *black persons* in the islands of America! Ah, my lord, these wild schemes send us back to *first principles*; set men to thinking, compel them to think, and make them *prepare to act*, in relation to principles which never before occupied a space in their minds.

Beyond, therefore, the mere flinging away of twenty millions of money; far beyond this, and far beyond the loss of the colonies, too, this measure may, and inevitably will, add to the hostile feelings in the United States against this kingdom; and, my lord, do you think that the *burning of the Parliament* house, when the news of that shall arrive in the United States, will not call forth the exclamation of 'Ah! that was the house in which George the Fourth bragged of, and in which the members applauded to the echoing of the roof, *the burning of the Congress-house at WASHINGTON'?* The shouts of the people of

London, the laugh that was heard from Westminster-bridge to the thing called W A T E R L O O - B R I D G E; the shout after shout that were heard during the progress of the flames; even those shouts were less stunning than will be the shouts in the great cities of America. 'It is nothing, may it please your Majesty, but the shouting of the foolish soldiers, on Hounslow-heath, for the acquittal of the bishops', said the courtiers of JAMES the Second. 'And, do you call that nothing?' said the King. He felt that it was *something*; and, if he had *instantly* profited from it, his descendants would now have been upon the throne. It was something, and so was the shout of the people, 'that another P O O R - L A W B I L L would never be passed there'.

This is the other measure which you owe entirely and solely to BROUGHAM. The history of this bill, beginning with the declaration by BROUGHAM, of his readiness to maintain the principles of MALTHUS to their full extent, a declaration made in 1819; the appointment of the commissioners; the character of those commissioners; the appointment of their runners; the character of those runners; the non-official book laid on the table of the House of Commons, a year before the bill itself appeared; the character of that book; the pushing on of the bill to a second reading, before the reports and the evidence were laid upon the table; and before it was possible for any one member of the House to have read one tenth part of the papers; the desertion of all its defenders except yourself, who were left at the last discussion with ten speeches against you; not one for you, and you avowing that he must be a bold Minister who would bring in the same bill again; the bare history of this bill would swamp any Ministry that ever existed. It might reel along; but reeling along is not existing; and in that reeling state it has now placed even your lordship, in spite of your character for good sense and integrity.

Your colleague has the quality of being indefatigable in an exemplary degree. As the mountain would not come to MAHOMET, MAHOMET went to the mountain; so your colleague, as SALISBURY, with its 11, 672 inhabitants, would not come to him, he would go to SALISBURY: as the little town of FAREHAM in Hampshire, with its 1,500 inhabitants, and its '*Mechanics' Institute*', would not come to him, he would go to the '*Mechanics' Institute*' at FAREHAM, and almost faint away under the praises of *three-and-forty* young fellows, who were biting their lips to smother a laugh, while the Lord Chancellor of England was 'tipping' them a speech on the blessings of *useful knowledge*. Ah! my lord! but it is SALISBURY that presents the melancholy spectacle. He had got upon the back of poor Lord RADNOR, and he stuck to him like a weazel that has its body on the back, and its muzzle in the poll, of a hare. In vain did he flee from London to Longford castle. The poor hare runs with all her might, but at last down she comes. And there is Lord RADNOR; so good, so kind, so considerate, in his nature; so beloved, and so justly beloved, by all around him; brought down to be one amongst a contemptible group of huzzaers, while his pursuer was haranguing them from the window of a public-house; and there he is now to exist under the reflections, accompanying the recollection of having been a party in this gotten-up and most ridiculous and contemptible drama, the reporters of the account of which have been hired to suppress the fact, that there were, even at SALISBURY, men with spirit enough to cry, '*We do not want coarser food; put on one of your* workhouse dresses!' and the like. The mayor of SALISBURY acted a very becoming part in refusing the use of the council chamber to this operator, and it must have been pleasant to my Lord RADNOR to reflect, and to have it known to the whole nation, that he was refused, and that such was the objection to his companion that he was refused admission into the council-house, built at the expense of his own father, and given by him to the city, being at the same time his own home, and the place of his birth! Thus it is to endeavour to palm upon the people a man like BROUGHAM. Wealth, ancient family, great benevolence in a neighbourhood, deservedly high character; these can do much; but even these are not sufficient to bear you up under the swamping weight of such a man as this.

No, my lord, not even you; even you must go down; or get rid of this colleague. He is the weazel, he is the nightmare, he is the indigestion, he is the deadly malady of the Ministry. He swamped Lord GREY, he swamped Lord RADNOR even, which is a great deal more; and he will swamp you, if you do not swamp him.

To conclude, when he was at SALISBURY he ranted away about many things; said how much good he had done, and how much more good he intended to do; did not say anything about *coarser food*, and workhouse dresses, and about separating wives from husbands, and both from children; but said a great deal about *useful knowledge*, and about the numerous good things that he had done; but the main drift of his speech was to make the people believe that he was *remarkable for his* C O N S I S T E N C Y. I wonder that my lord RADNOR was not ashamed to stand and hear this in silence! His neighbours of SALISBURY, he knew well, were incapable of detecting the falsehood; but he himself knew it was a falsehood, and the most glaring and impudent falsehood ever uttered by mortal man. He knew that there were scores of instances of the grossest inconsistency of this very man; and your lordship's memory must be very short if you do not know it, too. If you have forgotten every instance of it, it is necessary that you should have one laid before you at full length, in what I am about to address to the people of SALISBURY, to whom I shall clearly show the consistency, at any rate, of the man whom Lord RADNOR thought proper to bring down amongst them as one worthy of their praise.

I am,
Your lordship's most obedient,
And most humble servant,
W M . C O B B E T T .

Political Register, 8 November 1834.

To Charles Marshall, Labourer, Letter No. VII

*Normandy Tithing, Parish of Ash,
Farnham, Surrey.*

Dublin, 4 November 1834.
MARSHALL,

I dare say that my letters have made you stare; but, staring is not all that they ought to make you do: they ought to make you think about how you would like to have a naked wife and children; how you would like to have no shoes or stockings, or shirt, and the mud spewing up between your toes when you come down the road to your work of a morning. They ought to make you think about what you shall *do, all of you*, to prevent this state of starvation, nakedness, and filth, from coming upon you. Do not think that it is I M P O S S I B L E that it should ever come upon you. Do not think this; for there is no *reason* for your thinking it. The countries are very close to one another. The county of Cork is but a very little way from Somersetshire. I am not so far from you now as I should be if I were at Morpeth in the county of Northumberland. The same Ministers and the same Parliament who keep this people in this state, after having got them into it, are the same Ministers and same Parliament who have got the power of making laws, and of employing soldiers and policemen in England. This miserable people have been brought to this state by little and little, and for want of beginning in time to *do the things which they ought to have done in their own defence*; to make use of the faculties which God has given them; that is to say, in legally and constitutionally, and according to the good custom of our wise and brave forefathers, petitioning the King and the Parliament, and otherwise legally doing that, which the laws of our country bid us do, sanctioned as those laws are by the laws of God.

MARSHALL, I told you that you had as much *right*, as clear a legal right to parish relief; that you had as much right to relief out of the produce of my farm, in case of necessity; in case of illness in your family; in case of inability in yourself to work; or in case of your being unable to get work. I told you that, in either of these cases, you had as clear a legal right to relief out of the produce of my farm, as I had to the rest of the produce; or as Mr WOODRUFFE had to his rent. To *prove* this to you, and to all of you, will require one long letter; and I have not time to write that now; but I will mention a few things just to prepare the way for giving you such proof.

You will observe, MARSHALL, that I shall attempt to say nothing about the matter which I cannot prove to be according to the *laws of England*; those laws which we owe to our wise and resolute forefathers. I could tell you (and Farmer HORNE ought to tell his congregation), that the Holy Bible, which you know, MARSHALL, is the word of God, commands, from one end of it to the other, that the working man shall receive his full hire; that provision shall always be made for those who are too poor to help themselves; that the widow, the fatherless, and the stranger, shall be taken care of, and that all manner of curses shall fall upon the rich, *if* they do not take care of them. Farmer HORNE should take care to read to his congregation those passages of the New Testament, in which our Saviour and his apostles warned the rich of the curses that shall alight upon them, if they despise or neglect the poor. He ought to read to them the fifth chapter of St JAMES, which begins thus: 'Go, you rich men, weep and howl for your miseries that shall come upon you: the rust of your gold and silver shall eat your flesh as it were *fire*. You have by fraud kept back the hire of your labourers who have reaped down your fields; and their cries have entered into the ears of the Lord.' He should read to them the passage in the 15th chapter of DEUTERONOMY, which tells the farmer, that, when the labourer has served him faithfully for a length of time, and when he sends him away, not wanting him any more, he is not to send him away empty, either as to belly, back, or hands: he should read to them, this: 'When thou sendest him away thou shalt not let him go empty: thou shalt furnish him liberally out of thy flock, out of thy floor and out of thy wine-press. Of that wherewith the Lord thy God hath blessed thee, thou shalt give unto him.'

Now, MARSHALL, this is the word of God; and it is the business of the parsons and of Farmer HORNE to read these things to you and to me, that we may know our duty. It is my duty to give a good and faithful servant plenty of meat from my flock of sheep, or my drove of hogs; to give him plenty of flour or bread, coming from the wheat that shall be thrashed upon my floor. In the country where God promulgated his law, grapes grow naturally in the fields, and the climate is too hot for the keeping of beer. Therefore, they drank wine, as we drink beer; and as it was their duty to supply the labourer out of the wine-press, so it is our duty to supply him out of the mash-tub. Not a hint is here given about infamous potatoes and salt. The law of God forbids to muzzle the ox while he is treading out the corn. In those hot countries they make use of cattle to tread out the corn, the corn is so dry. It was, and is, the custom in those countries, to employ oxen, or horses, to tread the corn out; and in order that the farmers should be merciful and just, even to the animals that they employed, God commands, in the 25th chapter of DEUTERONOMY, 'Thou shalt not *muzzle* the ox when he treadeth out the corn'; that is to say, thou shalt not pinch him, thou shalt not take from him a share of that which he has caused to come. And what can be more just than this? For what would any farm be good for, and how would Mr WOODRUFFE get any rent out of it, if it were not for the labour that you and the rest of you bestow upon it; and how are you to perform that labour, unless you have out of it a sufficiency to eat and to drink and to wear?

Such, then, is a specimen of the laws of God. The laws of England say, that nothing can be law of man, which is contrary to the laws of God. It is the very first principle of the laws of England; and this principle is laid down by all our great lawyers in all ages, that any rule, regulation, or call it what you will, which is contrary to the laws of God, cannot be law in England. Begging you to bear this in mind; begging those who can read it, to read it to those who cannot read, I shall conclude for the present, promising you that, in another letter, I will show you, that the laws which were left us by our forefathers, and which are the birthright of us all, are in perfect agreement with these laws of the King of kings and of the Ruler of the rulers of the earth.

Hoping that you are all well, and that you will not let me see a weed on the farm by the time that I get back; and in full confidence that no half-drunk and half-mad vagabond will be able to induce any body to do any thing that shall take away your shirts and your shoes and your stockings, make you live upon *lumpers*, and sleep upon hog dung, covered over with dirty straw: thus trusting, and trusting also to your own sense and own spirit, to make that lawful use of your rights, which will prevent so great a disgrace falling upon England,

I remain,
Your master and friend,
WM. COBBETT.

Pilot, 10 November 1834.

Mr Cobbett's Lecture on Repeal

On Saturday[6] evening Mr Cobbett addressed a very numerous auditory in Fishamble-street. The question proposed by him to lecture upon was 'the Repeal of the Union.'

Mr Cobbett went upon the stage about seven o'clock, and was received with the most enthusiastic cheers. He then proceeded to address them thus – Gentlemen, when I had the honour of addressing you before, not having seen the country, I declined offering a distinct opinion on the subject of a repeal of the Union – (cheers) – on the ground that though I had formed an opinion upon the subject, yet it could not be as well founded in reason as it might and it ought to be before I returned to Dublin again. (Hear.)

I have seen the country now, and the first thing that struck me, and that must strike any other man who sees the country is this – things cannot remain as they are. (Hear, and cheers.) Repeal of the Union or no Repeal of the Union, whatever be the consequences, a change there must be in the management of the affairs of Ireland. (Hear.) Having then made up your mind upon that point, you next set your mind to inquire what sort of change there should be? I confess that after as much deliberation and attention as I am master of – after bestowing upon the subject all the time I could spare, and as much time as I ever gave to any subject, my deliberate opinion is that there ought to be a separation of the legislatures of the two countries. (Hear, and long-continued cheers.) Be so kind as to hear my reasons for that opinion, for the opinion is not worth a straw unless there are reasons to support it.

This subject that we are now talking of – the very mooting of it has been looked upon as a sort of sedition or treason in itself! (Hear.) It has been thought to be a crime to talk of it; and some gentlemen, I remember, when the Coercion Bill was brought in, introduced the question of Repeal, and spoke of it as if the stirring of such a question was treason. It was the real ground for passing that Bill, and the attacks upon Mr O'Connell; and they represented that the talking of a Repeal of the Union was something approaching to an attempt to repeal the Bible! – to repeal the sun, or something of that sort.

They said it was a thing not to be talked of but as a crime, and those who spoke of it should be put to death without trial! What a monstrous proposition, said they, is this of Mr O'Connell – what madness to discuss it – it is a thing 'to be resisted unto the death!' (Hear, and laughter.) 'Resisted unto the death!!!' Resist what? The repeal of an Act of Parliament! Why, any Act of Parliament can be repealed. There never was any Act of Parliament before, which could not be repealed by the same legislature that passed it – the same power that *made* can *unmake* it. What a terrible thing is this then to be resisted unto the death? – just as if an Act of Parliament was never repealed before; and this is said, too, when we can find five hundred Acts of Parliament in which Magna Carta itself is repealed in part.

I can find another Act of Parliament in which the Triennial Bill is repealed. When was that Triennial Bill passed?[7] It was an Act between the King and the people – it was an Act securing to the people their freedom, and giving to a certain person the throne – it was an Act for securing to the people triennial Parliaments, and these kingdoms to the House of Hanover; and yet there was a Parliament elected for three years. Here, indeed, was fraud and baseness! – and this Parliament, elected for three years, repealed the Triennial Bill, and ordained that it should sit for seven years. That was not resisted to the death, though it was, indeed, an Act to be so resisted. Yet it was not, and no one ever accused of high treason those who had proposed to repeal that Bill.

There was an Act of Parliament which was in force for a couple of hundred years – for nearly three hundred years.[8] It was an act for enforcing residence on the part of the clergy of the Church of England. If any parson absented himself from his parish for so long a time in the year, or if he lived out of the parsonage for so long a time in the year, he should forfeit a certain sum. This was to prevent them from staying away from their parishes, through any inadvertence, for they could not have any desire to neglect their duties! It was to prevent the clergy of that church to which I have the honour to belong from absenting themselves from their parishes. Here was an Act of Parliament, a long time in existence – An act that was enforced: several actions were founded upon it, verdicts were obtained in several cases, and judgments given in others – and yet what was done?

The Church found itself in danger. What did it do? Here was an Act not only in existence for three hundred years, but it had gone into effect, and there were the decisions of the Court of King's Bench upon it. They could not repeal that Act – they could not repeal it, *then*? Yes, they could. They first stopped all the actions, and there were several brought at the time – they then stayed them again for another year – they then made the informers lose all the expenses of these suits; the next year they passed an Act quashing all the actions brought, and the next year they repealed the Act altogether. (Hear, hear.)

Well, then, an Act of Parliament can be repealed without resisting it unto the death. (Hear, hear, and cheers.) I remember all these proceedings myself – they occurred in 1802; the Bill for repealing that old Act of Parliament was brought in by Sir William Scott, the brother of the late Lord Chancellor. Nobody then talked of resisting the repeal of an Act of Parliament to the death. The Church was in danger, and was an Act of Parliament to stand in the way of clergymen straying away from their flocks without anybody knowing why? (Hear, hear, and laughter.)

This, then, shows than an Act of Parliament can be repealed. This (the Union) is an Act of Parliament only thirty-four years in existence; only think of that. (Hear.) But another Act of Parliament was repealed much more solemn in its character than the Act of Union. It was an Act of Parliament for setting aside the family of the Stuarts, and seating upon the throne another family. If ever there was an Act of Parliament that should be considered solemn and absolute in all its parts it was that act. How did that act begin? It was an act for limiting the crown, and for the better preservation of the liberties and religion of the people of England. Now, there was an Act in which the rights of the crown were referred to; but the main object was to preserve the religion and the liberties of the English people.

There was a most solemn Act of Parliament – it was an Act by which the House of Hanover came to the throne. In that Act it was expressly provided that no person employed by the crown as military or naval officers – no person receiving the public money in any sort of way, should sit in the House of Commons; and there is now the House of Commons full of them! One good half of that House consists of persons who are receiving the public money in one shape or other.

There were no officers to sit in that house, and there they now sit, whole rows of them, before me when I am in that house. When I sit there beside the Irish members, I see a whole row, as long as that opposite to me, of admirals and generals. (Laughter.) They have now got 450 generals and 250 admirals. They have got four generals and a half for every regiment of infantry and cavalry, and they have five admirals for every ship of the line! (Laughter!) They have a pretty good show of them, and these persons, not having anything to do in the fighting way, come now and busy themselves in the law-making way. (Hear, and laughter!) There they are, whole rows of them, in the very face of that Act of Parliament. Aye, but that Act of Parliament *was repealed*, in so much as it related to their being members. When the question was for putting their hands into our pocket – when that was to be done by their having a seat in the House of Commons – when they were to get the power of putting their hands into our pockets – when that only was the question, there was no 'resisting to the death' for any one talking of a repeal of that Act.

There is nothing so sacred in an Act of Parliament as not to admit of its repeal. (Hear, hear, and cheers.) There was the Bank Charter Act – how often was it repealed?[9] (Hear.) Now, nothing has been declared to be so sacred as a charter, and you might expect to hear some of those persons say, 'My God! do not violate a charter.' Yes, but they could and they did violate the Bank Charter in 1797; they first violated it by an Order in Council, and without the consent of Parliament at all. They were not punished for doing this; no – the Parliament said the motive was so good that we cannot call the act criminal. In your case we will judge of the motive by the act, and the act was so good that your motive must be good. They violated that Act, and for what purpose? We see all the ruin which from that day to this has fallen upon the country from paper money, and of which I spoke to you last night. (Hear.)

It is then, you perceive, no crime to propose the repeal of an Act of Parliament; and here is an Act of Parliament which for thirty-four years has been found to interfere with the happiness and prosperity of an entire people. (Hear.) I do not pretend to more candour than the rest of my countrymen. I know that they are ambitious – that they are arrogant, greedy, fond of power, and of dominion all over the world. I do not pretend to be less greedy or arrogant; but with these feelings in my breast, I am friendly to Repeal, because I am as sincerely anxious for the honor of England as I am for the happiness of Ireland. (Hear, and cheers.)

It has often been said that the end can never satisfy the means; and I must say, that, considering the means by which the Union was carried, the horrible crimes that were perpetrated to effect it, (if) it was one of the wisest measures ever carried, I should still take my stand upon this, that the honor and morality both of the King and the people demanded its repeal. If any body remembers or reads the transactions of those times – if he learns the means by which the Union was carried, he cannot do so without a shudder of horror; and when he finds there was so much of violence and bribery used, he cannot but believe that no good could ever come of it – he cannot but be confident that a mischief must befall any nation that would use such dreadful means as were employed to accomplish the Union. (Hear.)

And yet, after all, they say that the Union was for the good of Ireland. Mr Spring-Rice says it was good for Ireland; England did not want the Union – Ireland required the Union – her necessities demanded it. If then, the Union be truly for the benefit of Ireland, why not let Ireland take her choice? (Hear, hear.) I believe, if it were put to the vote, there would be a very small minority against the Repeal measure. (Hear, and cheers.) There is something odious in this hypocritical pretence. You know that this hypocritical sort of reasoning prejudices a person even against what might be fair arguments in defence of the Union. (Hear, hear.) The terms of the Union show the kind of work that was going on when the Union was made. (Hear.) But I have said some change must take place, and I am sure it must. If there were nothing beyond the foul conditions of the Union, it would be impossible for Ireland to continue a consenting party to the trickery used towards her.

What is your number of representatives in the *imperial* Parliament? – for you are so lucky as to belong to an empire. Every thing is now grand and imperial! Now, for my part, I would sooner have beer and bread, and live under a king, or even in a republic, than eat *lumpers*, and belong to an empire! (Hear, cheers, and laughter.) I never yet knew a people to be greater or happier from any fine names that their sovereigns had. (Laughter.) I say, as to the number of your representatives in the imperial Parliament, you can have no real representation at all. There are your hundred of Irish members on one side, and 558 on the other.

Parliaments are held at the court and in the seductions of the metropolis: suppose that all your members (and this would be too much to expect) were every one of them too old to be won over by the ladies – then he is not young enough to do the work he ought. (Laughter.) He is not young enough to sit up until twelve at night and fight for you. (Hear, hear.) But, suppose they were all men of the greatest integrity and talent – suppose that they were all perfect that you sent there, what would your 105 members be able to do with the other 558 members? It was offered to the Americans, at the time of their rebellion, that they should send members to the Parliament in London. They were not, indeed, at first offered this: they were told they should submit to pay whatever was demanded from them, and that the Parliament should tax them as they pleased. The Americans said, 'No, we will not be taxed but by our own representatives.' They then offered to the Americans to send over their representatives to London. The Americans said they would not let their pure drop into our corrupted bucket, and it would have but a poor chance when it got to London. (Hear.) Ireland should refuse, upon the same grounds, to send her representatives to that all-corrupting place. What are they to do there against four to one? Why has not Ireland more representatives?

I dare say you have very frequently heard a comparison of the distribution of the members that are representatives in both countries; but you are hardly aware of the fact which I am now going to state. There are three counties in England, Buckinghamshire, Bedfordshire, and Berkshire, and in these counties there are 386,000 persons; in the county of Mayo there are 366,000 – that is within 20,000 of those three English counties. These three English counties have twenty-four members to serve them in parliament; the county of Mayo has but two! (Hear, hear.) Tell me what they will, Ireland may be made to submit to this – but are we safe? Can she ever be contented in such a state of things? (Hear.) What security can there be for England, while a population like that of this kingdom is thus treated? What can be more odious than this, that 349,000 persons in England should send 105 members to Parliament, while 8,000,000 of the Irish people should send but the same number. Three hundred and forty-nine thousand English people have as much weight in the legislature as the eight millions.

Now, I say that this is not a thing to endure – it may for a while. A wise governor, a prudent minister would tell his King – 'The Irish subjects will not long remain contented with this state of things – it is my duty to endeavour to preserve the permanency of your Majesty's throne. I do not know what may be the consequence of this ill treatment; and I, therefore, recommend to you to consider the state of Ireland, in order that there should be a change in the management of her affairs.' – (Hear, hear.) That Act of Parliament has been in part repealed. If partly, why cannot it be wholly repealed? I do not seek to repeal any part of the Act of Settlement – that might be dangerous; but if an Act be repealed in part, it can be on the whole. (Hear.)

A bargain was made by the Act of Union – a certain sum was to be paid in taxes by Ireland – Ireland was to have a share of the debt – she was to pay the interest of her own debt, and the accounts were to be kept separate. (Hear, hear.) For a very few years the accounts were kept separate; but upon examining them it was thought, perhaps, they might get to disputing, and the people get too much from the squabbling of both. Well, at last, they say – 'We will take your debt, and we will put equal taxes upon you, and we will be all alike.' Whatever motive there might be for it, I really believe that the motive was want of diligence and ability in keeping the accounts. But they did repeal the Act of Parliament in part, and how then can they talk of resisting the remainder to the death? They have repealed one part, and let us repeal the rest as soon as we can. (Hear, and cheers.)

There was a wrong done to Ireland, as I have frequently expressed and contended. It was provided that she should pay a share of the debt. My opinion is that there is not any share of the debt that belongs to Ireland. I am aware that there are persons who have estates in Ireland, and helped to make Acts of Parliament for contracting the debt; but as for the people of Ireland – the people whose industry creates and produces everything – those who make Ireland worth something, and without which it would be worth nothing – I cannot see how it can be said that they owe a single farthing of that debt. (Hear.)

Let us now ask what was that debt contracted for? Let me not be answered by any loose expressions – such as that 'it was contracted for the maintenance of the power, the glory, or the renown of the kingdom.' Oh! don't talk to me with these loose descriptions. Let us not be carried away by intentionally deceitful and eloquent descriptions. Was this debt contracted for the benefit of Ireland? I was going to say I wish I was an Irishman, and I would wish it were I not an Englishman. (Hear, and cheers.) If I were an Irishman, I would, to the last breath in my body, contest for Ireland being exonerated from her share of the payment of that debt. (Hear.)

What was that debt contracted for? Troops to put down the Catholic religion in Ireland, as well as in England. Ireland cannot owe much for that. (Hear, and laughter.) Now that professedly was the purpose for which the debt was first contracted – any one who looks at the Act of Parliament bears me out in stating this. The first shilling of that debt was contracted, it is expressly stated in the Act of Parliament, for the purpose of putting down Popery, and keeping it out of the kingdom – for crushing Popery, and for preserving his Majesty's crown and people against it.[10] However benevolent and kind the object might have been, there can be no question that Ireland owes not one farthing of money on that ground. (Hear.)

The next portion of the debt was contracted to pay for a long and expensive war to uphold the Dutch King, William the Deliverer. I presume Ireland owes nothing upon that score; I think they paid dear enough for that. (Hear, hear.) The next portion of the debt was to defend Hanover. About £100,000,000 was contracted on that ground. Now, I do not know what interest Ireland had in Hanover, or what she had to do to defend that country from France. There is certainly no great connexion between Hanover and Ireland. I certainly have no affection for Hanover – it is enough for me to have a regard for the House of Hanover. I do not want *the country*, as *the family* is enough for me. (Hear, cheers, and laughter.) Not a farthing does Ireland owe upon that score. (Hear.)

The next great heavy item in the debt was the war for seven years with America, to compel the people of that country to pay taxes without having representatives in Parliament. Now, let me relate an anecdote relative to that war. The American war was really protested against by the people of Ireland. At that time Colonel Sherman and others protested against that war being carried on, particularly if it were to cost Ireland anything.[11] In carrying on that war, that part of the army which never flinched from General Washington, as other parts of it did – the permanent and useful part of that army was the Pennsylvania line; they were the regular troops. Now, I assert, upon my word – and there are many persons here who know I would not state it if it were not true – the greater, if not more than one-half, of that Pennsylvania line, in number about 20,000, were Irishmen. (Hear.) That is always acknowledged by the Americans themselves, and hence it is that Irishmen are received with so much favor and kindness in the United States. (Hear.) This shows that Ireland had nothing to do with the American war.

The next great item to the debt was the expensive French war; and did the poor of Ireland desire this war? I would desire any one to look at the transactions of '98, and the year preceding, to show that Ireland did not wish for that war. What was that war undertaken for? What was acknowledged by those who carried on that war – by the Duke of Portland, Lord Spencer, and another nobleman, when they joined Mr Pitt to carry on that war. They declared they entered into the war, that the nobility and the established church should not be overthrown. (Hear, hear, and cheers.) The French had abolished tithes, and if we, do not put them down, the Irish might abolish tithes. These noblemen joined, with this object, Mr Pitt, to carry on this war, not with his own inclination.

Ireland did not desire that millions upon millions – that hundreds of millions, should be expended to uphold an established church, and maintain the power of collecting tithes. She did not desire that money should be laid out for that purpose. (Hear.) If any body did desire that church establishments and tithes should be maintained, it certainly was not the Irish people. The debt was not contracted for them

– they should not be called for. (Hear, hear.) It is something like the war which the Turks carried on against the Tartars. (Hear, hear.) After invading the Tartars, they insisted they should pay tooth-money. Unless the Irish are to pay tooth-money, as the Tartars did, I cannot see how you owe a single farthing of that debt. (Hear.)

Now, as to the evils of this Union – I may differ with you as to the extent of mischief which it has done to manufactures. I may care very little about manufactures, and, indeed, I do care very little about them; but, as to the evils of absenteeism, there can be no doubt how much the Union has promoted them. Before the Union, absenteeism did exist, and great miseries were the consequence of it.

Now, Mr Peter M'Cullagh, a Scotch philosopher, who has seen Ireland, contends that absenteeism is no evil at all. There is, he says, no harm nor loss in a man taking £10,000 a year in the rents of his estate; and laying it out elsewhere. If the rents of the estate were brought back to the people, and laid out amongst those who raised that rent, then absenteeism would be no harm at all. But now it is taken away, and never finds its way back in any shape or form. For instance, Lord Egremont takes £10,000 a year, and has it carried to Sussex. What does he do with it? He is a generous nobleman: he is so spoken of in Sussex and lays out very nearly £3,000 a year there in various charitable institutions, while upon his estates in Ireland not a half-penny is expended.[12] There, then, is a generous landlord for you! (Hear.) I have seen the Irish tenants of that nobleman – I wish I could take up the house of one of those tenants – the father, the mother, the daughter, and the pig all sleeping together! They pay thirty shillings for that. There they are lying together in a place in which there was a fire, and without a chimney.

I wish I could take up that cabin, ground floor and all – I wish I could enclose them in something – I wish I could take them altogether, and place them down in Sussex, and say to the people, there is one of the Irish tenants of your generous Lord Egremont! (Hear, hear, and loud cheers!) It is a very good maxim, 'Be just before you are generous.' There is a poor wretched man (I have his name down) paying 30s a year for half-an-acre and a miserable hole, and which a Sussex man would not put his pig into – there is an old man, eighty years of age, or sixty at least, with his wife and daughter; there they are sleeping all together. Lord Egremont takes 30s a year from that man, and he gives his thousands away in Sussex. (Hear.) What right has he to do that? Why, he should send his £3,000 to the miserable Irish, who pay him four times as much rent as his tenants in Sussex do. (Hear, and cheers.)

I do think that you would be able to prevent such things being done if you had a domestic legislature sitting in Dublin. (Loud cheers.) Englishmen have always had steady heads, though they have kind and compassionate hearts; and therefore is it that I should so much wish that the tenants of Lord Egremont should see the Irish farmer. Englishmen always try to take care of number one. All the rest of mankind we found looking to self; but the Englishman first tries what he can do best for himself, and then the next question is, cannot I do something for England?

Now, look to the opinions of Englishmen upon the subject of absenteeism. I do not inquire as to their opinions in newspapers and books, but as they have practically proved them. For about seven hundred years there were priories in England − I suppose they were not all priories, but convents, monasteries, and such other institutions − they were called 'alien priories.' The persons belonging to these priories lived generally in Normandy − they were subjects perhaps of the King of France, but still their revenues were taken from England and spent abroad. Perhaps they had one of their community as a factor in England, to receive the revenue, but the great body remained abroad, and spent the revenues of the different convents there. This was a subject of great complaint for many years. There was a growling and a grumbling about it. Whenever the King met his Parliament to ask money from them, they always raised an outcry about these alien priories collecting revenues in England, and spending them in France. At last, after many growlings and complainings of this sort, in the reign of Henry V, they suppressed for ever the 'alien priories.' (Hear, and cheers.) If gentlemen remember the ancient statute to which I allude, they will find that it runs something in this way − 'Whereas great injury and injustice has been done to our loving subjects by their labor being carried out of England and spent in foreign parts ...' (Hear, and continued cheering.)

When peace was made with France, were not great fears expressed about the loss to England of gentlemen going abroad and spending their money in Paris. How many speeches were made about it – how many complaints were uttered that the museum formed by Bonaparte would attract such considerable numbers of English gentlemen to expend English money in visiting the exhibition of fine arts in Paris. (Hear, and cheers.) I have ventured an opinion in print upon this subject – it is in the life of the late King.[13] My serious opinion is there given, and I would like to see it contradicted – that Bonaparte was brought back a second time for the further demolishing the power of France, and in particular, of breaking up that museum.[14] (Hear.) When he was back a second time, 'Oh,' said at the time Mr Bankes, Member for Dorsetshire, and one of the trustees of the British Museum, 'I trust that the allies will not a second time leave the monuments of the fine arts in Paris as a temptation to our young men of fortune to go there.' What was the result? The museum was dispersed – the laws of nations were violated to effect this object. We have here the motive recorded – that of preventing Englishmen of fortune going to Paris, and spending English money abroad instead of at home. (Hear, hear.)

But, again, look to the rule in the army and navy with respect to halfpay officers. They cannot spend their pay in a foreign country without a special licence, and such licence is not given but for very particular reasons. – Why is such a regulation made? On the ground that they have no right to receive the public money to carry it out of the country and spend it abroad. (Hear.) But, I say they have just as much right as a man has to receive rents in Ireland and spend them in England. (Hear, hear, and cheers.)

Another most striking fact upon this subject is this – in the report of the Poor Law Commissioners which was laid on the table of the House of Commons this fact is stated. They sent circulars to the gentlemen in the different parishes, inquiring whether the poor rates were not a very great injury? Numerous parishes answered 'no' but from one of these parishes, Broadway, in Worcestershire, they received from Sir Thomas Phillips and two of the overseers this answer: 'No, the poor rates are not an injury but rather a benefit, for that which was given to the poor remains to be spent in the parish, whereas if the poor had it not, the absentees would spend it in London, Paris, or some where else.' (Hear, and cheers.) Is that reasoning to be good in England and nothing in Ireland? (Hear.)

They are dreamers who say that absenteeism is good. The argument used there can be most usefully employed in Ireland: for if there was a necessity in one parish out of the thirteen hundred in England of keeping some of the money there, and to prevent it going into other parts of the same country, how much greater must be the necessity upon a whole country of preventing the whole of the fruits of the soil being carried away and spent in a foreign counry, and no return ever being made to it. Why, a domestic legislature could not but find means to remedy this. Such an evil could be corrected by them. They would discover the means; but such means never will be adopted until the laws are made on this side of the water. (Cheers.)

Gentlemen may think the present state of things will continue. If the country were as small as one of the Swiss cantons – if you had only as many people as you have members, 105 – if there were only 300 or 1,000 persons here, it would not make much matter; but this is too great an evil – it is too great and too fearful an evil for eight millions to continue as a colony to twelve millions, and to feed four millions of that twelve at the same time. (Hear.) They talk of the patience of Job in enduring human sufferings. Why, if you continue to bear it, the reading of the proverb must be changed, and 'Irishman' placed there instead of Job. (Hear, and loud cheers.)

It has been said, and it is one of the most monstrous pieces of impudence that I have ever heard – and it has been told to me even by absentees themselves several times – 'Oh, Mr. Cobbett, they want capital in Ireland.' (Hear, hear.) What is 'capital'? It is a nasty word, for it is used to delude. 'Capital' means money in land, to be laid out in business. They say to me, 'they have no capital in Ireland.' What! can the people of Ireland want capital? You have no money? Why, you have hogs, and butter, and wheat – you have these in abundance; how can you be in want of money? I know that in times of scarcity you send four times as much wheat to England as comes from all the rest of the world. We pay three or four millions a year to foreigners. Why not to Ireland, and how can she be in want of 'capital'? It is so contrived that she does not keep that capital.

When your hogs are sent to London or to Surrey – in Surrey a hog is worth forty shillings the two hundred weight at this time – if that forty shillings came back to Clonmell, where the pig was sent from, it would do good there; but it is laid hold of by my Lord Middleton in Sussex, and he lays it out there, and the forty shillings never returns to Ireland for the hog. You would have capital to be seen if you did one thing – that is, to 'hold fast.' (Laughter.) Not to let the hog without the money. You have not that power at present; and I confess that there is but a domestic legislature to find a remedy for it. (Hear, hear, hear.) That they would shortly do, without the slightest act of injustice to property, or without incurring the least breach of the law. (Hear.)

Always bear in mind that the most distant parts of an empire, as it was well proved by the republic of Rome, are always the worst treated. Those who are nearest the seat of government have always the best chance. The people of London made Lord Althorp take off the house-tax. If they had been in Ireland they would have been a long time calling for it before they should be relieved. The farther you are off from government the nearer you are to the cat's claws, and it is much safer to be under her belly. (Hear, and laughter.) It is very easy to send a force to the extremities, and there are always to be found reptiles in all countries to act as proconsuls, and do the worst bidding of their rulers. (Hear.) Such a country as this ought to have the protection of a domestic legislature. (Hear.)

But they say you want capital. What is capital? What does it come out of? How is it created? Capital is not oblong bits of paper made by a fellow who has not perhaps a dozen of shirts. Capital is something tangible, and proceeding from labor. A man who cultivates the land has no capital – he gets lumpers, and contrives to live on them until the crop of apples comes in. (Hear.) He has a wife and a boy to assist him, and he just lives as a pig would in a sty. He spuddles up the ground with their help, and he contrives to grow about three-quarters of wheat. (Oh! Oh!) He sells that wheat for five or six shillings the barrel – he gets some potatoes – he lives on them. Next year he has a little more money, and he is able to have butter, and to get goods, and he has more and more every year. Thus he acquires a capital. But what is the landlord to do all this while? I confess if he is to take *all* away – if every over-farthing that man makes, beyond what will barely sustain life, is to be taken away, no comfort can grow up in Ireland. (Hear.)

Ireland fairly treated, and allowed to keep her own money at home, would be one of the richest and most beautiful countries on the face of the earth. (Hear, and cheers.) I believe it is the finest spot of land in the whole world beyond all comparison – taking one part with another. I am sure that it is so – that it might be made ten times as good as it is if properly cultivated, and the money raised in it were devoted to its improvement. That, however, cannot be, as long as the present system lasts. That the present system is injurious to Ireland there can be no doubt, and it cannot be for your interests that it should continue.

Now, as regards the interests of England, I must say that if I did not see that the interests of England were as much affected by it as Ireland, I decidedly would not be for the change that you seek; but when I behold a system at work producing effects that are fatal, and bringing into jeopardy all that I wish to uphold, I cannot see it continue without an anxious desire to put an end to it. Remark, too, that I am bound by an oath to uphold, as far as I can, his Majesty's authority, throne and dominions; and it is impossible for me to see a state of things which endanger these without exclaiming against, and as far as I can putting a stop to it. I am satisfied as I am here that these dominions will be endangered if some great change is not adopted as regards Ireland before long. (Hear, and cheers.)

I wish to state here the way in which the people are treated – the tenants are squeezed so much that they are pushed to starvation, and some of them have actually died of starvation. (Hear, hear.) This fact, too, can be proved, that while largesses of money and meal were sent from England to the Irish poor, these very poor were obliged to pay rent for the year in which they got that charity. (Hear, hear.) This is a fact which, if not capable of proof, could not be believed – that in the same year in which the Irish landlords or their agents distributed to the poor the charitable donations sent from England, in that very same year they made those unfortunate tenants pay their rents to the uttermost farthing ! ! ! (Hear, hear, hear.) Then the landlords in this country contend that they have the right to turn their tenants off their estates.

I deny the right of any landlord to free the people from their bonds of allegiance. I deny the right of landlords to endanger the peace of the kingdom – I deny the right of any man to do this – for there arises the question of reciprocal ties between allegiance and protection; for can there, I ask, be allegiance where no protection is given? (Hear, hear, and cheers.) The landlord, by his merciless conduct, forces on that crisis at which all allegiance ceases. Has, I ask, any man a right to do that? Has he a right thus to dissolve the ties between subject and sovereign – that sovereign under whom he himself holds property – for there can be no property except under a grant from the crown. (Hear, hear.) But, then, landlords say that they will turn the tenants out on the road to starve if they do not emigrate. (Hear.) Has any man in this kingdom, I ask, a right legitimately to compel the King's subjects, that they shall be exonerated from their allegiance in sending them out of his dominions, and to do this, too, upon pain of starvation? There is no such right. I know that it is a crime at common law to do any such thing. They say to a man 'If you do not go to America, and here is five pounds for you, and if you do not you shall perish for hunger and cold.'

I say that this is a crime at common law. If I were Prime Minister I would call upon the Attorney-General to indict men guilty of such conduct; if he would not draw up the indictment, I would get another Attorney-General to replace him; and if I found him equally incapable, I would apply to Parliament to make such an offence punishable. If the Parliament would not do it for me, then I would let them have another Minister to propose to them to make laws for the King. (Hear, hear, hear, and cheers.) The landlord has a qualified right, and not an absolute right; and when he comes to expel a part of the King's subjects, and free them from their bonds of allegiance with a threat of the danger of starvation – I say that if there is no law to punish him, and I had the power, I would cause him to be punished to a certainty. (Hear, hear.)

The number of deaths that occur on emigration are not unknown to you. There have been horrible instances, just as they were about to embark, of fathers dying, and leaving their children beggars. (Hear, hear.) There is one scene in particular which I have to tell of an Irish landlord, but which I shall reserve for another place than this, and where it can be done with more safety. (Here one or two cried out 'name, name.') I will not name *him*, that you may depend upon. (Hear, and laughter.) Some of those men who have been thus infamously treated do get across the Atlantic; and what is the consequence of that to England, for there you touch them? Perhaps 20,000 annually go out to the United States, or they are sent to Canada, the road to the United States – the filtering-stone which takes all the good, and leaves all the dregs behind.

As a caution to the poor people, towards whom the most monstrous and infamous delusions have been used as to the land which they could procure in Canada, the assembly in Canada passed, the year before last, an Act for imposing a tax on all emigrants. This was done for checking emigration there, which was carried to such an extent as to be injurious, and also for providing a fund to preserve from hunger and cold the Irish emigrants brought to their shores by absentee landlords, who thus banish them from the fine soil of Ireland to till these swamps. The legislature of Canada would check you from going there; but in doing so they do not act half so barbarously as those who send you away – for they, at best, would keep you from starving when you go amongst them. (Hear.) Is not this a pretty situation for a country like this, in which the land is not one-tenth part cultivated, and in which it is so rich? In Limerick I saw four times more land than there were laborers to till it, and yet in such a land they are lessening the number of laborers!

This, however, is not the most serious part of what are the effects of this treatment of the Irish poor. (Hear, hear.) When they are thus driven from their country – when they are thus starved out of it, they serve in the army and navy of foreign powers. When they are in a foreign army or navy they have not only no incentive to fighting which all soldiers and sailors have, but also that of fighting against a land in which their fathers were persecuted. (Hear, and loud cheers.) Ought the King's government to stand quiescent, and see the landowners sending off yearly forty or fifty thousand men thus influenced to fight against them? (Hear.) Ought they ever peaceably to sleep until they had devised the means of making Ireland a land to be envied in the whole world – the happiest, as it might be, on the face of the earth, but in which the people now are not suffered to remain without danger of starvation?

I believe I may mention now a fact which is stated by Mr James, the historian, in his account of the naval war with America.[15] After the *Guerrière* had been taken by the *Constitution*, Dacres and his crew were taken on board the American (for our ship was demolished in twenty minutes by the Yankees). Dacres saw in the enemy's ship a sailor, who was sitting quietly under an awning upon deck, and making buck-shot. 'What are you doing that for?' said Dacres – for he adds, 'he saw that I knew him; and I said to the *Irish* ruffian, "Don't you know me?" "Yes, I do," answered he. "And, then," I added, "are you not ashamed to be making that, to fire off against the faithful friends of your country?" "No, by –," said he, "but making shot to fire off against the *faithful enemies* of *my* country."' (Hear, cheers, and continued laughter.) This is a notorious fact.[16] Mr James, the historian, acknowledges that whenever we were beaten, (and we often did get a good thumping,) he always says it was by *British* sailors we were beaten. He does not say *Irish* sailors: therefore, taking him at his own word for a very disgraceful fact, here we have sent from Ireland men to beat us at sea – and beat us they did to some tune.

Now, mark this very singular fact: in the last American war there were not only Irish sailors but Irish soldiers fighting against us.[17] In what proportion they formed a portion of the forces of the enemy it may be guessed from this – that, in a body of about one hundred of the enemy that were taken prisoners in Canada, there were twenty-three Irishmen. Our commander-in-chief said, 'those twenty-three men must be punished as traitors.' So that you see that they would hold you to your allegiance, after tossing you from the land into the sea. Though Mr Stanley told us he would exercise that right,[18] and say to his tenants – 'Go; turn off; I deny you any right to a single portion of this land – to a bit of potato to eat to save your lives' – yet they are thus treated – are to be held to their allegiance – and are not to be allowed to fight for the people who feed them. (Hear.) All nature cries out against that. (Hear, hear.)

These twenty-three Irishmen were however, found in the fact of fighting against Old England, and they were considered as traitors, and to be tried for high treason! What was the consequence? The moment the American general was apprised of what was about being done, he shut up twenty-three Englishmen, who were prisoners, and let the English general know he would put every one of them to death if a hair of one of the Irishmen's heads was injured. (Hear, and loud cheers.) This was communicated home to England, to our big sovereign the Prince Regent, who was so very fond of his Irish subjects, that he told you he had an Irish heart! (Hear, hear, and laughter.) This annoyed his Irish heart, for, in order to show he was determined upon executing the Irishmen, he clapped into prison forty-six American officers; and Earl Bathurst by his desire wrote that these forty-six officers should all be put to death, if the twenty-three English soldiers were molested.

It fortunately happened, to spare the effusion of human blood which might have followed in such a dreadful quarrel, that Commodore Macdonogh (an Irishman) beat the British on Lake Champlain.[19] (Cheers.) Major Grogan, too, an Irishman, in a fortress of Canada, with 160 men, and only a single six-pounder, beat off an English commander with 700 men, and a full supply of artillery.[20] He not only defended the fortress, but routed the English. These successes too were quickly followed by the victory over the English of General Jackson – (loud cheers) – that General Jackson, who was the son of an emigrant Irishman, probably a poor emigrant Irishman, very likely an Irishman insulted by an English landlord, who had driven the father to starvation off his land to go to America; and gave to the United States a son who was to conquer an English army. These victories secured a peace; after them there was not a word of executing the Irish 'traitors', and the twenty-three Paddys were sent tramping back to New York. (Great cheers and laughter.)

Now this is a serious matter; it is one full of danger – it is one which I would not wish, if I could, to incur; for I could make the Irishman stop at home by convincing him there was not a better nor a happier one upon the face of the earth. And on that ground, above all others, I contend for a repeal of the Union! (Hear, and long continued cheers.) I do not believe that men would ever talk of separation unless they had good reason for it. I never met an Irishman who did not unaffectedly deny it. (Hear.) I do not think that England has a right to preserve her greatness at the expense of the happiness of Ireland. (Hear, and cheers.) It is quite right that we should unite together, and it is because I boast of the liberties of my country that I would like Ireland to have her full share of them. This would be true policy as well as justice. (Cheers.) Now, I am of opinion that you cannot have that happiness which you ought to have, unless you have the legislature in your own counry. (Hear.) I am satisfied that it would be for the good of England as well as of Ireland that a repeal of the Union should take place. (Cheers.) For this and the other reasons I have stated to you, and which you have been so kind to listen to with so much attention for so long a time, I am for a repeal of the Union, being quite satisfied that it is necessary to uphold that connexion which will bind Ireland as well as England. (Hear, hear, and repeated cheering for several minutes.)

When the applause had subsided, Mr Cobbett again presented himself, and read the following as his address to the citizens of Dublin, for the kindness with which he had been received:-

GENTLEMEN OF DUBLIN, ...*

* The text of Cobbett's address was published in the *Register* of 15 November, and is to be found in Chapter 8, p.209.

NOTES

[1] Thomas Cochrane, Earl of Dundonald, the great sailor-democrat and fearless activist who had once carried a barrel of gunpowder to defend Burdett's Piccadilly house against the troops. He had fought in South America alongside the revolutionaries seeking independence from Spain.

[2] Peel's deflationary Bill had restored cash-payments by cancelling paper-money. Though this brought down some prices, it lowered wages, increased unemployment, and raised the real burden of the National Debt – a debt Cobbett sought to repudiate in part.

[3] Cobbett insisted on no compensation being paid to the ex-slaveowners.

[4] Cobbett took neither coffee, rum, nor sugar produced by slave-labour in the West Indies. (Spater op. cit., p.205.) 'I hold all slavery in abhorrence' he said at the time of Fox's bill for the abolition of the Slave Trade. Cobbett's frame of mind was normally of the earth, unfrequented by universal or visionary gleams. The issue of the abandonment of black slavery in the West Indies, when he reckoned that one eighth of the working people in England

fared worse than the slaves, seems to have struck him as evangelical and hypocritical. His view of slavery in the USA was unreservedly reactionary.

⁵ The oblique glance is, of course, towards Ireland. Cobbett reckoned that there were at this time half a million volunteers under arms in the USA, willing to sail for the Irish ports.

⁶ 8 November 1834.

⁷ The Triennial Act of 1694 was repealed in the crisis of 1715, and replaced by a 'Septennial Act'. Cobbett's vigorous support for annual Parliaments was to become a key demand of the Chartists.

⁸ Cobbett is referring to the Uniformity Acts.

⁹ The charter had been granted by William of Orange in 1694 to a new financial trading company, by name 'The Governor and Company of the bank of England'. It had been set up in response to an Act (1692) inspired by the King, short of money for his war with France; and offered inducements of 'Certain Rates and Duties upon Beer, Ale and other Liquors' (the title of the Act) 'to such Persons as shall voluntarily advance the sum of Ten Hundred Thousand Pounds towards carrying on the War against France'. The loans, ever renewed, and the growing interest on them, became known as the National Debt, which stood in 1801 at £579,931,447. The wartime (still a French war) Bank Restriction Act of 1797, which Cobbett fairly describes as violating a provision of the company's charter, made paper money inconvertible by this 'Bank of England' into gold. (Cobbett's *Paper Against Gold* which he enjoyed writing in 32 letters, mainly written from Newgate Prison between 1810-12, makes good reading even today. See also Cole's *Life of Cobbett*, Ch.XII.)

¹⁰ The Penal Codes of Elizabeth and James I under which Catholic priests and religionists had been put to death charged with high treason, were followed by those of William of Orange, after his military victories in Ireland. A number of Acts passed by the (all-Protestant) Dublin Parliament abolished or restricted the rights of Catholics in Ireland to land-ownership, inheritance, mixed marriage, apprenticeship, teaching, voting, press ownership, and taking part in municipal and parliamentary elections. The Catholic hierarchy was proscribed under the penalties for high treason, and the work of the parish priests made difficult and dangerous. English Catholics in the reign of William III suffered somewhat less severely. Things did not improve much for Catholics in either country until, after 1778 and the American revolutionary war, the Penal Codes began to be amended and relaxed.

¹¹ Roger Sherman, the son of an immigrant radical (probably Irish) shoemaker, was one of the signatories to the American Declaration of Independence. In 1787 he drafted the 'Connecticut Compromise', which set up two houses of Congress, one to represent each state of the union equally, the other to represent each state in proportion to its population.

¹² George O'Brien Wyndham, the third Earl of Egremont, was as munificent a spender in West Sussex as he was niggardly on his Irish estate, and it is likely that the sum of £3,000 a year was a considerable under-estimate and that the total was nearer £20,000. Arthur Young had been a frequent visitor to Egremont's Sussex home, between Upperton and Tillington, where he kept open house to painters, poets – including Shelley –

and architects. A liberal in regard to India, the colonies and America, he remained opposed to Catholic Emancipation.

[13] In his *Regency and Reign of George IV* (London 1830-34) Cobbett vigorously defended the right of the French to retain the treasures of the Louvre, including those brought into France by the republican armies.

[14] Cobbett remained convinced, and produced evidence for believing that the British government had connived at Napoleon's escape from Elba in order to crush more thoroughly all the social gains of the Revolution. This had left France unburdened by a National Debt and state religion, her peasantry free of tithes and in possession of their own land, under Napoleonic laws that also provided for the economic independence of Frenchwomen, and equal inheritance for their children. It was undoubtedly in the British Whig and Tory interests to impose a Bourbon on the French people, in order to teach the well-fed French artisans and peasants a salutary lesson.

[15] William James's *A Full and Correct Account of the Chief Naval Occurrences of the Late War between Great Britain and the United States* was published by Egerton, the Admiralty booksellers, in 1818. The naval historian's pro-British fervour led Cobbett to refer to him as the 'hired' and 'slave' historian.

[16] The British frigate *Guerrière*, commanded by Samuel Pechell, had boarded an American coaster between Portland and New York, and seized an American citizen for impressment into the Royal Navy. Britain was already at war with France, and had declared a blockade of all ports of all countries deemed under French control. Repeated impressments of this kind, of Irish-American 'rebels' serving on American ships, were a factor leading to the declaration of war on Britain by the Act of Congress of June 1812. The British Government made no reply to this declaration, but 'You will now see your friends, the Yankees, done for,' Cobbett was informed in Whitehall. 'We shall demolish their towns upon the coast; and harass them and divide them, and break up their jacobin government,' (*Regency and Reign of George IV*, Ch.VI) The re-colonisation of America, Cobbett felt sure, was Britain's real object in the war. As for the US navy, it consisted, according to Canning, of 'six fir frigates, with bits of striped bunting flying at their mast-heads.' In the second month of the war *Guerrière* (now commanded by James Dacres) boarded the American passenger ship *John Adams*. He wrote on the ship's register a challenge to any American frigate, 'for the purpose of having a few minutes tête-à-tête'. Dacres' encounter with Isaac Hull, captain of the US frigate *Constitution*, was to end after thirty minutes with the *Guerrière* 'dismasted and cut to pieces', and Captain Dacres on board the *Constitution* in conversation with an Irish-American seaman 'busily employed in making buck-shot cartridges'. (James: *Naval Occurrences of the Late War*.)

[17] The British-American War was fought between June 1812 and December 1814, when a 'Treaty of Peace and Amity' was signed at Ghent. The final battle of the war took place a few weeks later with the victory of the Americans at New Orleans, under General Andrew Jackson, the future President.

[18] Edward Stanley, Cobbett's Whig opponent and the victor of the Preston election in 1826. As Earl of Derby he was to become Tory Prime Minister in three administrations.

[19] Commodore Macdonogh (or Macdonough as his name is spelt in US official reports) captured a British squadron under Captain Downie on Lake Champlain, forcing the survivors to flee to Canada.

[20] Major Grogan (spelt Crochan in US reports) played a major part in the defeat of a British force under General Proctor at Sandusky Fort, on Lake Erie.

CHAPTER 8

Political Register, 15 November 1834.

Address to the
Gentlemen of Dublin

The following address was read by me to the audience in the theatre at Dublin, after my lecture on the Repeal of the Union, on the evening of the 8 November.

'GENTLEMEN OF DUBLIN, – In taking my leave of you, and about to take my leave of Ireland, I cannot content myself with a mere verbal expression of the gratitude which I feel for the kind and generous treatment that I have experienced at your hands; but I think it proper in me to avail myself of the occasion to communicate to you, and through you, to all our fellow-subjects, these, the following statement and observations:

1. That I have seen eleven Prime Ministers come on the stage, one after another, and be, one after another, snatched off by death, or turned off it by the more lucky actors; that all these have been my enemies, each causing as much mischief to be done to me as he could; and, that I am convinced that the one who is now upon the stage is most cordially disposed to act up to the example of his predecessors.[1]

2. That these men, having always millions at their command, and always a hungry pack of mercenary writers in their pay, began their hunting of me at a time when I had but just quitted the red coat and sixpence a day; that, in 1820, the present Lord Chancellor[2] laid it down as a *maxim*, that Cobbett must, at all events, be *run down*; and that these clever fellows have been at

the work of *hunting* and *running down* for now more than thirty years; until they have at last fairly run me into a seat in Parliament, and into a set of circumstances which have led to all those marks of honour which you and your countrymen have been pleased to bestow on me.

Gentlemen, I am proud of being the representative of free men; I am proud of my constituents, and of the station in which they have placed me; I am proud of the applause of my countrymen; I am, above all things, proud of the manner in which I have been received in this part of the kingdom, to which I came alone, and in which I was an utter stranger. I enjoy these things exceedingly; but oh, how sweet are they, when taken in conjunction with a reflection on the mortification, the impotent rage, that are burning up the souls of the haughty and empty-headed men, who, have been so long endeavouring, if not to destroy me, to cover me with indelible disgrace.

Still, however, there are considerations beyond these arising out of this visit to Ireland. The malignant men who have been so long employing a hireling press for the purpose of degrading me, know full well the attachment of the people of England to me; and they know also, that the kind reception given me by the people of Ireland will have a tendency to encourage a mutual friendship between the two people. '*Divide and govern*' has, in all times, been the maxim of tyrants: 'Unite and be free', ought to be the maxim of the people. The present state of things never could have existed had the people of England and Ireland known one another as well as I know both. The great object of my visit was, to be able to promote this desirable union in sentiment of the people of the two countries; and, gentlemen, you may be assured that if it be in the power of man to effect that object, it shall be effected by me.

Gentlemen, it is impossible that Ireland can be suffered to remain in its present state! What! vessels laden with provisions ready to sail for England, while those who have raised the provisions are starving on the spot where they have raised them! What! landlords living in England, having a 'RIGHT' to drive the King's subjects out of this island, on pain of starvation from hunger and from cold! What! call upon England for meal and money to be sent in charity to save the people of Ireland from starving, and make the relieved persons *pay rent the same year*! What! demand allegiance from a man whom you toss out upon the road, denying that he has any right to demand from any part of the community the means of sustaining life! Tell him that there is no law even for the protection of his life, and yet that he owes allegiance! What! give to 349,000 of the English people[3] as many representatives in Parliament as you give to the whole Irish nation, and bid the latter be content!

Gentlemen, there must be a change: these things cannot continue; and let me be permitted to hope that the knowledge which I have now acquired, and that the support which I shall receive from you may enable me to do something, at least, in the accomplishment of that change; and thereby, besides the performance of my duty, demonstrate that gratitude which I shall ever feel towards all Ireland, and particularly towards you, the gentlemen of Dublin.

Political Register, 15 November 1834.

To Charles Marshall, Labourer, Letter No.VIII

*Normandy Tithing, Parish of Ash,
Farnham, Surrey.*

Shangana Castle, 10 November 1834.
MARSHALL,
 Since I wrote to you last I have learned that, when the charitable, and most benevolent Catholic priests have contrived to collect a little money to give to poor creatures who are sick and even in danger of dying; when the poor sick person gets a sixpence or a shilling in this way, intended to buy him some little comforting thing, the poor creature is frequently obliged to give the bit of money thus obtained to pay the rent of the place where he is, for fear of being flung into the street by the agent of the great lord to whom the house belongs! There are poor women, who, having got a few pence by begging from shopkeepers and other persons in the middle rank of life, purchase herrings and tobacco with the pence, then go to the country and *swap* these for potatoes; then come into the town, eat some of the potatoes, and sell the rest to pay the rent of the great English landlord. A Catholic priest informs me that *dung* is constantly made in cellar-rooms, *under the bed* that the poor creatures lie on! The other day this Catholic priest (whose name I shall be ready to state to the House of Commons) informed me, that he had just been to visit a sick man on his death bed, expected every hour to die. He found an ass tied to the foot of the bed, which was laid on a frame of old rough boards; man, ass, pig, and family slept, and had the dung-heap, in the same room! In the country it is a common thing to see the farmer's cow sleeping in the *same room*, with the pig and the family, with a heap of dung, as you know there must be, MARSHALL, in such a case, every morning!
 MARSHALL, I have a great deal more to say to you another time; and a great deal more to say to the whole nation, in a

little book; and still more to say to the Parliament when I shall meet it, on the subject of this condition of this kind and good people who inhabit the most fertile country upon the face of God's earth; who themselves, while they see the oxen, the hogs, the sheep, the butter, the corn, sent away out of their country in hundreds and thousands of ship-loads, never taste either bread or meat themselves; but see it all taken away from them, while they are reduced to live upon the very worst sort of potatoes and salt at the very best. I shall have a great deal more to say to you and our neighbours and to the nation and to the Parliament upon this subject; but, at present, I will point out to you what the law of God is upon this subject. I shall, in a short time, publish a BIBLE FOR POOR MEN;[4] but I will just show you here what God has said upon this subject, in one instance or two. You will bear in mind, MARSHALL, that it is the business of the parson to read the Bible to you and to me; that this is his principal business, and that he gets the tithes for this. You will also bear in mind, that there are Bible societies making great collections of money to distribute about the Bible amongst us. Therefore, into this Bible we ought to look, and see what God has told us to take for our guide in these matters; to see what he says shall be the fate of the oppressors of the poor.

In the tenth chapter of ISAIAH, verses 1 and 2, we are told this: 'Woe unto them that *decree unrighteous decrees*, and that *write grievousness* which they have prescribed; to turn aside the needy from judgment, and to take away the R I G H T of the poor of my people, that the widows may be their prey, and that they may *rob* the fatherless.'

Now, MARSHALL, a decree is a law; and 'writing grievousness', which has been 'prescribed', means just such writings as are now coming from the Scotch vagabonds that I have so often mentioned; and it is very curious that the great object of these infamous writings is to take away the *right* of the poor, and to rob the widows and the fatherless!

But, MARSHALL, what is to be the end of those who put forward unrighteous decrees; those who write grievousness, as the Scotch vagabonds are now writing; those who 'turn aside the needy' when they apply for justice; those who strive to take away the R I G H T of the poor; those who are manifestly seeking to make the 'widows a *prey*', and to 'rob the fatherless'?

What is to be the end of these Scotch vagabonds, and all those who assist and uphold them, let them be who they may? God says, that he will raise up a man to destroy them, to spread desolation amongst them, to make them feel the effects of his indignation at their conduct, to strip them of their property, and to *'tread them down like the mire of the streets'*. This is what God says shall be done to those who are the oppressors of he poor, or who try to oppress them.

In the fifth chapter of the prophet AMOS, the oppressors of the poor are denounced in these words, in verses 11 and 12: 'Forasmuch as your treading is upon the poor, and ye take from him burdens of wheat: ye have built houses of hewn stone, but ye shall not dwell in them; ye have planted pleasant vineyards, but ye shall not drink wine of them. For I know your manifold transgressions and your mighty sins: they afflict the just, they take a bribe, and they turn aside the poor in the gate *from their right.*' You see, MARSHALL, how all the prophets and all the apostles agree as to this matter. The villains, the Scotch vagabonds, are not, however, to profit from their villainy in the end. 'They take a bribe.' A bribe means money given to people to do wicked things; and here the word of God points directly at these Scotch vagabonds, for they are notoriously hired and paid, 'to turn aside the poor *from their right*'. But, MARSHALL, what is to be the fate of those who take bribes? In the book of JOB, chapter XV, and verse 34, we are told, that 'the congregation of hypocrites shall be desolate, and that F I R E shall consume the tabernacles of B R I B E R Y '! Now, MARSHALL, a *tabernacle* means a house in which people live. God has told us before, that there shall be 'woe unto those that take a bribe to turn aside the poor from their right'; and he here tells us, that the tabernacles, or houses, of the bribed villains shall be *consumed by fire*.

Now, MARSHALL, if we believe the Bible to be the word of God, as I hope we all do, this is what God says upon the subject; and this is what will assuredly come to pass, if these Scotch vagabonds be not speedily put to silence, as I trust they will be put to silence, by the good sense and the humanity and the justice of English gentlemen.

Tell Farmer HORNE, or get Mr DEAN to tell him, that I say this is the sort of matter for him to lay before his congregation. Tell him that I say that it is a shame that the people of

NORMANDY should be imposed upon by those who pretend to collect money for the 'conversion of the heathen', which is a false pretence, and a gross and infamous lie from the beginning to the end; tell him that I say that I am very sorry to see an honest and good man like him thus imposed upon. Tell him that not a farthing of the money is ever applied to the purposes of real religion and piety; and that the fellows who get the money into their hands up at London spend it upon themselves, or their wives, or their girls; and that not a farthing of it is ever applied to any good purpose.

Hoping that you and your family and all of you are well, and knowing that you will be glad to hear that I am the same,

I remain,
Your master and friend,
WM. COBBETT.

Political Register, 15 November 1834.

To the Earl of Radnor

Shangana Castle, 10 November 1834.
MY LORD,
 I am sure that it is unnecessary for me to say that I heard with extreme pain of the serious accident which has recently happened to your lordship; and if I had not felt that pain, I should have been an unnatural and most ungrateful monster. But, my lord, the accident has taken place; no one can prevent that which has happened; and, like wise men; men, at any rate who ought to have some portion of wisdom, seeing that we have the happiness of millions confided to our care, let us endeavour to draw some good even out of this great evil.
 My lord, three of your ribs, it appears, were broken, and your collar-bone was dangerously fractured, by a fall from your horse in hunting. We are informed, and I dare say very truly, that LADY RADNOR had flown to the spot where it was necessary to lodge you, and had been in constant and most anxious attendance upon your person, day and night. Every one that has the pleasure to know you and her will be sure that this is true; and will also be sure, that this attention on her part must have greatly tended to mitigate your sufferings.
 Now, then, my lord, suppose my man MARSHALL, having a wife and eight children, the eldest, I believe, only twelve, were to have his ribs broken, and his collar-bone fractured in just the same manner; not by an accident arising from enjoying the sports of the field; but by a fall from a rick or a mow, or by the running away of a wild horse, dragging a cart over him, or flinging him headlong down some deep and craggy place; suppose him (as would necessarily be the case) to apply for *parish relief*; would you have him and his wife and children taken to a workhouse; *his wife separated from him*, and the children separated from both; all of them cut off from all communication with friends and relations out of doors; and all of them stripped of their own clothes, and have the odious workhouse dress put upon them?
 The reader shudders at the thought, and exclaims, 'How

could you put such a cruel question to such a man?' It is a cruel question; but the cruelty is towards him who knows it to be his bounden duty to put it. I know that your lordship will shudder at the thought: I know that you will say, that it must be in a savage breast that the design to execute such cruelty was first generated. But, my lord, I beg you to recollect, that you, in your place in Parliament, *praised* the system of PARSON LOWE of BIRMINGHAM, in Nottingham; that you *praised the practice* of this church parson; and that you defended the Poor-law Bill on the ground that, without it, there could not be the practice of PARSON LOWE adopted in every parish in the kingdom; and, finally, I beg you to recollect, that according to the practice of this Parson LOWE, MARSHALL and his family would, in case of such an accident, have been treated in the manner that I have described.

Never to be forgotten is the precept of 'doing to others as we would be done unto'; and if this accident, which has happened to your lordship, should induce you to make the labouring man's case your own, even this accident, which has filled with sorrow any one who has any knowledge of your character, may produce the great good of making you reflect on the horrible nature of that measure, in the adoption of which your sanction had much more to do than that of all its other advocates put together. You were misled; you were blinded by the Scotch impudence and jaw; you were *fastened upon*, and held up to the mark by excessive cunning and incessant importunity, to say nothing of brazen falsehoods and infamous libels on the people of England. Left to your own good sense and benevolent disposition, this species of enchantment will, I trust, be broken, and you will be again the man you heretofore were; and that you may feel that the words of the psalmist apply to you: 'Blessed is he that considereth the poor; the Lord will deliver him in time of trouble: the Lord will strengthen him upon the bed of languishing: thou wilt make all his bed in his sickness.'

With sincere and ardent prayers for your complete restoration to health,
I remain,
Your lordship's grateful,
Most humble and obedient servant,
WM. COBBETT.

Political Register, 15 November 1834.

To Lord Althorp

Shangana Castle, 10 November 1834.
MY LORD, – There was one lucky circumstance belonging to the mad scheme about the negroes, produced by the crack-skulled county of York, and by the scandalous impostors who have lived upon this cant about humanity for the last almost fifty years. It was twenty millions of money flung away: it was eight hundred thousand pounds a year laid upon our backs for ever; but, it was putting an end to the thriving imposture; it was like putting an end to NAPOLEON, who was made use of as the means of robbing the people of England for so many years. The negro-scheme, bad as it was, put an end to this most abominable, this shameful, this at once ridiculous and scandalous imposture. Other BROUGHAMS and other WILBERFORCES, if it should please God in his anger to afflict England with more of the breed, may be sent forth to play their tricks in the face of high heaven, and to insult the sensible part of this nation, and to cause their ruin at the same time. By that crack-skulled, that canting, that hypocritical, that fanatical, that conceited, that bragging, crew, forty thousand of whom ran away once at the sight of twelve dragoons and their sergeant, and knocked down crowds of women and children in their flight; this crack-skulled and light-headed and talking and bothering crew, who send thirty-seven members to Parliament, while the greatly more valuable county of CORK sends only eight, while it feeds one-half of the cracked-skulls at the same time; this fanatical and presumptuous and meddling and mischievous crew may possibly find out other WILBERFORCES and other BROUGHAMS to fasten upon us; but they never can again, thank God! have the base and hypocritical pretence of sending them; of sticking them upon us with the weazel-like claws and muzzles, under the base and hypocritical pretence of obtaining 'FREEDOM FOR THEIR FELLOW - MEN IN THE WEST-INDIES'.

The scheme has been, thus far, productive of all the

consequences, which I, you well know, told you to anticipate from it; Mr STANLEY's flashy speeches; and the small talk between him and FOWELL BUXTON, in the month of May last, I think it was, intended to send about the country the news of the '*complete success*' of the scheme; small talk arising from FOWELL, under the pretence of wanting information as to how they were going on amongst the negroes. This drew from the Right Hon. *superintendent of some Irish estates that I have seen*, and about which I shall probably talk of to his face; this drew from him (as the thing had been contrived between them beforehand) a description of the *glorious success* of that '*great measure of humanity*'!

It is very true that the loss of the money given to the sharpers who have mortgages on the West India estates; it is very true that the loss of this money is a good deal; it is very true that the ridicule which will fall upon Mr STANLEY, yourself, and FOWELL cannot come again with his petition signed by two hundred and seventy-eight thousand females: he cannot again play off this farce of humanity. It is a curious fact that, in the small talk of FOWELL and STANLEY, the former asked the latter whether the usual quantity of provisions had been sent to the West Indies *from Ireland*, for the negroes to eat; and STANLEY 'had great pleasure in telling the honourable FOWELL, that he believed there had been no diminution in the quantity usually sent for that purpose'. In a few minutes after this answer had been given, Mr SHEIL, member for the *county of Tipperary*, rose, and asked Mr LITTLETON if the Government had received any intelligence, relative to the fact of there being, at that moment, in that country, four thousand persons IN DANGER OF BEING STARVED ON ACCOUNT OF THE SCARCITY OF POTATOES? To which Mr LITTLETON replied, that the Government had been informed of the circumstance, and that it would take care to adopt measures of precaution!

Now, my lord, let me ask whether it be 'humanity' for a Government to stand by and see the meat and the flour and the butter sent away from the poor Irish who raised them, to be eaten by these black fellows, who do not raise them. If ever there were any thing in the world more shameful than all other things, such is that thing; this is that unparalleled shame. My lord, *protection* is necessary to maintain the claim of *allegiance*.

Have men, who are proprietors of land, a right, I mean a *legal* right, to act thus towards those who till the land? In the ownership of land it seems always to be forgotten in the present day that there are two parties: the landholder, and the chief of the commonwealth, who, in our country, is a king. In every estate, there is proprietorship, and there is dominion. Your lordship has the proprietorship in your estate; but your estate forms a part of his Majesty's dominions; and you are not to use the proprietorship in such a manner as for that use to be manifestly dangerous to the *dominion* which his Majesty has in the estate.[5] I know very well that Y O U would not, and do not, so use your proprietorship; but, placed in the station in which you now are, it is your duty, and your bounden duty, too, to prevent the wrong being done to his Majesty by persons who may be proprietors of other parts of his Majesty's dominions. And, will any one pretend to say that his Majesty's dominions are not mis-used, and that danger to his royal rights may not arise, and, in the end, must arise, from misuse so flagrantly outrageous as that which takes the food from those who raise it, exposing them to starvation, which carries that food out of the country, and which causes the poor creatures who raise it to receive nothing in return?

It is very easy to talk of a landholder having 'a right to do that which he likes with his own'; very easy for him to tell the people who are living on the estate, or near it, that they may go away from it if they please; and that it is their own fault if they continue to be there. It is very easy to say all this; and the arrogant and insolent pretension of the main part of the present landowners, especially the Irish, is well enough expressed in this sort of language. But will you contend, my lord, or will any one but a half-drunk, half-mad, greedy, cormorant, monster, seeking to aggrandize himself by flattering the sordid propensities of landholders; will any one but a hideous monster like this, stepping forth with the howl, and almost the figure, of Satan; will any one not cursed with depravity equal to that of the Jews,[6] dare to stand forward and assert this; namely,

> That, supposing the whole of the land of the kingdom to have for proprietors one thousand men, that one thousand men have a R I G H T (each being able with his family to

live upon the fruits of five acres of ground) to refuse to let any of the rest of the land be cultivated or used, and thus to cause all the people to die, or to quit the kingdom?

Let us have no shuffling here. Let the Scotch vagabonds[7] not attempt to shuffle or explain. Let them say that they are ready to maintain and stand by this proposition, or that they are not; if the former, what *dominion* has the King? What *subjects* has he? What *rights* has he? What protection is there in the laws? Yet they must not flinch; or what becomes of the right of Scotch and Irish landlords to clear their estates? What becomes of their right to toss the King's subjects out upon the road to perish, while they send out of the country the food raised upon their estates? What becomes of their right; or rather, is it not a *crime* in them to give to any portion of his Majesty's subjects the choice of perishing in Ireland, or of quitting the kingdom for ever? And finally, what becomes of the principles laid down by BROUGHAM in defence of the Poor-law Bill?

Ah! my lord! We have as yet only a glimpse of the consequences of passing this bill. I have been laughing today at the appointment of those illustrious brother-members of Parliament of ours, the sublime Messrs GROTE, WHITMORE, WARD, CLAY, *Colonel* TORRENS, and Mr SHEIL's H I L L, one of the members for the town of HULL, in the cracked-skull county of York; I have been laughing at the appointment of these, our *brother-senators*,[8] to be C O M M I S S I O N E R S under an act for establishing a new colony in the neighbourhood of Botany Bay, or in the Botany Bay country; which appointment has carried my recollection back to the zeal and devotion with which these our brethren defended the Poor-law Bill; and especially that part of it which provides for the *taxing of parishes for the sending of the working people out of the country*, at the very moment when we had, under your hand, a report telling us, that a great part of the lands of England lay uncultivated for the *want of a sufficiency of hands employed upon them*; at the very moment when, by way of weakening an argument of mine, you yourself declared *that you did not believe there was a surplus of labour in the country*!

Ah! my lord! A government does not get along: it may live: it may boggle and justle about: it may exist amidst shuffles and expedients; but it must produce intolerable evils at last; it must become insufferable in time; when means like these are resorted to prop it up. Mr Commissioner HILL appears to be a great favourite, and nearly upon a level with WOOD, emphatically called JOHN. The rest of these eloquent squires, who so poured out their souls in praises of the Elysian fields in the south seas; and that Lord of the Shannon, who promised me so faithfully a bill to amend the stamp-laws, and, who, in his right of sovereign, collects a revenue from the sea-weed thrown up by the tide;[9] even his enlarged soul, too, poured itself forth, in almost evangelical strains in praise of the blessings to be found on the borders of the Swan River. Never shall I forget the cogent arguments, the ponderous eloquence, of the squires, GROTE and CLAY; and as to Squire WHITMORE, he seemed to have caught the spirit of DEMOSTHENES himself, when he was speaking of the 'vast regions', the 'fertile lands' of which, were about to be brought under cultivation by your wonder-working bill.

I shall take care that no persons emigrate from England, who have arms to defend her, and who are not such base, spiritless, or imbecile creatures, as to be of no value. I shall teach the able men, that it is their right as well as their duty to remain in England; and a proper sense of your duty would teach you, that you ought to expose the various tricks and contrivances by which his Majesty's subjects are deluded or driven away from their country and their allegiance. In the meanwhile there are other effects proceeding from measures, and out of a state of things produced by an inattention to the doctrines which I have above laid down relative to the rights of dominion and proprietorship. A disregard of those doctrines and principles has led to a sort of treatment of the working people which has finally produced that which my lord STANHOPE lamented, several years ago, as being likely to be produced, namely, a feeling of universal and bitter hostility of the poor against the rich. Far away as I am from my home, complete as is my lack of all private information from England, I gather from the bare newspapers, that the scenes of the fall of the autumn of 1830, are now again renewed. I renew, in this address to your lordship, and beg leave to be understood as again expressing, all that I said upon the subject in the fall of that year, and in the commencement of the next. I then fully explained to you and your colleagues, that, great and terrible as was your power; dreadful as had been your proceedings in Hampshire, Wiltshire, and Berkshire, terrific as were the examples at BRISTOL and NOTTINGHAM; you had not the power, and never could have the power, to prevent, or to check the progress of the F I R E S, by any physical force, or by any punishments of any sort that you could possibly inflict. I then told you that you had *moral* power enough, not only to check it, but to prevent it: I exerted you to employ that moral power: you not only scorned my advice, but sought my destruction; or, at least, the destruction of my character and influence, as a reward for having given the advice; and I verily believe that it was mainly owing, or, at least, in part owing, to that endeavour on the part of you and your colleagues, that induced my sensible and just fellow-subjects of OLDHAM to place me in that station, which will now enable me to give you the advice, and to urge the Parliament, in the name of the peace and harmony and happiness of the country, to adopt those measures which shall once more bring back Englishmen to that cheerful obedience to the laws; to that veneration for courts of justice, for which they were formerly so renowned throughout the world; and which, of all the features in the character of a people, is the most valuable, conducing as it does, in every possible way, to the prosperity and greatness of a country. I am by no means sanguine in my expectation that your majority would listen to my advice, much less act upon it; but a man must not be deterred from doing his duty, by even the certainty of failure in his efforts. I shall do mine, at any rate, proceeding upon the maxim of Major CARTWRIGHT: 'Do what is right, and leave the rest to God';[10] I am not one of those who hunt about the Scriptures to find out prophecies to fit the times in which we live; but it is impossible for me to recollect that which I have read in those matchless writings, and to view the things that are before me at this moment, without being seriously impressed with the fear that we are doomed to experience the evils contained in denunciation more than three thousand years old. Our rulers appear to be incapable of profiting from any lesson, in however awful a form and manner it may come. The means of effectually obviating, or staying, the terrible and disgraceful scourge of which I have been speaking; these means are so clear to my eyes; they are so infallible, if adopted; and they are so easy of adoption; they are so perfectly costless, and so inevitably effectual; that it seems to me raving madness that these means should be not only rejected, but that others should be resorted to, which, as sure as the sparks fly upwards, must augment the evil tenfold.

My lord, it is easy to talk of doing things *in spite of the people*. But pleasing as it may be to men of arrogant and insolent disposition, to entertain the notion that they have the power to do this; and though, in certain cases, and for a certain time, they may do it; in the end such attempts must always fail. It is not given to man, possess what power he may, to set the voice of the millions at defiance. Nor is it right that he should be able to do this; it is not right that any man, or any few men, should be able to enjoy security and happiness in despite of their hundreds and thousands of neighbours. It is what never was, and what never can be. If it could be, the life of man would be a curse: God would have made him to suffer evil upon the earth, instead of participating in the enjoyment of its fruits.

It is very natural, and indeed every moral sentiment calls upon us to deplore the commission of those acts to which I have alluded; but, my lord, it becomes us, whose bounden duty it is not to lose a moment in seeking for a remedy for the evil, to look carefully into the *causes of it*; and not to waste our time in useless invectives against the acts themselves, or against the perpetrators. The elaborate report laid before us by your lordship and other gentlemen, tells us that the riots of 1830 and 1831 arose from the *lowering of wages*; it tells us that the fires succeeded the forcible suppression and the punishment of the rioters; it tells us that the fires were put a stop to by the raising of the wages; and, everywhere, we now see that the fires are rekindled by the lowering of the wages, to which must be added the opinion naturally enough taken up by the working people, that this lowering is now contemplated to be acted upon as a system.

The defence of the farmer is, his inability, with the present rents and prices, to pay wages sufficient for the good-living of his working people. This defence is founded in truth; and he might add his inability, with the malt and hop taxes in existence, to supply, in considerable part, the place of money payments by payments in kind, and by the having of inmates in his now half-empty and half-useless house. But, my lord, while the farmer's defence is good, as against the landlord and the tax-gatherer, it is good for nothing against the labourer, whose wages are now hardly, in any case, sufficient; and who would be taught by the light of nature, if he had not the law of God, and the law of the land, before his eyes, and if he could forget all the knowledge that he has derived from tradition; he is taught by the light of nature alone, that he is not to suffer from hunger, thirst, or cold, while his life is spent in causing to produce abundance of meat, drink, raiment and fuel. The farmer is the person that comes in contact with him: it is *for him* that he has ploughed and sowed, reaped and mowed, hedged and ditched, attended the sheep, and cut down the coppice: it is *for him* that he has risen before the sun, toiled through the day, and dragged his weary limbs home in the dark: it is *for him* that he has left a wife in a sick bed, while he has been working and sorrowing in the fields to procure them the necessaries of life. To the farmer, therefore, he looks for a reward for his cares and his toils; and he recollects that God has told the farmer to give him that reward; and by no means withhold it from him a minute, for that he has set his heart upon it. Thoughtless, hectoring, and arrogant, and unfeeling bullies may call the people of England the 'peasantry', the 'lower orders'; may speak of them as of insensible beings, while these bullies are taking such tender-hearted care of the blacks; but, my lord, fatal, indeed, is the delusion of those who assume that these lower orders, as it is thought wise to call them, do not well understand the rights which nature and which God has given them.

Thus it is that the *homestead* becomes the object of vengeance; and this, too, from the dreadfully dangerous opinion that the vengeance is inflicted without crime! To prevent, or to check, by physical force, is impossible. No punishment is of any effect in the way of prevention, if the perpetrator's punishment do not excite general acquiescence in the justice of the punishment; and if the suffering of the perpetrator excite *compassion*, it does harm instead of good; instead of deterring it encourages. In this state of things, we who are charged with the making of the laws, ought to enact such laws as will take out of the hearts of the people the desire to inflict this species of vengeance, seeing that we have not the power of prevention by any other means; we ought to consider how we can dry up the current of mischief in its source, and not how we can dam it back when it is grown to a torrent, or a flood. It is to us that the farmer has to look for protection; and not to any other means that are in existence, or that can be brought into existence.

The danger from this cause was very great in the years 1830 and 1831. It is much greater now; and just now the difficulty of the currency comes and makes its prodigious addition. Not only cannot the farmer receive any relief from higher prices; but the prices *must be lower*, unless you adopt the course of legal tender for all bank-notes of every description. I warn you of your danger, if you do that; I have warned you of that danger before; it is a measure that cannot be adopted and endured without first abolishing the sinecures, the pensions, the grants, the half-pay; without a temporal application of the clerical revenues; and yet, if this be not done, the proprietorship of the land must change hands as completely as if by an act of general confiscation, and a new granting of all the lands from the crown. The only course of justice and of safety is the one that I have so often recommended; and, while I have not the smallest hope of seeing it adopted, I am sure the whole country will bear me witness that the consequences, be they what they may, will no part of them be attributable to me.

I am,
Your lordship's most obedient
And most humble servant,
WM. COBBETT.

Political Register, 15 November 1834.

The Cobbettites

Shangana Castle, 12 November 1834.
MY FRIENDS, – I have this moment got news from NEW YORK, which tells me that my LIFE OF JACKSON had been published there at the price of SIX CENTS; and that TEN THOUSAND COPIES HAD BEEN SOLD IN ONE DAY! Talk of a long arm, indeed! The Bank villains were all frying alive; just like so many sharks in a frying-pan on a lake of fire. I dictated this LIFE OF JACKSON to my secretary, during one single day, while I was lying in bed to rest myself, after a night's fighting of the army estimates.[11] Base enemies of mine; base Tories and base Whigs; base reptiles with *nick-names*, do you recollect when BOLTON FLETCHER and his companions put JOHN HAYES into prison ten weeks for the *crime* of having gone round the town of BOLTON with a bell, to inform his townsmen that 'WILLIAM COBBETT had arrived at LIVERPOOL in GOOD HEALTH'?[12] I wrote the 'LIFE OF JACKSON' *to smite the rich ruffians, and the nick-named reptiles of England!* I did, indeed, wish to do honour to that wise and brave man, and to do good, at the same time, to his brave and virtuous countrymen: but, my principal object was, to lend my aid in upholding him against the perfidy, malignity, and bribery, of the infamous villains, *on this side of the water*, in whose hands the scoundrel bankers in America were the mere tools? And, did I forget the imprisonment of JOHN HAYES; and did I forget the THOUSAND POUNDS FINE? I remember, that, when I finished the dictating of the last sentence, I said, 'There! Lord ALTHORP is famous at *expunging*; let him expunge *that*'![13] Every creature in America old enough to read, or to understand reading, will read, or hear read, the last chapter of that LIFE OF JACKSON; and, though this reading and this hearing are three thousand miles off, they will give a heavier blow to CORRUPTION than any which she has received for many a day. Aye, that reading and that hearing *will lower the price of the bushel of wheat in England*, strange as that may appear

to imbecile, stupid, fraudulent, rapacious and ferocious CORRUPTION! I give you joy, my friends, on this news, and remain

Your faithful friend,
WM. COBBETT.

P.S. I know the *three* bank-villains, who are now in London, *from America*, negotiating with villains in London, to obtain the means of upholding the bank-villainy in the United States. I will send their *names* to a friend at New York immediately.

NOTES

[1] King William IV had dismissed Grey's Whigs in mid-November. Peel, the most impressive Tory, was to accept the office of Prime Minister within three weeks (though without a majority in the House) and was in this sense 'upon the stage'.

[2] Lord Henry Brougham; 'Botheration Brougham' to Cobbett and, at this time, 'Lord Crack-skull.'

[3] An estimate of the population of Yorkshire, culled from his *Geographical Dictionary of England and Wales*, which his secretary Gutsell had brought to Dublin.

[4] The proposed Bible never took shape.

[5] Cobbett is relying, as he frequently did in the course of his writings, on Blackstone's awesome constitutional authority. The judge had written in his *Commentaries on the Laws of England* (Book 2, Ch.7): 'The word allodium, the writers on this subject define to mean every man's own land, which he possesseth merely in his own right, without any rent or service to any superior. This is property in its highest degree ... This allodial property no subject in England has; it being a received, and now undeniable principle in the law, that all the lands in England are holden mediately or immediately of the king.'

[6] Cobbett's fierce dislike of 'Jews and Quakers' was not, strictly speaking, racialist nor religious. It was an expression, however unpleasantly misdirected, of that general peasant hatred shown to all merchants, middlemen and shopkeepers, in particular towards cattle-dealers, corn-dealers and even millers, who bought and resold what the land-workers with great pains produced. As for the upper tiers of commodity-speculators: bankers and other money-gatherers and lenders, Cobbett described them in the round as 'Jewish Christians' without a strictly racial or religious bias. On this point George Spater has reminded us (op. cit., p.441) that for Quakers who themselves tilled their acres, as did those 'broad-brimmed Jews' farming in Pennsylvania, Cobbett had nothing but respect.

[7] Cobbett's 'Scotch vagabonds' were of the same general order as his 'Jews

and Quakers'. Cobbett would have been as surprised and angered as would Samuel Johnson at any charges levelled at him of the 'patriotism' that was the last refuge of a scoundrel..

[8] Grote, a banker, then a radically-disposed historian, Whitmore and company, with Rowland Hill were all MPs.

[9] The sea-weeds were (and are still) highly valued as fertilizers for the potato-patch. Edible varieties, such as the carragheen, still form a part of the coast-dwellers' diet, in soups and puddings.

[10] John Cartwright, the grand old man of English radicalism, had laboured for parliamentary reform since before the revolution in France. When it came, he warmly welcomed it. To the end of his long life the 'Old Major' maintained a stalwart radicalism.

[11] Earlier in the year Cobbett had published his *Life of Andrew Jackson*.

[12] The Bolton Town-Crier. With voice and bell he had proclaimed Cobbett's return to England from the United States in November 1819, and suffered imprisonment for his enthusiasm. When Cobbett revisited Bolton in 1830 he arranged that this now 'poor but very industrious man' should receive an award of £5 on a regular basis.

[13] On his return from Ireland Cobbett had moved a vote of no confidence in Peel, the new Tory Prime Minister, as the 'strongest man amongst all the blunderers.' His provocative motion had the support only of John Fielden and four other radicals. Althorp moved, to applause, that the offending motion be 'expunged' from the parliamentary records. (These records – originally Cobbett's *Parliamentary Debates*, had since been taken over by Mr Hansard. But the deletion of Cobbett's motion serves as a neat example of how even the small print of history can get written by the winners.)

CHAPTER 9

Political Register, 22 November 1834.

To Charles Marshall, Labourer, Letter No.IX

*Normandy Tithing, Parish of Ash,
Farnham, Surrey.*

Shangana Castle, 15 November, 1834.
MARSHALL,
    You must needs think that I hear about the F I R E S that are going on in England. Indeed I see accounts of them in every newspaper that comes from England. There is no man more sorry than I am, that my country should be in such a state; but I cannot join with those who call the working people of England *'lazy and sturdy miscreants'*; being, besides, quite satisfied that, to call them by such names, never yet was, and never will be, the way to make them cease to do any thing, in the doing of which they are engaged, however wrong it may be to do that thing.
    I will endeavour, MARSHALL, to explain to you, why it is that the farmers are unable to pay the wages that they have been paying for some time past. The greater part of farms are still paying as much *rent* as they were paying when wheat was, on an average, ten shillings a bushel. Besides, they pay nearly as much in poor-rates: they pay more in county-rates, in church-rates (taking England and Wales all through); in road-rates; in malt-tax (which is heavier than all the other taxes); in sugar, tea, and tobacco tax; and they pay full as much as they ever paid for all articles of clothing; and they pay as much for fuel as they ever paid.

Now, you know, that fat hogs used to be from twelve to fifteen shillings a score; that mutton used to be from four shillings to five and sixpence a stone at SMITHFIELD; that beef used to be from four shillings to six shillings a stone; that butter used to be at GUILDFORD, from fifteen to twenty pence a pound. You know that now fat hogs are about eight shillings a score, I suppose; and you know, that even the fine wheat, that grows on your little patch, is hardly worth five and sixpence a bushel.

Therefore, MARSHALL, if the farmer have to pay the same rent, and the same taxes, he must be ruined if he pay the same wages that he paid before; and, I am sure that there is none of you who would wish to see Farmer WEST, or FAGGOTTER, or HORNE, or any of the rest of the farmers brought to ruin. They have all families as well as you; and, besides this, if they be brought to ruin, their labourers must either come to ruin and starvation, or there must be an end of all law, and all security even for person. Yet, MARSHALL, the labourer and his family must live; they must have meat, bread, beer, clothing, and a bed to lie on, and fuel to warm them; and there is no reason, seeing that their labor is as great as ever, why they should not live as well now as they did before. There is a miscreant who publishes a paper called the *Brighton Gazette*, who says, that the wages of the labourer ought to be lowered, in proportion to the fall in the *price of wheat* and flour; so that, according to him, a man ought to have six shillings a week, instead of twelve. This, MARSHALL, is a *real miscreant*, who, if he could have his will, would set the whole country in a blaze.

Let us see, then, how this matter stands. Suppose a man to have twelve shillings a week. He is no *corn dealer*, and no bacon merchant; and the question with him is, not the price of *wheat*; not the price of the *whole fat hog*; not the price of *barley*; but the price of the *bushel of flour* and of the *gallon loaf*; the price of the *three or four pounds of bacon*; and the price of *the pot of beer*. The wheat, the bacon, the barley, have to go through the hands of the corn-dealer, the miller, the baker; the bacon has to go through the hands of the bacon merchant and the shopkeeper; the barley has to go through the hands of the maltster and the tax-gatherer and the brewer and the public-house keeper: through all these hands they have to pass before they come to the labouring man; every one of them respectively, comes loaded with a share of all the enormous taxes, of every sort, paid by the corn-dealer, the miller, the bacon merchant, the shopkeeper, the maltster, the brewer, and the public-house keeper; and, at last, the low prices which ruin the farmer, produce very little effect in lowering the price of these commodities to the labouring man; and this you all find to be the case.

If this is the case with regard to the mere food, how stands it with regard to other things necessary to the decent existence of yourselves and your families? The sugar, the tea, the tobacco, the rent, the fuel, the soap, the candle light; all these; every article of clothing; all these put together make twice or three times the amount of the mere bread and bacon: as to the drink, that is still as dear as before; for five parts out of six of the price is *tax*, or *monopoly* arising out of tax. Put the drink, then, to the rent and these other things, which are all full as dear as they were before; and then see how unjust this BRIGHTON miscreant is, in proposing to lower your wages in proportion to the fall in the price of W H E A T ! The single man, too:[1] has he not still as much to pay for his *lodging*, for his *washing*, for his *clothes*, as he had to pay before? Has he not as much to pay for his *tobacco*, for his *soup*; and, in short, for every thing except a mere trifle on the loaf, and on the pound of bacon? He must lament that the farmer is ruined; but is he to *starve* because the farmer is ruined? The farmer has been ruined by the arbitrary changes made in the value of the circulating money of England, and by the heavy taxes which the farmer has to pay. But was it the labouring man that caused this arbitrary change in the value of the money? Was it the labouring man that laid on the malt-tax, on account of which the working people of England pay twice as much as the amount of all the parish relief that they receive? Was it the labouring man that laid on taxes, which make the tea cost three shillings instead of one; which make the sugar cost two shillings instead of threepence? The labouring man did none of these things. He must be sorry to see the farmer ruined: it would be unjust in him to wish that the landlord should receive no rent for his land; but if the farmer lose all his money, and the landlord lose all his rent, the labouring man has not been the cause of it. The law of God and the law of the land, say that he shall not starve, as long as there is food in the country; and, if you will speak to Farmer HORNE, he will show you, that St PAUL tells TIMOTHY that 'the husbandman that *laboureth* must be the *first* partaker of the fruits.'

I do hope that good-will and good neighbourhood will prevail in the west of Surrey, at any rate; that landlords, farmers, labourers, will all have consideration one for another, and that the farmers and landlords will particularly have great consideration *for the single young men*; and that, whenever they possibly can do it, they will take them into their houses, make them part of their families, and bind them to them by the ties of mutual benefit and kindness; and not drive them away from their doors as if they had no right to be upon the land whereon they were born.

Now then, MARSHALL, so much for that; and now I have to talk to you about another matter. You know that there has been a P O O R - L A W B I L L passed, which, whenever it shall be put into execution, will make a *total change* as to the situation of the working people. It was a SCOTCHMAN of the name of BROUGHAM who proposed this bill to the House of Lords; and he said that such a bill was necessary to prevent the poor from S W A L L O W I N G U P T H E L O R D S' E S T A T E S. Now, MARSHALL, it is a command of God, that those who have the ability to do it shall plead the cause of the poor, the widow, the fatherless, and the stranger. I have the ability to do this, as well as to teach you how to rear fields of cabbages; and it is my duty to obey this command, and not to waste my time in feasting and drinking, and in snoring in bed. After having taken time to consider in what way I can best perform this duty, I have determined to write and publish a L I T T L E B O O K, in such form and size that any working man can carry it in his waistcoat pocket, and at the price of FIFTEEN PENCE; so that all the working men may read it, or hear it read. And I shall have it bound in leather, so that it shall not easily be worn out; and that it may be read, not only by the men of the present day, but by their children, and their great-great-grandchildren.[2] I have sent the first part of it to London, and shall send the rest in a few days. If the *landlords* and *farmers* have any sense left, they will be the first to read it, and to C O N S I D E R I T W E L L ; and if they do not choose to read it, they may just let it alone. I will here give you the TITLE of it, MARSHALL, and the TABLE OF

CONTENTS; and when the book is printed, which will be in the course of a fortnight, some copies of it will be sent down to Mr DEAN, and I shall request him to send one of the copies and give it to the man who now lives in the house in which I was born.[3] The Title and Contents of this little book are as follows:

COBBETT'S
LEGACY TO LABOURERS;
or,
What is the Right which the Lords,
Baronets, and 'Squires, have to
possess the Lands, or to make the Laws?

In Six Letters addressed to the Working
People of the whole Kingdom.

With a Dedication to
SIR   ROBERT   PEEL

BY WILLIAM COBBETT, M.P. FOR OLDHAM.

CONTENTS

Dedication to Sir ROBERT PEEL; stating the reasons for writing the book, and also the reasons for dedicating it to him.

Letter I. How came some men to have a greater right to parcels of land than any other men have to the same land?

Letter II. What right have English landlords to the lands? How came they in possession of them? Of what nature is their title?

Letter III. Is their right to the land *absolute*? Is the land their *own*; or, are they *holders* under a superior?

Letter IV. Have they *dominion* in their lands? Or do they lawfully possess only the *use* of them?

Letter V. Can they do *what they like* with their lands?

Can they *use* them in any way that shall clearly tend to the injury of other men, or to that of the King, or Commonwealth?
Can they *use* them so as to drive the natives *from* them?
Can they *use* them so as to cause the natives to go *from* them?
Can they *use* them so as to cause the natives to perish of hunger, or of cold?
Letter VI. What right have the Lords, Baronets, 'Squires, and rich men, to *vote at elections* any more than working men have?

You are not to suppose, MARSHALL, that I am going to die, because I have awarded you a legacy. You are to have it first or last; and the sooner you have it the better; and if I see it in your hands in my life-time I shall be sure that you have got it. Since the vagabonds have dared to assert that the *poor have no rights*, it is high time to see what are the *rights of the rich*. When you get the little book be sure to send one of them over to the chaps at PURBRIGHT, and tell them to go to the parson at CHOBHAM, and ask him what *right* he had to libel me; and to tell him that I will call him to account for that before this winter is over.

I have nothing more to say to you at present, only that, if all of you work as hard as I do; if you be as diligent (as I hope you are) with the ploughs and the spades and the dung-prongs and the bill-hooks as I am with the pen, you will have the farm in most excellent condition before I get back. I hope that all of you and your wives and families are well, and

I am,
Your master and friend,
WM. COBBETT.

Political Register, 22 November 1834.

To The King's Servants

Shangana Castle, 16 November, 1834.
MY LORDS AND GENTLEMEN,
   I recommend to you, in the terrible time of the special commissions of Hampshire, Wiltshire, Berkshire, and Buckinghamshire, the measures which I thought ought to be adopted for effectually doing away with the discontents of the country people of England, and, especially, the *working people*, including, as Mr LOCKE most judiciously does, all the various tradesmen employed in conjunction with the husbandman in the producing of a loaf of bread; for, surprising indeed is your mistake, if you imagine that low wages, deprivation of relief, and the hardships arising therefrom, do not appertain to tradesmen, as well as to those that are more immediately engaged in tilling the soil. I recommend to you those measures, so easy of adoption, and execution, and so perfectly *costless*, which I was S U R E would restore tranquillity and contentment to the millions of Englishmen and Welshmen. Instead of the thanks of you, and of those colleagues who are now out of power, I had to endure the effects of your endeavours to shut me up in jail for the probable remainder of my life, from which end I was preserved by an honest jury; and by that jury alone.
   I will now offer you the advice again, and, if you reject it, I, at any rate, shall have done my duty. I have just quoted the remarks and recommendations of a writer in a London paper. He does not understand the subject, but, apparently, his wishes are good. This gentlemen talks of checking the destructive deeds, which he very properly describes, as far as relates to the deeds in themselves considered; but, when he is loading the perpetrator with hard names, I am sure he does not know the consequence of that, supposing these hard names to reach the eyes of the parties.
   His recommendation of instituting an *inquiry into the* causes, by agents sent from you, shows that he is totally ignorant of every thing connected with the matter; and shows, that,

however good his motives, he is wholly unfit to advise. And, with regard to the associations of farmers and others in the country, they are the mere effect of passion, operating upon irritated minds. It is baffled power: it is power and undisputed domination filled with resentment on seeing itself reduced to a state of impotence. Did you never dream (you are very likely to have such dreams) of having some man standing before you; some unfortunate underling, on whom you wished to pour out a torrent of censorious expressions; and that, somehow or other, you could not speak? I once had such a dream; I thought I had got an opportunity of laying it well on upon old SIDMOUTH; and that I could not utter a single articulate sound of all the expressions (which were not of the mildest sort) which I had prepared for him. Just much about such is the situation of these agricultural chieftains: they would swear like troopers: oh, how they would swear! but they do not know whom to swear at: they would execrate and blaspheme; but they do not know on what object to pour out their execration and their blasphemy: they would cut, flay, shoot, hang, quarter; but they do not know on whom they would exercise these terrible inflictions; while, perhaps, and most likely, the very persons that they employ (for they are compelled to employ some to aid and assist them in their work of detection) are the persons who have perpetrated the deeds; and that nothing short of an extirpation of the people, by whom they are surrounded, and on whose labour they depend, will give them security, without taking the hostile disposition out of the hearts of the people. This was my opinion before, and it is still my opinion.

I will not act the hypocrite, nor will I act the fool; and it would be acting the fool in a manner the most staring to affect to *deplore* the existence of the evil. What would be thought of me, if I were to affect to *deplore* the present confusion in the West India colonies, which confusion I so clearly foresaw and so distinctly foretold, and to prevent which I laboured so earnestly? To affect to deplore these evils is as ridiculous as it would be to deplore that Christmas is so near at hand, unless he who deplores is able to show that he has done everything in his power to prevent the evil from happening; that he has had some power to exercise in the case, and that the evil has come in despite of his laudable exertions.

Men of sense and sincerity seeing the evil, and knowing, or thinking they know, the causes of it, will propose a remedy, not wring their hands, tear their hair, and sit down and cry; not, as a great privy councillor is said to have done at the time of the panic, violently clasp his hands together, turn up his eyes, till you saw nothing but the whites, and exclaim, 'My God! what shall we do!' This is not the way to govern nations; it is not the way to govern the English nation at any rate. 'Get up, you lubberly dog!' said JUPITER to the wagoner, 'apply your hands to the whip, and your shoulders to the wheel; and do not lie there worrying me with your exclamations!' Pray, my lords and gentlemen, do not think that I recommend the whip to be used by you in this case, nor the racking-wheel by any means; just the contrary, as you will presently learn, if you should be condescending enough to do me the honour of reading this address, which is entitled to your attention, because, long before any fires at all took place, I, being afraid that such would be the end, discharged my duty in suggesting measures of effectual prevention.

Come, come! It is time to get the better of your pride and haughtiness, and of your apparent vow, recorded in heaven, to perish rather than to listen to me. It is time to get the better of this prodigious and absurd perverseness; and then let me ask you whether, if I foresaw this terrible result of what my Lord RADNOR, in his evidence before the Poor-law Commissioners, calls the harsh treatment of the labourers; whether, if I clearly *foresaw* this result, and so clearly foretold it to his tenants, amongst others, at SALISBURY, in the year 1826; whether, this being the case, it is not your duty to your master to attend to me now?

... One, if not two, of the most terrible fires that have taken place, was the act of a son, whose father had been transported for rioting by the Special Commission at Winchester. In this very list of burnings, which I have inserted above, we find, that, while a farmer was gone to an examination before the magistrates, of persons *suspected* of having set fire to his *stacks* and *barns*, his *farm-house*, which had escaped before, took fire and was *burned to the ground*; and that this also was suspected to be a wilful act! will nothing open your eyes? A *rural police* is talked of. The newspapers tell us that WELLINGTON asked MELBOURNE, whether it was intended to establish a *rural police*; and the same newspapers tell us (I hope falsely), that the latter seemed to answer in the affirmative. Gracious God! a rural police in a village of Wiltshire, or Hampshire, or Berkshire, or Sussex, or Kent, to protect corn ricks, standing out in the fields, each, on an average, a mile from any house! There will be another time and place for talking of this matter; therefore I shall say no more about it here.

I repeat, that there are no means of prevention but that of taking the disposition to do the thing out of the hearts and minds of the people; and, if I had the power that you have, out of their hearts and minds I would take that disposition in the course of one month on pain of being racked on the wheel in case of failure. That is to say, in one month after the Parliament should meet; and I would have it together in fourteen days, the time limited by law, if I called it together in a tavern, or a play-house. Now, then, let me tell you *what I would do*, if I had the power; first laying down the principles upon which I would proceed, and stating shortly the notorious facts which call for, the application of those principles.

It is notorious that the working people, in town and country, the latter especially, are in a state of great and general discontent. As Lord RADNOR says, in his evidence given to the Poor-law Commissioners, this has been produced by harsh treatment, of long growth, and, as my Lord STANHOPE observed, a year or two ago, has at last produced a hostile feeling in the poor towards the rich. Laying the facts out of the question, though they are indubitable, reason tells us that this must be the case; because, if it were not so, there could not be generally prevalent this simultaneous disposition to commit these acts; and, besides, if this were not the case, numerous detections would take place. I will engage that, for every fire that is wilfully set, there are, on an average, forty persons, who could either give evidence of the fact sufficient for conviction, or who could furnish a clue to the obtaining of such evidence. Thus, in ordinary times, it is very rare that an act of arson escapes punishment. It is so terrific an act, it excites such general alarm, that the common feeling of self-preservation sets the whole neighbourhood at work; puts the whole country in motion to discover the perpetrator. How is it that this is not the case *now*? How is it that, now, instead of every creature running to help to put out the fire; instead of women and girls forgetting their sex, working, as if for their lives, to extinguish a fire; instead of this, instead of being ready to risk their lives in the work of extinguishment, how comes it that we see men, women, girls and boys, standing by, and laughing at the destruction they behold; and how was it with you; what were your thoughts, when you heard the laugh from Westminster-bridge, re-echoed from Waterloo-bridge, when the Houses of Parliament were burning? And, will the '*rural police*', though armed, as in Ireland, with pistols, swords, daggers, carabines, and muskets, sent to remove the discontent; tend to take the resentful and revengeful feeling out of the hearts of the people?

Come! come down, proud stomach! It is useless to storm; it is useless to rage. It is useless to revile the thunder and the lightning; it is time to think of a reconciliation. For, when men cease to regard the wilfully setting of fire as a crime richly deserving of death; and when the death of the perpetrator ceases to be acquiesced in, in the manner that it formerly was, it is obstinacy, it is madness, it is power in a passion, not to think of the means of bringing the people to their former way of thinking upon the subject. I would bring them back to that former way of thinking, if I had the power; and now I will tell you what I would do to effect that desirable purpose. I will state my measures to you; and, as you will see, they are all within your power. I will state them one by one; and, if I had the power they should be adopted within forty days from this time.

1. A complete, absolute, and entire, repeal of every part of the new Poor-law Bill.
2. A repeal of STURGES BOURNE'S Bills which gave to the rich a plurality of votes in the vestries; and which then gave them the power of forming select vestries; and the power of nullifying the old powers of the real overseer, and of the magistrate, and also the power of introducing hired overseers, strangers to the parish, which bills of STURGES BOURNE were the principal cause of the riots in 1830 and 1831.
3. A repeal of the new and severe Game Laws, which authorize the magistrates to transport for seven years men found, in the night time, in pursuit of pheasant or hare; those wild

animals which the common law of England holds to be the common property of all mankind.
4. A repeal of PEEL'S new trespass-law, which punishes the trespasser without trial by jury; a repeal of PEEL'S new felony laws.
5. A repeal of the malt-tax.
6. Pass an act to restore young people to the farm-houses, by indirectly giving inducements to the farmers to have yearly servants as formerly.
7. Repeal the new law giving magistrates power to shut up foot-paths without setting out others in their stead.
8. Repeal PEEL'S BILL, and pass an act on the NORFOLK PETITION.
9. Abolish the Bourbon-like Police.

I think I see you sitting round a table, and *bursting out in laughter at this being read to you.* Happy to see you so merry, gentlemen; but not being ambitious to be the subject of your mirth, I put on my hat and take my leave of you. Those are the things that I would do; those things you can do, if you like. I cannot make you do them; and if you will not do them, you must leave them undone. You call me '*innovator*', and 'revolutionist': I propose to you to do nothing but to *remove innovations*, the oldest of which, except the malt-tax, is only of sixteen years' standing, and one of them the work of the 'REFORMED Parliament'! I ask for nothing for the people, but to bring them back to *the laws of England*, such as they were only twenty years ago. However, *you* have the power, and *I* have not the responsibility; follow, you, your course, being assured that I will follow mine.

WM. COBBETT.

Political Register, 22 November 1834.

Turning Out The Whigs

To THE KING

Dublin, 19 November, 1834.
SIR,

I was grateful to your Majesty for your assent to the Reform Bill; but I am much more grateful to you for having driven from your councils and presence, a set of servants who have used their power for the purpose of procuring to be passed a bill which has abrogated the greatest of the fundamental laws of the kingdom, and that, too, upon the express allegation, by them made, that the labouring part of your subjects, when brought by misfortune into a state of indigence and want, have *no right to relief* out of the land upon which they were born, and which they alone make worth any thing; and upon the further allegation, that even assistance to the old and infirm was bad and mischievous, when provided for by law.

I most heartily and humbly thank your Majesty for having dismissed from your councils a set of servants, who, when the House of Commons had resolved upon the repeal of a part of the malt-tax, threatened to quit your service and leave your Majesty without servants, unless that vote were rescinded; a set of servants who sent out the special commissions of 1830 and 1831; a set of servants who have expended twenty millions on a project, which has thrown into utter confusion the most valuable of your foreign dominions; a set of servants who have introduced bands of commissioners, and a sort of mongrel government, carried on in detached parcels, by creatures of their own, irresponsible as well to your Majesty as to the Parliament; a set of servants who have commenced making innovations in every thing, giving a shake to every institution of any standing, finishing nothing, tossing all rights and principles of government into the air, till, at last, no man knows what to expect.

But, may it please your Majesty, it is of the *severities* of this set of servants, that I most complain. It is impossible for an Englishman to look at their deeds in almost every part of the kingdom, without shuddering; it is impossible to behold their conduct with regard to the press; with regard to other things connected with the sufferings of the people: it is impossible to look at these, or to think of these; without being grateful to your Majesty for having put an end to their power. To your Majesty it belongs to choose your own servants. It is our duty to leave you the free exercise of that prerogative, and carefully to abstain from every thing like an attempt to thwart you in your choice. If that choice should unhappily (which we ought not to presume likely) be such as to be hostile to our liberties and happiness, we must rely on our representatives in the House of Commons to protect us against any evil that may be likely to arise from their counsel; and, if we do not choose representatives that will discharge this duty towards us, the fault will be in ourselves, and not in your Majesty. At any rate, the first feeling of your people, upon hearing that you have driven from your presence a set of men, amongst whom he, who is technically held to be keeper of your Majesty's conscience, has openly and loudly declared himself to be a disciple of the merciless MALTHUS, and has inculcated the justice and the necessity of ruling the poorer part of your subjects upon the principles laid down by that barbarous man; at any rate, the first feeling due from us towards your Majesty, upon this occasion, is that of gratitude.

I am,
Your Majesty's faithful subject,
And most obedient humble servant,
WM. COBBETT.

NOTES

[1] These last two years Cobbett had himself been living as a single man. Anne and the daughters had never set foot on the farm at Normandy. After leaving the Kensington house in January 1833, just before the opening of the new reformed Parliament, the family joined Cobbett in the house he had rented at 21, Crown Street, just off Westminster Hall. Following a family crisis that summer (for the full story of which see George Spater's biography, pp.518-23) Cobbett never again lived with the family, but when in London put up at the rooms in Bolt Court. He had no other home now but Normandy, his family having themselves moved to 10, Red Lion Court. The eldest son, William, did come to the farm at first, but was not happy with the choice of farming land nor with his father's increasingly egotistical

behaviour; and he left at some date early in 1834.

[2] *Cobbett's Legacy to Labourers*, the most passionate and uncompromising of his political works, ran to three editions, each about the size of an army pay-book, bound in black leather as he had promised, though priced 1d more than he had bargained for. The fourth and last edition appeared in 1872, from Griffin, London.

[3] The 'Jolly Farmer' pub, at Farnham, in Wey Street. Now the 'William Cobbett'.

CHAPTER 10

Political Register, 29 November 1834.

To The People of Oldham.

Dublin, 21 November, 1834.
MY FRIENDS AND CONSTITUENTS,
   There has arisen in our national affairs a state of things of a very interesting and important character, and which, in all human probability, will lead to events affecting, and deeply affecting, our liberties and our happiness. At such a time it must be one of the duties of a Member of Parliament to offer his opinions to his constituents upon the subject generally, and particularly with regard to the manner in which he deems it right to act in this new light of things. In the discharge of this duty I now address myself to you.
   The King has made a change of his servants; has turned one set out, and has taken another set in. If it be proper to maintain the kingly government, it is also proper in us to allow that he not only possesses the right to do this, but that he ought to have the right to do it; for, if the House of Commons, or the people at large, were to appoint the servants of the King, there could be no such thing as responsibility anywhere. If the House of Commons were to choose the minister, he would be their servant. They would be the absolute sovereign; and a pretty sovereign we should have had in those who brought in and pushed on the Poor-law Bill. The Americans have taken all the precautions possible upon this subject; they have given as little power as possible to the President and the governors; but, for their own *safety's sake*, they have left the appointment of all

executive officers to those chiefs of the several republics. Therefore, I deem it my duty scrupulously to abstain from any act which should seem to call in question the King's entire freedom to choose and appoint his own executive officers, knowing that I possess the right to call in question, in your behalf, any misconduct on the part of those officers; and, distinguished as you have made me, it is my duty also, to make my opinions, as to this matter, known as extensively as I can.

What were the motives of his Majesty for dismissing his late servants, it is impossible for me, at present, to say. But, if I had been King, I never would have retained a Ministry one hour, who thought proper to retain amongst them the man who had draggled the great seals, the insignia of royalty, from the Highlands of Scotland to the Isle of Wight; then back again to north Lincolnshire; and who had, in harangues from a public-house balcony at SALISBURY, and at another public-house, in the little village of FAREHAM, been pouring out, amidst masses of insufferable nonsense, his bragging about his friendship for me, and my friendship for him. Had there been no other reason than this, this would have been sufficient. The King had lived through the time of THURLOW, of LOUGHBOROUGH, of ELDON, of LYNDHURST.[1] He had seen his father and his brother with Lord High Chancellors, who, whatever might be their politics, had not run about the country in this wild manner; and it was not reasonable to expect that he should be able so far to master his natural desire to keep up the dignity of his throne, as not to be enraged upon hearing this man promise his associates at a dinner, that he would write to the King by that night's post, to tell him with what cheers his health had been drunk by about threescore of people.

However, be the King's motives what they might, he had a right to do that which he has done; and it is for us to take care to do our duty, to protect ourselves against any evil consequences that may arise from the change. The newspapers in London, which are the property of, and are managed by, persons living on public money allotted them by the Whigs, are naturally endeavouring to stir up the people, to do something or another, that shall force the Whigs back again to the King. The *Morning Chronicle*, which is said to be the property now of a little band, making a part of those numerous hordes of commissioners, which the Whigs have stuck upon our devoted backs. These pensioned and sinecured reptiles are naturally desperate at the prospect, and, indeed, the certainty of being deprived of their means of living luxuriously on our labour, while they have assisted to push on a law, intended to reduce us to live upon COARSER FOOD. They endeavour to alarm us with the sound of *soldiers* and *police*; and to make us believe that the Duke intends to establish a military government in England. I shall by-and-by show you, that the Duke could not do this, if he would, any more than I could pluck the sun from the sky. But, suppose we grant the *coarser-food* gentlemen, that the Duke has this foolish intention, how is the change for *the worse?* The Whigs, or, to give them their proper name, the COARSER-FOOD MINISTERS; and let this be their name; the '*coarser-food Ministry*' began their career by augmenting the number of the standing army, which, upon all occasions, they have employed with more vigour than any of their predecessors. And, as to POLICE; why, just before the Parliament separated, MELBOURNE, the head of the coarser-food Ministry, declared in his place, in the House of Lords, that it was his intention to establish a police in the villages; that is to say, what he called a 'rural police'. Besides this, was he not Secretary of State for the Home Department, when the spy POPAY was employed? Was it not proved, that he himself received written reports coming from that spy, of things that passed in private families, as well as at political and public meetings? Was it not proved before a committee of the House of Commons, that POPAY received extra pay for acting as a spy? and was it not proved that the money came from the office of this very Secretary of State? What more, then; what worse, then, are we to apprehend as to military and police?

But the Common Council of London, a set of as great oppressors as any in the kingdom, as Mr WILLIAM WILLIAMS has most amply proved: this set, and here and there a cluster of people that have been put in motion by the army of commissioners, are holding meetings to address the King, in which address they purpose to express a fear, '*that all reforms will now stop*'. Why, their Lord Chancellor of the coarser-food Ministry has been flying about, from one end of the kingdom to the other, asserting, that he and his colleagues had gone *too fast* in the work of reforming; that they did *little*, it is true, during the last session of Parliament; and that, in the next, they should *do less*. We may console ourselves, then, on this score, I think. But, what have they done, or attempted to do? The only thing that they have attempted, in the way of church reform, has been, to pass a bill in the House of Commons for permitting *Dissenters to take degrees in the universities*; a thing of no sort of value at all to the great body of the Dissenters; of no value to any but a few rich men; and of very little value, even to them. The *church-rates*; the *marriage* rites and expenses; the *tithes*: these are the things of value. The marriages they proposed a measure to adjust, so insolent that the Dissenters rejected it; and, indeed, it was perfidious, as well as insolent; for it would have subjected the Dissenters to rules which would have given to the Government the power of limiting the number of their places of worship, and, indirectly of choosing their ministers. With regard to the church-rates, they have done nothing, and declared their intention to do nothing; though it is as unjust to make Dissenters pay church-rates in Ireland; and, be it known, that they were not taken off in Ireland, until there must have been a hundred thousand men in arms to collect them, and could not do so any longer. With respect to the *tithes*, which is the great burden of all, they have *talked* of nothing but merely altering the *mode of payment*. The regulation might prevent the parson having the power of coming and taking the tithe in kind, he, the dissenter, would still have as much to pay in money.

But, I do beseech the Dissenters to bear in mind the following undeniable fact; namely, that, collectively and individually, the coarser-food Ministry, including Lord GREY, have distinctly declared, that they would never agree to a *separation of church from state*; which is the great thing that the dissenters prayed for, and that they want; and that, since the church is come into its present state, every churchman must want too, on grounds which I have heretofore fully stated to you. The separation of church from state takes away the maintenance of the church, except by voluntary contribution, and leaves the teachers of religion to be chosen by the parents of those who are to be taught. Will the Duke's Ministry agree to this? I do not T H I N K they will: I do not think that, until urged on by more pressing events, they will yield to this separation of church from state. But I K N O W that the coarser-food Ministry will not yield to it; I might nearly say, that I K N O W that the Duke and his Ministry will not yield to it; but the coarser-food Ministry have positively told us, collectively and individually, that they will *not* yield to it. What danger is there, then, that this change will produce any injury to the cause of church reform? And is it not clear, that all the talk of such reform on the part of the coarser-food Ministry, was intended merely to amuse the Dissenters, and to get their support to measures relative to other matters, deeply injurious to the people at large?

As to the church in Ireland, they have proposed, and caused to be passed, bill upon bill; they have voted a million of our money to be given to the parsons of Ireland, to keep them till tithes could be collected; and still they have done no one thing to remove the burden from the Catholics of Ireland, or to restore peace and tranquillity to that country, to supplant the endless broils and violences, arising out of the exactions of the Protestant established church. What, then, have the Dissenters to apprehend from this change? Above all men living, why should *they* be afraid of the change? I should like to know how it is possible, in the first place, that the WELLINGTON Ministry can *do less* for the Dissenters and Catholics, than the coarser-food Ministry did; and, in the next place, I would ask the Dissenters, whether those who repealed the Test and Corporation Acts, and who passed the Catholic Emancipation Bill, are *less likely* to abolish the connexion between church and state, than those who have done nothing for the Dissenters or Catholics, and who have positively declared, collectively and individually, that they will *maintain* the connexion of church and state.

Then, as to the nation in general, Dissenters, Churchmen, Catholics, and altogether; what are those '*reforms*'; what is that which is meant by the '*carrying out of the Reform Bill*', which is a favourite phrase of *pis-aller* PARKES and the rest of the horde of commissioners? Is the commission for inquiring into public charities, which has cost a hundred thousand pounds or more, and which has done nothing; is this one of the '*reforms*'? Is the corporation commission another 'means to an end'? Yes; the means of enabling *roaring* RUSHTON, *pis-aller* PARKES, and a whole band of commissioners, to drink champagne, eat turtle, and loll on sofas, instead of drenching down bits of bullock's liver with small-beer, and curling their carcasses up upon a whisp of straw, which is the fare and the lodging that anything that they could honestly earn would supply. Is this thing; this insolent flinging away of our money, one of the 'reforms' that *pis-aller* PARKES and his crew are afraid of seeing stopped? Certainly it is; and I trust it will be stopped. The fellows now acknowledge that they could do nothing effectually; that the corporations set them at defiance; and that there is no law to punish them for setting them at defiance. Why, then, were they appointed? Why were fifty or a hundred thousand pounds of our money to be thus squandered away for no purpose, except that of feeding *pis-aller* PARKES and his crew, while hundreds of thousands belonging to the families of weavers and labourers, who toil from morning till night, have not, upon an average, three pence a day each to exist on.

The hangers-on of this coarser-food Ministry are insinuating, and, indeed, saying, that that part of the press which refuses to join in the howl of lamentation for turning out of these Whigs, is corrupted. What! must I be corrupted because I do not howl; because I laugh, instead of howling, at the turning out of those, in the reprobating of whose deeds I have bestowed more time and labour, than I ever bestowed on any other subject in my life! Let me state *some* of the deeds of this coarser-food Ministry; let me set them down in the form of distinct propositions; and then let me ask, whether I must be *corrupted*, because I do not howl at their disgrace. I say, then,

1. That they proposed and got passed the Coercion Bill for Ireland, which provided for the administration of justice by military officers, instead of a judge and jury.
2. That they augmented the standing army, in time of peace.
3. That they sent out special commissions, by which upwards of three hundred countrymen were transported for rioting.
4. That they rejected the numerous petitions in favour of the poor Dorsetshire labourers.
5. That they armed and called out the Irish yeomanry.[2]
6. That the NEWTOWNBARRY affair took place in their time; and that nobody was punished for the slaughter on that occasion.[3]
7. That they proposed and carried a vote of twenty millions

of money, to be given to slaveholders to cease the commission of the deed of keeping their fellow-creatures in slavery.

8. That they rejected a proposition to put the landholders upon a level with the farmers and the tradesmen, with regard to the stamp taxes.
9. That they displaced a taxing man, and gave him eight hundred a year for life to retire, in order to make a place for WOOD, emphatically called J O H N, and that this was no more than a sample of their proceedings in this respect.
10. That they opposed and set aside the Factory Bill of the considerate and humane Lord ASHLEY.
11. That they opposed the repeal of that act of the Six Acts, which related to cheap publications.
12. That under this act, they sent more than three hundred men to prison in one year, for selling cheap publications; a thing which their predecessors had never done at all, and under an act, which they, at the passing of it, had represented as hostile to every principle of English liberty.
13. That they opposed a motion for a repeal of the Septennial Bill; and for the shortening of the duration of Parliaments.
14. That they surrounded themselves by bands of commissioners, of various descriptions, some of whom were merely students at law, the rest chiefly going under the name of barristers: and that they thus formed a sort of establishment of gossiping and tale-bearing supporters, haunting the coffee-houses and all the other places of public resort.
15. That they made a King's counsel of that H I L L,[4] who, as he himself confessed, '*incautiously*' made a statement about Mr SHEIL.
16. That having before them a report from a committee of the House of Commons, proving that the lands of England were daily becoming *less valuable*, for want of sufficient labour being bestowed upon them, they brought in and passed a bill for establishing a new colony, in a country called Australia, and passed, at the time, a law to enable the vestries of parishes to raise taxes on the whole of each

parish, to defray the expense of sending away the labouring people out of England; and that they appointed the above-said King's counsellor, HILL, together with GROTE, CLAY, TORRENS, and WHITMORE, *commissioners* for the affairs of the said colony.

17. That they proposed no measure whatsoever to redress the crying grievance discovered and proved, by the committee who examined into, and reported upon, the allegations respecting the spy POPAY, though it was proved before that committee, that the spy had received money for spying from the Secretary of State, through the commissioners.

18. That they opposed and set aside a motion for inquiring into the grounds for giving pensions to prodigious numbers of men, women, and children, on the pension list, alleging tht it was '*indelicate*' and '*ungentlemanlike*' to make such inquiry.

19. That the House of Commons having agreed to a motion to repeal the half of the malt-tax, they proposed, and carried a motion for the RESCINDING OF THAT VOTE.

20. That they proposed, and passed, what they called the 'POOR-LAW AMENDMENT BILL'; and that BROUGHAM, when he proposed the second reading in the House of Lords, asserted, *that the poor had no prescriptive right to relief*; and that *all legal provision for the poor was bad*, and that he proceeded upon the principles of MALTHUS, which were worthy of the admiration of the world.

These things I know; these things I know of this coarser-food Ministry; and is there upon the face of the whole earth so base a wretch as I should be; so corrupt and villainous a betrayer of the trust which you have reposed in me, if I were not to do every thing in my power to prevent the possibility of these men ever again possessing the confidence of the King? and yet the bands of commissioners; those hungry bands; who, like the locusts of Egypt, threaten, not only to snatch the meals from our tables, but to devour up every thing in the shape of human food: those voracious bands accuse me, amongst others, of corruption, because I do not weep at an event that chokes them off from their cormorant repasts. Villains! They swallow up as much in a month, as the poor of a large country receive in the way of relief, in a year! Savage monsters! And am I to be called corrupt, because I do not weep at the prospect of seeing them brought down to that bodily labour, for which nature fitted them, and their desertion from which can be justly animadverted on only by the vagrant act, applied by an impartial justice of the peace!

But, have I forgotten Lord DURHAM?[5] Might not he be brought in? And so, by being infused into the body of the coarser-food Ministry, make it endurable? In the first place, what *power* has he? what *talent* has he? what has he ever done? He said that we owed the Reform Bill to Lord GREY! I know that we owed it to the people; and that the ten-pound suffrage, in preference to the twenty-pound suffrage, we owed to my timely exposure of the whisperings of *pis-aller* PARKES, followed up immediately, as that exposure was, by the thundering petitions from GLASGOW, NEWCASTLE, LEEDS, MANCHESTER, and other great towns. Lord DURHAM, let it be recollected, most positively declared to the Dissenters, to their faces, that he *was not for a separation of church from state*; what, then, have the Dissenters, or any of us, to expect from him; or, rather, what should we have to expect, if he had any power, or any talent? neither of which he has; besides, what is the extent of his professions? Let us see. 1. To reform all *acknowledged* abuses in the church, whether in England or Ireland. 2. To give householder suffrage. 3. To give triennial Parliaments.

This is the extent of his professions. The first amounts to nothing at all: it is perfectly indefinite; for, *who* is to *acknowledge* the abuses? And, if not acknowledged by himself, I suppose, they are not to come within his definition. The Dissenters say, and I say, that the *connexion between church and state* is a great abuse. He says that that is no abuse. So that this profession amounts to nothing at all.

The second is by no means definite. It does not say, that *every man holding a house* is to have a vote; it does not say, that there are not rents and taxes to be considered; and, if the right to vote is to depend on these, in any degree whatsoever, it is not worth a straw. If it be householders, *paying scot and lot,* and thus shutting out all the hardest working people in the country, as well as in towns, the thing may as well remain as it is. I have just sent to the press a little book, entitled, *Cobbett's Legacy to Labourers*; in which I have shown, that *labour* is not only *property* in itself, but that all other property must be founded on labour;[6] and that the labourer, or weaver, or carpenter, or smith, has a *clearer right*, founded on the property which he has in his labour, to vote at elections, than any landlord can have, founded on the property which he has in his estate. Why, then, talk about *householders*; why talk about a thing that has no *principle* to rest upon? The capacity to labour is a man's property, in whatever state of life he may be. Is it not infamously impudent to assert, that *pis-aller* PARKES, for instance, who swallows up out of the fruit of the labour of working men, as much as the whole earnings of seven or eight of them; and who gets into '*a house*' (what a shame!) by the means of such swallowings; is it not infamously impudent to assert, that he has a right to vote, while those seven or eight working men, out of the fruit of whose labour he lives, have no right to vote; which would be the case, under a law to the full extent of Lord DURHAM's professions if they happen to be single men?

With regard to triennial Parliaments, if we were *sure* that we could get them by supporting him, I would take them as part of our due; but annual Parliaments are our right; and, when we are stating our right, for them we must contend. I could very clearly show, as I have shown before, not only are annual Parliaments and universal suffrage the people's right, but that the *full enjoyment of them would be the security of all the orders and institutions of the country*. If Lord DURHAM could, indeed, come at once and give us householder suffrage and triennial Parliaments, I should say, let us take him; but as he does not bring us the most distant chance of his ever being able to give us any thing, why am I to give up a *principle*; why am I to give up the assertion, and the hope of justice, in order to grasp at this little beam of moonshine? In short, he brings us nothing; he is worth nothing to the people, in such a state of things; and all the effect that can possibly be produced, by sticking him up, is to favour delusion in fools, and a lingering hope in the hungry dependents of the coarser-food Ministry.

Now, then, as to the Duke, ... I know that he cannot

completely overset the local and domestic governments of England. Things which have stood since the days of ALFRED are not going to be overset by him. We may hear loose talk, and impudent menaces, but sheriff, coroner, justice, constable, tithingman, quarter-sessions, judge, jury, vestry, overseer, churchwarden, court-baron, court-leet, hayward: these are not going to be overset by ten thousand heroes of Waterloo; and they must be overset before he can effect any thing more, by all the forces that he can muster, than a mere temporary strife, which must end in his own defeat; and *may end* in the overthrow of the *great* and more conspicuous and dignified institutions; but nothing that the Duke could invent, backed by the devil himself, could break up the governments established by ALFRED.

In the hope of seeing you soon, and of finding you all in good health,

I remain,
Your faithful friend
And most obedient servant,
WM. COBBETT.

COBBETT'S WEEKLY POLITICAL REGISTER.

Vol. 86.—No. 9.] LONDON, SATURDAY, NOVEMBER 29TH, 1834. [Price 1s. 2d.

No. X.

TO CHARLES MARSHALL,

LABOURER,

Normandy Tithing, Parish of Ash, Farnham, Surrey.

Chester, 25. Nov. 1834.

MARSHALL,

I shall not write any more letters to you now. I came from Dublin into Wales between seven o'clock last night and two o'clock this morning, and I am come eighty miles to this city along a country, nine-tenths of which are solid rock; mountains, like three or four *St. Martha's Hills* put one upon t'other; and all rock. I never could have believed that I was in England, if I had not, in a little village about as big as Ash, seen that necessary appendage to rural justice, commonly called THE STOCKS, which is peculiar to the villages of old England. I was afraid the coach was carrying us away into some foreign parts; but the moment I saw the STOCKS, I knew that all was right.

And, now, MARSHALL, as I shall not write any more letters to you, you must beg Mr. DEAN to read to you the LITTLE BOOK that I mentioned to you in my last letter; then you will know the rights of it all from the beginning to the end. I should not have written that little book, if the half-drunk, half-mad Scotch vagabonds had not had the impudence and insolence to deny that the working people, when in distress, had a right to relief out of the land. These vagabonds having done this, it is now time to inquire what really was the right that the landlords had to the land at all. So that, if the landlords do not like the book, let them thank the Scotch vagabonds for it; and thank their own folly for having let loose the tongues and pens of these vagabonds.

But, Marshall, I have the pleasure to tell you, that I do not think that we shall hear much more of the impudence of these Scotch vagabonds; for, I hear from London that the *pay* is going to be taken from these vagabonds; and, if they don't get pay, they will not write long; however, we shall know all about this in a few days.

I hope that you are all well, and all your wives and children; and, in the hope of finding, when I come home, all the farm nice and clean,

I remain,

Your master and friend,

WM. COBBETT.

TO

THE PEOPLE OF OLDHAM.

Dublin, 21. Nov. 1834.

MY FRIENDS AND CONSTITUENTS,

THERE has arisen in our national affairs a state of things of a very interesting and important character, and which, in all human probability, will lead to events affecting, and deeply affecting, our liberties and our happiness. At such a time it must be one of the duties of a member of Parliament to offer his opinions to his constituents upon the subject generally, and particularly with regard to the manner in which he deems it right to act in ——— of things. In the discharge of duty I now address my ———

The King has made ——— servants; has turned ——— has taken another set in ——— to maintain the kingly gov———

[Printed by W. Cobbett, Johnson's-court.]

K

Political Register, 29 November 1834.

To Charles Marshall, Labourer, Letter No.X

Normandy Tithing, Parish of Ash,
Farnham, Surrey.

Chester, 25 November, 1834.
MARSHALL,

    I shall not write any more letters to you now. I came from Dublin into Wales between seven o'clock last night and two o'clock this morning, and I am come eighty miles to this city along a country, nine-tenths of which are solid rock; mountains, like three or four *St Martha's Hills* put one upon t'other; and all rock.[7] I never could have believed that I was in England, if I had not, in a little village about as big as ASH, seen that necessary appendage to rural justice, commonly called T H E S T O C K S, which is peculiar to the villages of old England. I was afraid the coach was carrying us away into some foreign parts; but the moment I saw the S T O C K S, I knew that all was right.

    And now, MARSHALL, as I shall not write any more letters to you, you must beg Mr DEAN to read to you the L I T T L E B O O K that I mentioned to you in my last letter;[8] then you will know the rights of it all from the beginning to the end. I should not have written that little book, if the half-drunk, half-mad, Scotch vagabonds had not had the impudence and insolence to deny that the working people, when in distress, had a right to relief out of the land. These vagabonds having done this, it is now time to inquire what really was the right that the landlords had to the land at all. So that, if the landlords do not like the book, let them thank the Scotch vagabonds for it; and thank their own folly for having let loose the tongues and pens of these vagabonds.

    But, Marshall, I have the pleasure to tell you, that I do not think that we shall hear much more of the impudence of these Scotch vagabonds; for, I hear from London that the *pay* is going to be taken from these vagabonds; and, if they don't get pay, they will not write long; however, we shall know all about this in a few days.

I hope that you are all well, and all your wives and children; and, in the hope of finding, when I come home, all the farm nice and clean,

I remain,
Your master and friend,
Wm. COBBETT.

NOTES

[1] All were judges.

[2] For a glance at the background and particular savageries of the 'Irish Yeomanry' in this period, uniformed and armed with English money, see T.A. Jackson's *Ireland Her Own*, Lawrence & Wishart 1971, pp. 157, 198.

[3] Three years earlier, at the start of the Tithe War, a bloody engagement had taken place here (between Wexford and Carlow) when peasants defending their cattle from a police tithe-enforcement raid found themselves encircled by the yeomanry. Twelve Irishmen were killed there, and twelve died later from their wounds. (See Jackson ibid. a concise account of the Tithe War, and indeed of the Irish War as a whole.)

[4] Rowland Hill.

[5] Lord Durham, formerly John Lambton. When Lord Privy Seal in 1831, Durham had been subpoenaed by Cobbett at his trial at the Old Bailey on charges of seditious libel.

[6] Cobbett's practical perception that labour is 'not only property in itself, but that all other property must be founded on labour', though it looks forward to Marx, was not new. William Thompson of Cork, Cobbett's contemporary, had among others already recognized that labour under capitalist production must create property alienated from the workman; and that capital was at bottom nothing other than alienated labour-power. See Thompson's *Inquiry into the Distribution of Wealth* (1824); and, jointly with Anna Wheeler, feminist and socialist republican, their extraordinary *Appeal of One Half of the Human Race, Women, against the pretensions of the Other Half, Men, to retain them in Political and thence in Civil and Domestic Slavery*, 1825, republished 1983.

[7] St Martha's Hill, with its small church on the top, dedicated to the working woman saint, stands by the River Wey (the river of Cobbett's boyhood), at Shalford, near Guildford.

[8] It is an irony not without its sadness that by far the ablest, most lucid, feared and fearless writer of his day, a son and grandson of Surrey labourers, should have written such powerful letters to another Surrey labourer who could neither write in reply nor even read them.

APPENDIX I

Political Register, 5 April 1834.

Dedication,
to the Working People of Ireland

MY FRIENDS, Ever since I became acquainted with the nature and extent of the ill-treatment of the people of Ireland, I have availed myself of every opportunity to endeavour to show that I held their persecutors in abhorrence. I now dedicate to you a history of the life of the bravest and greatest man now living in this world, or that has ever lived in this world, as far as my knowledge extends.[1] It has given me pleasure, which I cannot describe, to find that this famous man sprang from poor emigrant Irish parents; and that he was born in the United States of America two years after the landing of his parents. You will read, with uncommon interest, the clear proof of his having been urged on to perform the wonderful acts of his life, by his recollection of the ill-treatment of his parents in their native land. For more than two hundred years, the laborious Irish people were scourged, because and only because, they would not apostatize from the religion of their fathers; and, even unto this day, every effort is made to keep them down, and to represent them as an inferior race. It is, therefore, in the name of truth and of justice, that I send this book forth amongst the people of this whole kingdom, to prove to them, that this ill-treated Ireland, this trampled-upon Ireland, has produced the greatest soldier and the greatest statesman, whose name has ever yet appeared upon the records of valour and of wisdom. According to all the laws of all nations, a man, though born in a foreign country, is a native of the country to which the parents belong. Thus the famous man is an Irishman; and, I beseech you to look at his deeds and to applaud that just Providence, which has made him an instrument, though in a manner so indirect, of assisting to avenge the manifold wrongs of ill-treated Ireland.

I am,
Your faithful friend,
and most obedient servant,
WM. COBBETT.

Bolt Court, 27 March 1834.

NOTE

[1] This dedication is to Cobbett's edition of the *Life of Andrew Jackson* (the then American President), by Senator Eaton, of Tennessee. Cobbett had abridged and rewritten the *Life*, which he published from Bolt Court in the summer of 1834.

APPENDIX II

Political Register, 17 May 1834.

Repeal of the Union

It is useless for me to repine at not having been present to vote in the minority on this question; but it may not be entirely useless for me to state the *reasons*, or, at least, some of them, which would have induced me to give that vote.

I have never been able, for one single moment, to look upon Ireland or Scotland, other than as parts of my native country, to which I am bound by all of those considerations, the observance of which, constitutes that which is properly called patriotism; and which is no more of kin to the base and servile thing called 'loyalty', than I, thank God! am akin to such a two-legged thing as WILBERFORCE was. I never have been able, for one single moment, to view an Irishman other than as my own countryman; and, I could appeal to the acts of my whole life, in proof of my practice having been consonant with my principle in this respect. Therefore, I have always considered the wrongs done to Ireland (and they are beyond all number, and beyond all calculations as to magnitude); I have always considered these wrongs as participated in by myself.

Thus viewing the matter, the question of repeal of the union, or non-repeal of the union, is, with me, a question of good, or of evil, to the *whole kingdom*; and not at all whether it be good for Ireland alone. Devonshire cannot suffer without England suffering: that fine county cannot be defaced, beggared, and degraded, without injury to the rest of England; and precisely the same must take place with regard to the beggaring and defacing of Ireland. I defy any man to show that injury can be done to Ireland in any way whatever, without that injury recoiling upon England. The question, therefore, is, whether a repeal of the legislative union would, or would not, tend to the peace, happiness, and *real* prosperity of Ireland; I am of opinion that it would, and for this opinion I shall give the reasons under the following heads, which will embrace an answer to everything worthy of attention that I have read, as having been uttered upon the subject, in the House of Commons.

1. A Repeal of the Union would do a great deal to put an end to the absenteeship.
2. It would give the Irish a legislature in which they would be really represented, and the members of which must, of necessity, have a deep interest in the welfare of the country.
3. It could save England the expense of thirty thousand troops, besides a Bourbon-like police, now found necessary to keep the people of that country in subjection.
4. It would, of necessity, prevent the misery, the famine, the human degradation which now mark that fertile land, and that laborious people.
5. It would remove the constant danger which England is in, during war, in consequence of the discontents of Ireland; and, particularly, it would remove that greatest of all dangers, the deadly and justly-to-be-dreaded hostility of the United States of America.

Now, before I enter upon any of these topics, let me trouble the reader with an observation or two upon certain doctrines put forth by the editor of the *Morning Chronicle*, relative to the *very nature* of the Irish people. And this very servile tool of the Whig Ministry has had the baseness to rip up all the old stories about the 'Wild Irish'; he has told his readers the vile things that SWIFT said of the Irish people; and has reminded the public that SWIFT, though an Irishman himself, said that he could not fix his eyes upon any piece of ground two feet square, in Ireland, 'without beholding something offensive to his sight.' All the world knows, that SWIFT was of English parents, he being born in Dublin, and that he says, in one part of his writings, that he does not belong to that vile country; but that he was merely dropped in it by accident. All the world knows, that he was an eccentric sort of misanthrope; and that, into the bargain, he was a disappointed politician of great ambition. In his early years he was patronised by Sir William Temple, lived a great deal at Moor Park (about six miles from where I am now writing),[1] one of the neatest and most beautiful spots in the whole world, and where the custom of the country renders it necessary to fair reputation, that the cottage floor should be as clean as a parlour in a palace. This was all that Swift ever saw of England; some parts of which he might have found not so very unlike that which he found in Ireland. In short, he is the worst of all possible authorities to quote in such a case, to say nothing about his description being in the exaggerated style of poetry; and yet even this is conjured up to show that the Irish were always *a miserable people.*

They have been a miserable people, and, perhaps more or less so from the time of the assumption of the sovereignty of England over Ireland. Certainly from the time of the Reformation, as it is falsely called, from the time that 'OLD BESS' sent over her Protestant parsons; from that time there has been great suffering on the part of the people of Ireland, and from a very obvious cause; but, what does this prove as to the native character of the Irish people? For three hundred years it has been a Catholic people, tyrannized over by a Protestant hierarchy: and unprovided, observe, with any of that relief for the indigent, which the Roman Catholic church so amply provided for them. It is notorious; it is recorded in the most authentic documents, that rebellion after rebellion was excited for the express purpose of forming pretences for confiscation. It is notorious that JAMES the First seized upon whole counties, as his property, unless the owners and possessors of the soil could produce the original grants from the crown; and that his Attorney-General ousted them by ejectments in behalf of the King, as sovereign lord of all the land. And, because a people became miserable under such Government as this; under such at once savage, cool, and hypocritical tyranny as this, having what they deemed a damnable heresy imposed upon them at the same time, as the sole condition of their preserving their property; is it surprising that, under treatment like this, a people should become miserable and almost barbarous?

It is not here that we are to look for proofs of the natural disposition of the Irish, or of their capability of civilization as great as the world ever knew, or ever can know. They were treated badly enough under the *Plantagenets* though of the same religion; but, the way to judge of the nature, or natural character of the Irish, is to look at what they were before the Reformation; before the confiscations began. And, here we have something like proof. Here we see that, as to monasteries, churches, charitable foundations, and all those proofs of solid wealth, of great industry, of piety, good order, good habits; here we see that Ireland was equal, not to Lincolnshire, not to Norfolk, not to Suffolk, not to Kent, not to some other English counties, but that she very far surpassed several of the English counties. Why monasteries could not be founded, the buildings erected, the monks and nuns residing there; cathedrals and churches innumerable; or, at least, not less than four thousand in number: all these could not be, and yet not '*two square feet of ground to be seen which did not present something disagreeable to look at*!' So that, proceeding upon the monstrous supposition, that what Swift said was literally true, instead of its being what it was, a poetical lie, told by him when he was in one of his most ferocious of humours, Ireland was not in that state till the end of *two hundred years of Protestant domination*. These monasteries and churches, as well in Great Britain as in Ireland, appear to have been erected for the purpose of giving the lie to those greedy monsters of the present day, who bid us be contented with potatoes and salt, by telling us that our forefathers were a set of rascally beggars, who lived upon dirt, and went about naked. Our forefathers seem to have foreseen the present times; and they seem to have said:

'*A time will come, seven or eight hundred years hence, when a set of greedy scoundrels will arise, and get power in their hands; and, in order to live in idleness themselves while our poor posterity will be made slaves to work for them, they will tell the poor souls, that, if they have roots and grass to eat, and smoky cabins to creep into to sleep, they ought to think themselves well off; for that we their forefathers were a set of poor lousy beggars, who had neither money nor goods; and, of course, not the means of living any better than the beasts that perish; and that, as to science, we did not possess enough to be able to erect a building sufficient to shelter our bodies from the pelting of the rain. Now, in order to provide our posterity with the means of putting this lie down, at once, let us erect churches, that time will hardly destroy; and let our posterity ask these greedy villains, how we came by the means of erecting these durable buildings. How we came to be able to carry the stone hundreds of miles for the purpose; how we came, without science, to discover the means of making the immortal cement that binds the stones together. The greedy villains will fly into a passion, and talk of our 'superstition', and of the 'priestcraft' that we submit to; but still our poor, slaved, and degraded posterity will answer, "Yes, they might be very superstitious, to be sure; but, if they had not had good victuals and some clothing, they never could have built these churches: a good deal of 'priestcraft', very likely; but the priests must have been crafty, indeed, if they could have made naked creatures find them money to build churches with." '*

Here stand these monuments, which even the present parsons have not been able to cause utterly to fall down: here they stand all over the kingdom, at suitable distances, constantly giving the lie to these greedy and all-devouring monsters; and there is enough of them yet left in Ireland to give the lie to all the blackguards who would persuade us that the Irish people are, in very essence, untameable barbarians; and yet this is a notion very general in England; and very industriously inculcated by the bands of miscreants who are pushed hard to find a justification for the treatment of Ireland. Whatever there is of bad in the national character of the Irish, has been the natural effect of most savage ill-treatment; which is proved beyond all doubt, when we look at them in the United States of America, where we shall have to take a view of them, before I have concluded this article.

Having bestowed these observations on the general charge against the Irish nation; a charge intended to still our consciences, when we are bidden to look at the deplorable state to which we have reduced that country; having made these observations, which I could not find it in my heart to suppress, I shall now proceed, under the several heads, as before stated, to give the reasons for which I should have supported the repeal of the union; for, in fact, to have voted for Mr O'Connell's motion would have been voting for that repeal.

1. *That a repeal of the union would do a great deal to put an end to the absenteeship.*

Nobody will attempt to deny that two houses of Parliament, sitting in Dublin every year, would put an end to the absenteeship, in a very considerable degree: nobody will attempt to deny this: no, say the prostituted knaves, in particular, who oppose the repeal of the union; but, 'there is no harm in the absenteeship'; and it does not signify a farthing to the working people of Ireland, whether 'the rents of Ireland should be spent in that country, or at Rome.' This monstrous proposition was first broached by PETER MACCULLOCH. It has since been universally scouted; but it is now revived again, for this especial purpose; and all the principles of all the statesmen in the whole world are set at nought for the purpose of finding out an excuse for oppressing poor Ireland.

What has been, for five hundred years, the main justification for the *game laws* of England?[2] That these laws are against the laws of nature everyone allows; that they are wholly unknown to the common law of England every lawyer knows well; that, upon the face of the thing, it is monstrously unjust to prohibit the enjoyment of so evidently a natural right, as that of taking wild animals, no man will attempt to deny; and especially to inflict bodily punishment upon him, who attempts to enjoy it. The game is no man's *property*, while it is alive and at large; and reason says, that you have no more right to prohibit the taking of it than you have to prohibit the breathing of the air. What, then, has been the apology for the passing and enforcing these severe laws? Why, this, and this alone: that the game could not be preserved in sufficient abundance, without these laws; that, if it were not so preserved, the *great inducement for gentlemen to reside in the country would cease*; that gentlemen residing in the country, was necessary to the well-being of the common people of the country, because, by expending their incomes there, they diffused happiness around; and that, therefore, in fact, the preservation of the game was necessary to the happiness of the common people themselves.

Now, I do not say that this argument has always appeared to me satisfactory, or that it ought to appear satisfactory to anybody. To a certain extent, however, it is true; and, at any rate, it has been made use of for five hundred years, and nobody ever doubted that it was true to a certain extent. Come, however, PETER MACCULLOCH and his Scotch crew, and they tell us, that it is just as well for a country, that all its meat and all its bread should be carried out of it, and eaten in other countries, while the people living in that country lived upon dirt and grass, or roots approaching to dirt, and herbs approaching to grass: and they have the audacity to call upon us to believe them. Why, one of the great evils existing in England at this time, is absenteeism. The Church of England totters to its base on this very account. If there had been no lay impropriations; no ecclesiastical corporations, also impropriators; if all the tithes had been collected by the clergy, and all spent by a resident clergy, the Dissenters, though well founded in reason and gospel, would never have had encouragement to *petition* for any one of those things for which they are now petitioning. This sort of absenteeship is general; the absentees have all the great livings; so that nine-tenths of the whole of the tithes, I might say nineteen-twentieths, are taken away from the parishes, carried away; come not back in any shape whatever, to renovate the labourer or the soil; come not back to give a hunch of bread to the destitute; but are actually taken away for ever.

Then there is *the breaking up of the small country gentlemen.* Is there a gentleman in England who does not see and lament this? I have never met with any one who did not, in the whole course of my life; and observe, in proportion as these gentlemen have disappeared, the manners and the morals of the common people have degenerated. It must be so: there is nobody left to be a guide: there is no standard of character: there is nobody for the bad to stand in awe of: there is nobody for the good to look up to, for friendship, or support, or encouragement: the *natural magistracy* is gone; the parental sway is at an end: force, sheer force, detested force, comes to supply the place; and all is misery; all disregard for character; all is changed. New men do, indeed, in some cases come: in thousands and thousands of instances the very houses of the small gentry have tumbled down, or have been converted into stables or cow-sheds. *New men* do, however, sometimes come; but they bring not with them the traditionary respect, the habitual obedience, which belonged unto their predecessors.

It is impossible that Ireland should ever be tranquil and happy, while she is drained, as she is now, by the proprietors of the land; while she is treated as a mere colony, out of which to squeeze as much as the planters can squeeze: this is impossible:

and as a native and resident Parliament would necessarily, in a great measure, put a stop to this draining of the country, I, were there only this one reason, should be very strongly disposed for giving her that resident Parliament.

2. *It would give the Irish a legislature in which they would be really represented, and the members of which must of necessity, have a deep interest in the country.*

A great deal was said about the native Parliament which the Irish had before the union, and about the bad manner in which they carried on the concern. Bad enough, sometimes, to be sure; but, is no account to be had of the change which has taken place in the consequence of the *emancipation* of the Catholics? Is it recollected, that the Parliament which the Irish had before was exclusively a Protestant Parliament, governing a Catholic people, that, in fact, it was an *Orange Parliament*? And, indeed, *this is what they are afraid of*; they would give them a repeal of the union tomorrow, if they could be sure, that the Parliament at DUBLIN would be as Protestant as the Parliament now is at WESTMINSTER. In short, the repeal of the union would be a repeal, a total repeal, of the Protestant church in Ireland. In 1829, just after the passing of the Catholic Emancipation Bill, I, wishing to have upon record, other than that of the *Register*, my opinion that the Catholic Emancipation Bill would by no means restore peace to Ireland, but on the contrary that that country would be as much or more disturbed *unless the Protestant hierarchy* were completely removed from Ireland; I, therefore, petitioned the House of Commons to pass an Act to nullify and set aside for ever that hierarchy. The Duke of Wellington and Sir Robert Peel asserted, on the contrary, *that Catholic Emancipation would tend to strengthen the Protestant establishment in Ireland*! Good God Almighty! Not choosing to call these gentlemen names, I expressed my fears, that they must have been labouring under a '*temporary delusion*'. It did seem to me such madness to entertain the notion of sustaining that hierarchy in future, except by mere military force: it did seem to me that a man must be absolutely mad to think of supporting that hierarchy after the passing of that Bill. The public know well; every man knows well, that, from the hour of passing the Emancipation

Bill till this hour, there have been thirty thousand soldiers, thirty thousand bayonets employed to uphold that hierarchy. Gracious God! what has this church not cost this nation? One king brought to the block; another king driven from his throne; a debt of eight hundred millions; and accursed paper-money that may send all by the board in an hour; fifty millions in taxes every year, instead of the three quarters of a million which JAMES the Second collected; a standing army of a hundred thousand men, in time of peace; a military *noblesse*, for the drawing up of whose titles the people are taxed to pay; last, and most horrible of all, a Bourbon-like police, which would have driven our fathers mad, if they could have ever entertained the thought of its ever existing in England. All this we owe to this Protestant hierarchy: all these have been produced by the divers monstrous efforts to uphold this church. The revolutionary scheme relative to the poor-laws is one of the consequences of these monstrous efforts. But now, thank God! this church has reached the length of its tether. Hitherto it has kept out of the battle, and made others fight for it, without knowing what they were really fighting for. But now, at last, the eight hundred millions of debt, contracted to uphold it, has *brought it up tight*. And, now, let its bands of pluralists; now let its clerical corporations; now let its Lord GUILDFORDS and Lord WALSINGHAMS come forth and fight its battles.[3] The Marquis of ANGLESEA [sic] recommends the *reforming* of it![4] Alas! my Lord ANGLESEA thinks that the church can be reformed now as it was in the reign of Henry the Eighth! It is a strange thing that my lord cannot see the wide difference in the two cases. The Parliament and the King reformed the church then BY TAKING EVERY FARTHING'S WORTH OF ITS PROPERTY TO THEMSELVES! I beg my lord to observe that if it be reformed now, its property will be TAKEN FROM THEM AND GIVEN TO THE PUBLIC. The noble Marquis, like lords GREY and ALTHORP, professed his sincere attachment to the *principles of the church of England, as established by law*. Why, so do I; that is to say, I am very sincerely attached to the religion of the church, always, however, excepting its having a King, or a little girl or boy, at the head of it. But, the 'principles of the Church of England', *as connected with its temporalities*, and as illustrated in its practice of pluralities and lay-impropriations: to these principles it is, I am half afraid, that these noble and respectable persons are so *sincerely* attached! The Dissenters mean, however, I perceive, to put this attachment *to the test*; to the test *in England*. Why, therefore, such a fright at the possibility of the oversetting of the Church of Ireland by a Catholic Parliament?

At any rate, the worst that they anticipate from the dissolution of the union, and a Catholic Parliament; the very worst that they can anticipate, is an oversetting, a total oversetting, of this Church in Ireland; and the choice of England is this: pay three millions a year for an army and a police, to uphold that church; or let that church be overset. This is the alternative, and the only alternative. That church has kept Ireland in a state of servile-rebellion for three hundred years, or thereabouts; a repeal of the union would put an end to it; and this brings me to my third proposition.

3. *It would save England the expense of thirty thousand troops, besides a Bourbon-like police, now found necessary to keep the people of that country in subjection.*

The annual cost of army and police, to say nothing about contingent expenses and secret-service money, amounts to more than FOUR MILLIONS A YEAR, sweated out of the industry of the people. The poor-rates, as far as go to the relief of the poor in all England and Wales, do not amount to *five millions a year*; and here are four millions a year expended to support this church in Ireland only! One wonders how the aristocracy can be so mad as to waste the money in this sort of way. Ah, faith! But there is something more than the bit of the church in Ireland; and the aristocracy knows surprisingly well, that a total repeal of the church in Ireland would soon take from them that much fatter thing, the Church of England, which my readers must now all understand, is the property of the aristocracy, who have the sense to perceive that lay-tithes never could exist, if clerical tithes were all abolished; and who must know, or, at least, verily believe, that the abbey-lands, which are held by precisely the same tenure as the lay-tithes, would be the next object to attract the attention of an over-burdened, a harassed, and a ruined people.

These are the reasons for opposing the repeal of the union; and these are amongst the reasons which would have made me vote for that repeal. However, as a matter of arithmetic, the plain question for England is, will you have a repeal of the union; or, will you continue to pay four millions a year to maintain an army and police to hold the Irish people in subjection? This the people of England should deliberate well upon. If they have no generosity; if they have no justice, they, at least, understand something of their interests; and, if they do not, time and sorrow will teach it them.

4. *It would, of necessity, prevent the misery, the famine, the human degradation which now mark that fertile land, and that laborious people.*

You are asked, first, why the mere passing of an Act of Parliament would be sure to procure effects like these. That Act of Parliament, be it remembered, would make a new government for Ireland; would give them law-makers of their own choosing, instead of sending 109 members in amongst the rest of the 658 English and Scotch members. I presume that it would give the Irish *good government*; and it is good government that makes a happy people. There is a famine to a greater or lesser extent every year. We have heard nothing publicly about any famine this last winter. A Catholic priest has written to me to say, that, during the last winter, great numbers of his poor parishioners were driven to live upon sea-weed; that he wrote to the absentee-proprietor, begging some little assistance from him for these poor creatures; that he not only got no assistance from him, but received a very insolent and abusive answer. He wrote also to the clerical tithe-owner, who takes six hundred a year out of the parish; and, like a true Levite, he gave him not one farthing. Now, I put it to any man of common sense, whether these ill-treated people are not acting *rationally*, in resolving to support that man who has made their ill-treatment known to the whole world and who has scorned to make a compromise with their enemies.

Of these ordinary *annual famines*, the English people hear nothing at all; but we have had, *since the union*, which was to make the Irish so happy, THREE GRAND FAMINES. And here is a spectacle such as this world never beheld, except in Ireland. What did we behold? Hundreds of thousands of living hogs, thousands upon thousands of sheep and oxen alive;

thousands upon thousands of barrels of beef, pork, and butter; thousands upon thousands of sides of bacon, and thousands upon thousands of hams; ship-loads and boat-loads coming daily and hourly from Ireland to feed the west of Scotland; to feed a million and a half of people in the West Riding of Yorkshire, and in Lancashire; to feed London and its vicinity, and to fill the country shops in the southern counties of England: we beheld this, while famine raged in Ireland amongst the raisers of this very food, to such an extent, that half the population of hundreds of parishes actually received the extreme unction as a preparation for death from starvation. Aye, and while this was the case, thirty thousand soldiers, ten thousand of them with fat horses, were kept in Ireland on full pay and full diet, IN ORDER TO PRESERVE THE PEACE! While Ireland was sending us provisions to choke up our ports, the begging-box was going forth from door to door in England, *by royal edict*, in order to raise the means of sending potatoes and oatmeal to the relief of these starving people, who had raised all this food by their labour! Talk of danger from a change indeed! Danger to the grinding absentees there might be, indeed; but, how is it possible for any government on earth to produce effects worse than these? Could a Parliament, with the devil for its speaker, produce effects more monstrous, more unnatural, more disgraceful, more cruel than these?

In answer to this, Mr SPRING RICE has his very neat tables of *exports* and *imports*; he tells us that these have gone on increasing since the union. It would seem that, in this gentleman's view of the matter, that the *people* and their happiness are objects pretty much beneath notice. Why, nobody will deny that the people of England, the working millions, are poorer, more miserable, more degraded than they ever were before; yet the exports and imports have gone on gradually increasing with their misery. The miseries of the people of England at this very moment threaten a dissolution of the Government; yet the exports and imports are seven times as great as they were when PITT began his fatal career. There is greater monopoly; greater riches in fewer hands; but what has this to do with the happiness of a people? Our exports and imports have prodigiously increased and are, perhaps, increasing at this moment; but the miseries of the people have increased to a pitch that makes it impossible that this frame of Government can continue to be what it now is. I suppose that lords think sometimes, as well as other men; and, if ours do think; if they do look at the change in their own situation and prospects, which has taken place since the beginning of the French war, what would they give to be *back again* to the year 1792! Yet the exports and imports are seven-fold now to what they were then.

This, therefore, is the shallowest, the most childish, the most contemptible, of all the arguments in support of the union. The sole question is: 'Is Ireland happy?' If that question is answered in the negative, as it must be, 'Can a repeal of the union make it more unhappy than it is?' My opinion is, that it must make it less unhappy than it is; and, therefore, I am for the repeal.

In answer to the general charge against the Irish people of laziness, negligence, carelessness I want nothing but the sight of the droves of live provision, that that country sends forth. British North America lives out of the produce of Ireland: the navy is provisioned by Ireland: West Indies, East Indies, the places in the Mediterranean, all fed by Ireland; besides, observe, when our ports are open for corn, Ireland always sends four times as much as the whole world besides. And can all of this come without prodigious labour? Can it be a lazy people who thus feed all the world? And can that be a good Government, under whose laws and regulations this laborious people are living upon roots, or weeds, or half-stinking mussels? No. Every reasonable man in this world will exclaim, No; it cannot be a good Government. *Ought this people to remain thus?* No: every just man will indignantly exclaim; and as it is thus, under a legislature in which Ireland has but a handful of representatives; why not let her have a legislature chosen by herself, among her own native citizens, under laws made by whom it would be impossible for her to remain in her present state of degradation and suffering.

It is not to be believed that a legislature, consisting, as it must, principally of Catholics, would suffer their poor countrymen, and of the same religion too, to experience the calamities which the laborious people of Ireland now experience.

5. *It would remove the constant danger which England is in, during war, in consequence of the discontents of Ireland; and, particularly,*

it would remove that greatest of all dangers, the deadly and justly-to-be-dreaded hostility of the United States of America.

I should not wonder if the sublime statesmen were to lift their lips upon reading of this; draw their nostrils gently up; give a shake of their heads; and perform all those antics which amount to what we call a *sneer*. Mr PAINE, in a letter to Mr JEFFERSON, written in the year 1795 or 1796 – and the main subject of which letter was the base policy of HAMILTON who,[5] in order not to disturb his FUNDING SYSTEM, prevailed upon WASHINGTON not to join the republican French in the war against England – in that letter, which I saw in Paine's handwriting in 1819, and which was not published until a year or two afterwards (if, indeed, it be published now), he described the sort of war that ought to be made upon England by the United States; and his grand stroke was, *an invasion of Ireland*. 'Ah! my dear sir', said he, 'five thousand Americans, with forty thousand stand of spare arms, *landed in Ireland, would make a great change* in the affairs of this whole world'! I shall never forget the words: they struck me forcibly when I read them; and I have never thought of them since, without dreading the consequences of another war with America, and with France at the same time, probably, *Ireland being in her present state*. Our statesmen may curl their lips, draw up their nostrils, and shake their heads; but I can tell them this, that an invasion of Ireland by the United States was seriously contemplated towards the close of the last war, though it was a war single-handed against England. We have a *great navy*; at least, we have one that costs a great deal. We have *more than three admirals to every ship of the line*: we have *more than two hundred admirals*: and the Americans have *none*. We had four generals and three or four admirals at *NEW ORLEANS; and the Americans had only a lawyer, the son of a poor Irish emigrant*! We know the result on that occasion; and the devil incarnate is not an object of greater terror to the enormously guilty sinner, than the name of that son of an Irish emigrant is to the 'sister services' of this *'mighty empire'*.

We can fit out great fleets; but we cannot employ them all in the watching of Ireland; and, if we could, it is by no means certain that there would always be a fleet in the right place; and if there were, who is sanguine enough to hope that that fleet would defeat the American fleet, of greatly inferior force. The gun-boats and other naval force stationed on the Irish coast, were employed, the newspapers told us, last year, in aiding the land forces in the collection of tithes! It is a pity that such gallant persons, who call themselves 'officers and gentlemen', had not something else to do, than to assist a christian clergy in 'collecting the oblations of the faithful'. An expedition, such as that recommended by PAINE, would give them something else to do; something very different from the 'heroism of the Peninsula'.

But, it is not the power of the United States; it is not the bravery of her people, though that surpasses all other bravery in the world; it is not the matchless skill and adroitness of her seamen; it is not any of these that we have most to dread: it is the hostility; the mortal revenge, of those, and the descendants of those, who have been *driven from Ireland to the United States*! Let our statesmen curl up their lips, reader; but I beg you not to believe that this is an imaginary danger, merely because the justly vindictive persons are three thousand miles off. I beseech you, in the name of prudence and self-interest, if generosity and justice have no weight with you; I beseech you, first, though I am the compiler of it, to read the *Life of Andrew Jackson*, just published by me. I beseech you to trace him from his poor Irish emigrant parents, to the time when he swept an English army back into the sea. I beseech you to look at him, urged on by his mother to fight against the English, in the first American war. Then I beseech you to view him at the present moment, striking at the very vitals of that paper-money system, which was intended, by the haters of American freedom, to accomplish that which they were unable to accomplish by arms. I beseech you, then, to read the extracts taken from American papers, and which extracts are in the present *Register*. In these extracts you see the full verification of all my opinions relative to the danger to England from this source. The state of things in America, however our statesmen may curl up their lips, is such that it must produce great embarrassment here. It has already produced great embarrassment; and that embarrassment is only beginning.

To say that the man, whose measures are producing this embarrassment, is the son of a poor ill-treated Irish emigrant is nothing: that might be *accident*; but it is not accident that thousands upon thousands of Irishmen are holding public meetings in America to support General Jackson against the partisans of England, and avowedly because it is against England that his measures tend. This *is* something. It appears that the Irish, and the descendants of the Irish, far more than one generation or two, perhaps amounting, very likely, to more than a million of adult males, are avowedly giving this support because they look upon the villainous banks as favourable to England, and the views of England. I beseech the reader to look at an account of a meeting which took place in New York, *to raise a subscription for* Mr BARRETT![6] Let our *statesmen* curl up their lips; but such a meeting, in such a city, will make every man reflect on ultimate consequences. Let the staesmen curl up their lips, but sensible men will not bestow a smile of contempt on the votes of thanks bestowed by the Irish throughout the United States to us who had the resolution to oppose the Coercion Bill. Never was there an object in this world so interesting; never was there anything so manifestly pregnant with mighty consequences as that which is now passing in the United States of America; and I must beseech my readers to withdraw their minds for a moment from things immediately pressing upon their attention, to contemplate the scene now exhibited on the other side of the Atlantic, and which I will endeavour to describe adequately with sufficient clearness, in as few words as I can possibly make use of; as follows:

1. That, after the establishment of the independence of America, there were certain certificates given to those who had served in the war, which certificates, as they were to be paid at a very distant day, became of little value in the hands of the poor men who held them.
2. That a Scotchman, of the name of Hamilton, who was a lawyer, who had been aide-de-camp to Washington during the war, and who was a great partisan of England, after the war, but who had gained a great ascendancy over the mind of Washington, conceived, secretly, the project of prevailing on the Congress to pay these certificates in full *after they had got into the hands of rich men.* This was the beginning of a sort of funding system, which was soon made to lean upon the funding system of England; and this was the real cause of

America not joining the republicans of France in the war against England.

3. That, after the last war, which was the people's war, a war which the people would have, the enemies of freedom seem to have given up the hope of destroying the American constitution and Government, by force of arms. They had caused France to be loaded with a National Debt; and a NATIONAL BANK, which had been so effectual in breaking down the English and depriving them of their liberties, was thought of as the certain means of finally effecting that purpose.

4. That in 1816, the Congress was prevailed upon, though in violation of the constitution of the United States, to charter a Bank, and to cause the *taxes to be deposited in this Bank*, after the manner of the English Government.

5. That the principal Bank share owners were *English noblemen*, gentlemen, noble ladies, and English loan-mongers! So that this institution was, in fact, an English institution, leaning upon the Bank of England.

6. That the evils of this Bank soon began to make their appearance. The Congress having violated the constitution of the United States, the state governments violated their constitutions also, and they chartered banks, called State Banks. The country was inundated with paper-money; and these pestilential money makers caused prices to rise and fall, stripped men of their estates, and robbed the working classes of the fruit of their labour.

7. That when JACKSON became President, he, who had always been an enemy of this paper-system, soon discovered a disposition to check it in its progress. This being discovered by the aristocracy, which had thus sprung up, and which was devouring the substance of the people, they, though there was no necessity for it, had influence sufficient to cause an Act of Congress to be passed by the two houses, for renewing the charter of the Bank, which charter expires in 1836.

8. That the President's four years were to expire, and he was to be re-elected, if re-elected at all, in a few months after this Bill was passed by the two houses. This Bill, therefore, was to put him to the test: if he gave it his sanction, he gave up all his principles; if he put his veto on it, the vile aristocracy

thought he would lose his re-election: he bravely put his veto on the bill, and appealed to the democracy for his re-election.

9. That he was re-elected by a great majority, notwithstanding his veto, and notwithstanding the hundreds of thousands of dollars which he detected the infamous Bank in having expended in bribery, to prevent his re-election.

10. That the law which established the Bank authorizes the Secretary of the Treasury to remove the deposits from the Bank when he pleases; and that the Secretary of the Treasury, who is chosen by the President, has removed the deposits, and left the Bank without the public money to sport with.

11. That this has compelled the infamous band of aristocrats to lessen the quantity of their paper-money; that this has caused thousands upon thousands of bankruptcies, and has actually broken about two hundred banks already.

12. That the infamous aristocracy set up a cry, that the President has caused all this distress. Begging deputation after deputation have been sent to him from all parts of the country, to beseech him to give way. He remains firm to his purpose; the paper-money is diminishing in quantity in a prodigious degree, and gold and silver are pouring in from all parts of the world, *particularly from England*, to the monstrous injury of the traders and manufacturers of England, who are compelled now to send money, instead of goods, in exchange for the produce of America.

13. That the whole of that immense republic is now in a state of agitation quite inconceivable, unless to an eye-witness; that the damnable aristocracy of paper, seeing their plunder about to be put an end to, and using every means in their power to oppose the industrious democracy; but that these latter stand firmly by the President, who is resolved to persevere till he has destroyed this aristocracy supported by England.

14. That, however, the most interesting part of this interesting history applies to our question of a REPEAL OF THE UNION; that the Irish, and the descendants of the Irish, have come pre-eminently forward to uphold the President; that they assert that it is for the *English Government* that the Bank was established; and that the banking system tends to

subjugate America to England; that, therefore, it is their bounden duty to stand by the President to the last; to crush the vile monsters that have been plundering them; and to *be avenged for the ill-treatment of Ireland*, by upholding the man who is giving the system a mortal blow.

This is a very brief history of this most interesting affair. Every man, who knows any thing at all of America, knows that in all the great cities and towns the Irish have it in their power to *decide the elections*; and it is the elections which decide every thing else. I do beseech the reader to go attentively through all the extracts which I have subjoined to this article. He will then perceive that, when the wretched people of Ireland are driven abroad by bad government, they are N O T D R I V E N O U T O F T H E W O R L D. They are still in the world; and there we see a million of them now assisting to inflict an injury, and a deep and lasting injury, on those from whom they have received the treatment which I have before described, and which Mr O'CONNELL has so much more forcibly described so many times before. I do beseech the reader to look well at the proceedings and the language of these emigrant Irishmen. All of them retain an ardent love for their native country; all of them resent every injury now inflicted upon her. Mr BARRETT'S imprisonment made no noise in England, but it has made a noise in America; made a noise in that country whence Ireland may be invaded at any time, in any future war.

Now, is it nothing to have continually before our eyes a danger like this? Is it nothing to know that there are five hundred thousand volunteers, under thirty years of age, always ready for the enterprise; and that a three weeks sail may bring them to the destined port. I have seen this danger for more than twenty years. In 1812, I described the danger to the Government and to the country. The danger is every day greater and greater, and there is no earthly way of putting an end to it, but that of making the people of Ireland contented with their Government; and contented with it they never will be, so long as they live under the domination of a Protestant hierarchy, and be deprived of a native and resident Parliament.

Thus have I stated some of the reasons which would have induced me to vote for the motion of Mr O'CONNELL; and which motion I should have liked still better if it had been, at once, for a repeal of the Act of Union.

Before I conclude let me beg the servile writer in the *Morning Chronicle*, to read the account of the proceedings of the Irish in America; and then to tell me, or, tell his readers, whether these are Swift's *barbarians*, who cannot make a piece of ground two feet square fit to look upon without producing pain. What! does the mere salt-water breeze change their nature? My reader must read their speeches, their addresses, and their resolutions, with admiration; he must observe with astonishment how clearly they understand, and in what a masterly manner they describe, all the intricate workings of that system of banking, of which not one English *gentleman* even out of one thousand, has any thing like a clear idea. What! were these men barbarians only the other day? I declare most sincerely, that their speeches have *taught me*, whom these men are condescending enough to consider as their teacher. The NEW YORK EVENING POST is the best-written publication that I ever read in my life, without one single exception: it is the voice of Ireland coming athwart the Atlantic; and, curl their lips up as long as they please, those who rule Ireland will, finally, be compelled to listen to that voice.

It would not be just for me to take my leave of this subject, without some remarks on the pitiful, nay, the *very base*, aspersions cast upon Mr O'Connell, on account of the pecuniary compensation for his mighty labours, which he receives from the people of Ireland. What! is it dishonourable for a man to be supported by the people; by their voluntary and free-will offerings; and that, too, when all the world acknowledges that the services which he has rendered that people, and which he is constantly rendering them, are beyond all praise? The Pittites used to caricature Charles Fox with a *begging-box tied to his girdle*; for he was kept by the contributions of a band of place-hunters: he was the paid mouth-piece of a faction: and that, too, for party purposes.

Is that the case of Mr O'Connell? Is he the tool of a party; or has he ever been? It is very curious that the two or three thousand hangers-on, though they have no pretence to ever having performed any service at all, pocket the earnings of the toiling people, without the smallest scruple; aye, and Mr Harvey was reproached with 'indelicacy', with a want of 'gentleman-like feeling',[7] because he moved for an inquiry into the pretensions of these receivers of the people's earnings, taken from them, observe, by compulsion! And, Mr O'Connell is mean, because, in lieu of his own great professional income, he receives the voluntary offerings of a grateful people, who have witnessed his twenty years of toil in their service.

All the world knows, all the world has acknowledged that he himself extorted Catholic Emancipation from its bitterest enemies. I remember that I said at the time, that every Catholic peer; every Catholic peeress; and every son and daughter of a Catholic peer, ought to have gone to him, thanked him for their restoration to their honours; and ought to have taken by the hand, and to have cherished, every member of his family. I am *glad that they did not* do it; I am glad that they gave proof of their ingratitude towards him, and left the gratitude to be shown by those whom the *Morning Chronicle* choose to represent as essentially barbarians.

A gentleman in Ireland wrote to me not long ago, ascribing Catholic Emancipation to my *History of the Protestant Reformation*. It is very true that that book broke down the prejudices of the people of England; and did a something to disarm the abominable efforts made still to misrepresent the Catholics and their religion. But, it was O'Connell's personal exertions and personal influence, amidst personal perils of every description, that brought the question to a speedy issue, and compelled its enemies to give way; and this, too, according to their own acknowledgements. Therefore he is entitled to every species of support, to every mark of gratitude which his Catholic countrymen can bestow upon him; and the difference between him, and the endless swarms who live upon us, is this; that he receives voluntary contributions; the oblation of grateful hearts; whereas they receive what they receive, by compulsion exercised upon those who yield it, coming to them with grudging and with curses.

More than this I need not say, and less than this would not have been justice to the man, who has made every sacrifice of what love of gain and ambition tendered to him; and who has bestowed a life of labour and an exercise of talent such as it was in the power of no other man to bestow. Eat! What should such a man want to eat for? Family! What should such a man want his family to be anything but beggars for? Quite ungentleman-like, to want to eat and to wear clothes, in him and his; but equally ungentleman-like to ask why the people should be compelled to work to earn carriages and silks and diamonds, to show off and to decorate the he and she pensioners. Two hundred and thirteen pounds a year given to a person who has two livings in the church, for five months' service, or pretended service, as *Chargé d'Affaires* at Florence; very ungentleman-like to inquire why the person should have this pension for one and twenty years, and why he should have it still: nothing 'mean' in the parson's continuing to sack this pension; but, horror of all horrors, for Mr O'CONNELL to receive from the Irish people, as a voluntary offering, that which is necessary for him even to continue his exertions.

I shall be told that Ireland contains other men besides Mr O'Connell. So it does; and very clever men too; and very brave, and very much devoted to their country; but, leaving his great and peculiar talents out of the question, where has she another man surrounded with twenty years of circumstances such as surround him? All the world must see that he himself has made a great change in the affairs of his country; and it is of the utmost importance in the times which are fast approaching, that he should retain his weight of character entirely undiminished.

WM. COBBETT.

NOTES

[1] As a boy, Cobbett had hoed in a hop-garden at Moor Park, William Temple's country house between Crookesbury Hill and Farnham. Here Swift, Temple's amanuensis, met his 'Stella'. An occasional visitor was William III, who during 1692-3 sought Temple's advice on how to get rid of the embarrassing Triennial Bill. On Ireland, Temple warned the Dutch king that 'to think of governing that kingdom by a sweet and obliging temper is to think of putting four wild horses to a coach and driving them without whip or reins.' (*Essay Upon the Present State and Settlement of Ireland*, 1701.)

[2] The game laws of the English landlords had been increasing in ferocity since American independence. But they were to become even more savage after the French Revolution accorded the peasants almost unlimited rights in the taking of game. A nadir was reached in 1816 when the Night Poaching Bill, carried without a word's debate, enacted that a countryman had merely to be discovered with a rabbiting-net in his possession, after dark, to suffer 7

years' transportation. Physical resistance to game-keepers was met with hanging.

[3] Frederick North, fifth Earl of Guildford, was probably better known in Corfu than Guildford. He founded the Ionian University on the island in 1824, and devoted much of his life to Hellenism. William de Grey (Lord Walsingham at the time of his death), the Member for Cambridge, was the judge in Wilkes's trial in 1768. He lived to become a reactionary Lord Chief Justice of the Common Pleas.

[4] Lieutenant-General Paget had fought in the Peninsular War with Sir John Moore. At Waterloo he lost a leg, which was buried with appropriate honours in a grave which is still tended. Paget was created first Marquis of Anglesey after the battle. In 1828 he succeeded the Duke of Wellington as Lord-Lieutenant of Ireland. 'God bless you, Anglesey, I know you are a true Protestant,' said George IV at his departure. 'Sir, I will not be considered either Protestant or Catholic,' replied the well-intentioned soldier, 'I go to Ireland determined to act impartially between them, and without the least bias either the one way or the other.' But three years later, with O'Connell now the victor in County Clare, the tithe war blazing, and Repeal again in the air Anglesey said, 'Things are now come to that pass that the question is whether he or I shall govern Ireland.' The Lord-Lieutenant was already asking for renewed Coercion Acts.

[5] Alexander Hamilton, George Washington's Secretary of the Treasury and the leading Federalist in the government, had by 1792 convinced the President of the need for a national bank and 'funding system' based on the paper money Paine (and then Cobbett) so abhorred. Thomas Jefferson, the Secretary of State, anti-Federalist, and a Jacobin-minded libertarian, disliked the bank plan as a gross concession to the Bank of England and the rich. He resigned his post. It is ironical that what Cobbett is here describing as Hamilton's 'base' policy of the 1790s was the same anti-Jacobin, pro-English policy Cobbett was furiously advocating in those years – and even more so after revolutionary France's declaration of war on England in 1793. As to the 'funding system', Cobbett had been won to Tom Paine's views on money as far back as 1803, when he first read the *Decline and Fall of the English System of Finance*. 'I took up the little essay of PAINE. Here I saw to the bottom at once. Here was no bubble, no mud to obstruct my view: the stream was clear and strong: I saw the whole matter in its true light.' (*Paper Against Gold*, Ch.XXV, Newgate Prison, 1811.)

[6] Richard Barrett, editor of *The Pilot*, Dublin.

[7] Daniel Harvey, journalist, leading reformer and radical MP for Colchester (1818-34), and Southwark (1835-40). He had started the *Sunday Times*, which for many years remained a serious newspaper, in 1822; and in 1833 took over the *True Sun*, then a radical evening newspaper. Harvey was a campaigning MP, and the first – and a popular – commissioner of the Metropolitan Police.

APPENDIX III

Political Register, 27 September 1834.

O'Connell's Welcome to Mr Cobbett

Derrynane Abbey, 11 September 1834.
To Edward Dwyer, Esq.

MY DEAR FRIEND, – I perceive by the papers that the far-famed Cobbett is on his way to visit Ireland. I wish we were able to give him a reception worthy of his talents and public services. He is really one of the most extraordinary men that the world ever saw. When one contemplates the station in society to which he has raised himself, and then looks back to his commencement in life as a labouring boy, enlisting as a private soldier, one knows not which most to admire, the value of that strong mixture of the democratic principle in British institutions which has allowed him to make such an advance, or the extraordinary and vigorous intellect which enabled him to overcome the many and numerous* difficulties which counteracting aristocracy threw in his way, and to become one of the most prominent and useful men now living.

I really think him, after all, one of the most useful men living. He has, it is true, changed his opinion of men and things with unaccountable rapidity and violence; yet when we look at his astonishing literary labours – when we see that he has published the very best and most practically useful books of instruction – that he has written the most pure English of

---

* 'numerous' is seemingly a misprint for 'onerous'.

any writer of the present day, and embraced and illustrated more topics of popular and sound politics than any other living, or perhaps dead author – that even his errors and mistakes are brought forward with so much distinctness and fairness, that they also advance the cause of truth and justice, by stimulating to and requiring most attentive and considerate discussion – in short, taking him all in all, I am convinced that he is of living men one of the greatest benefactors of literature, liberty, and religion.

Aye, of religion – for his *History of the Protestant Reformation* has all the interest of a tale of mere invention, whilst there is not one allegation in it but what can be sustained by the most ...[1] of contemporary and even adverse writers. With what admirable simplicity of style and felicity of effect does he describe the pious firmness and unaffected Christian boldness of the two friars of Greenwich – the Revd Mr Peto and the Revd Mr Elstow![2] What a specimen of truly English fortitude and frankness did not these two friars exhibit, especially when contrasted with the baseness, the servility, and the horrible profligacy of the court of that monster of rapacity, lust, and blood, Henry VIII; the first great author of that change of religion in England called the Reformation! and, then, his account of the tragic death of the Duchess of Suffolk![3] But in a book full of beauties one knows not what injustice one may commit by selecting in preference particular passages, because he who has not read the work through has not read the most interesting, affecting and JUST book in the English language. In fact, it can now be read in almost every cultivated language on the face of the globe.

I extremely regret that I cannot be in Dublin to meet him. You, my excellent friend, as secretary to the late Catholic Association, must supply my place. You must get up a public dinner to entertain him, at which he may receive the respectful attentions of the sincere friends of civil and religious liberty in Dublin. As he goes through the country he will, I doubt not, receive public testimonials of regard; and I hope he will go back convinced in his opinions that the people of Ireland do not deserve the cruel treatment they have received, and still continue to receive, from the British Government.

Do me the kindness to wait on him the moment of his arrival in Dublin, and hand him the letter I enclose, marked 'private'.

I beg of you to enforce for me the request it contains, that he will come to visit this mountainous district. Believe me to be, my dear friend, yours very faithfully,

DANIEL O'CONNELL

NOTES

[1] The print has been obscured by the government's 'Four Pence' surcharge. The lost word may have been 'meticulous'.

[2] William Peto was a Provincial of the Grey Friars. On Easter Sunday in 1532 he preached before Henry VIII at Greenwich a courageous sermon denouncing the divorce of Queen Catherine, on which the King had set his heart. The friar was rushed to 'a tower in Lambeth over the gate'. Peto later fled to Antwerp with his fellow friar Elston, where they published a defence of the Queen.

[3] Not the 'Duchess of Suffolk', but Margaret Pole, Countess of Salisbury, who refused to plead guilty to treason, or to lay her head on the block; and according to Cobbett's account was hacked to death by the royal axeman.

APPENDIX IV

Political Register, 27 September 1834.

Address From The Trades of Ireland to The People of England

WE CALL upon the people of England to consider the present state of the Irish people, unnecessarily labouring under almost every evil that can afflict men; last year millions of human beings were in a state of starvation, destitute of employment, while three million acres of waste land lie uncultivated, in the hands, for the most part, of absentee proprietors, capable of supplying the English manufacturers with as much corn and butter as they import from foreign countries; the finest fishing-stations in the world lie upon our coasts, and our people, deprived of capital, are unable to purchase boats or nets. The absentee landlords are not identified with the interests of the country, and the resident landlords, from the change in the value of money combined with the poverty of the people are, individually, without the means of employing the people; and we, the manufacturers, by working fourteen hours a day, can barely support existence, and in times of stagnation have no resource. The English poor-rates enable the English manufacturers to undersell us, and we regret to hear that the poor-rate of England is swelled by the migration of the destitute Irish seeking employment and food. The people give their labour to the lords of the soil, for permission merely to 'live, and breathe, and have their being.' If this be Irish independence, then it is forsooth all the evils of feudalism, without one of its advantages. Here the manufacturers have been ruined by the poor-rates of England; here three successive confiscations have transferred the land from Irish to English proprietors, and the natives are left to starve; here the Union has legitimised absenteeism; here we have the glorious independence of famine and fever, of gaols and hospitals, of police, soldiery etc ...

Dublin, 17 March 1828.

(The above is the opening paragraph of a long, impassioned 'address' reprinted by Cobbett in the *Register* to coincide with his visit to Ireland.)

APPENDIX V

Political Register, 11 October 1834.

Address of the Citizens of Kilkenny. To Mr William Cobbett, MP

SIR, With feelings of the deepest joy, we heard of your arrival on the shores of Ireland; and those feelings have been increased beyond adequate expression by your visit to our ancient city, to which, sir, in language too weak for the sentiment it would convey, we bid you the sincerest welcome.

When we see a man whose labours through a long life of industry have been devoted to the happiness of his fellow-beings, whose exertions in his own country have found their reward in the increased intelligence, and consequent comfort and well-being of his countrymen; and in that gratitude which nations owe to individuals who have conferred countless benefits on them; when we see one who has subjected himself to the hatred and persecution of the PEOPLE'S foes, because he had acquired the PEOPLE'S love; one whom Providence gifted with talents that have not been abused; with talents that have enabled him, in spite of the oppression of tyranny, and the opposition of bigotry, to raise himself to an eminence that renders him envied by the base, admired by the just, and loved by the grateful; when we see, sir, such a man amongst us for the purpose of acquiring that information which may guide and assist him in his future efforts for the benefit of our country, we are filled with bright anticipations of coming good which we hope soon to see realized.

You are not entirely unaware of the present state of Ireland; with the wrongs under which she suffers, the grievances she endures, and the burdens which oppress her, you are already acquainted; but the details of our misery are not familiar to you; our actual sufferings you have not witnessed; and, till you witness, you cannot know them. You cannot conceive how great, how agonizing to the heart of a philanthropist, how dreadful and almost unendurable they are. We need not tell you, sir, of the many evils which rack-rents, tithes, and absenteeism, have brought on this country. To the state of our own city alone we shall for the present direct your attention.

The Act of Union has proved the ruin of Kilkenny, not in that figurative sense, in which the supporters of the Union would pretend that we speak, when describing the effects of that fatal measure, but in a sense strictly (alas! too strictly) literal. If you walk through our streets and view our manufactories, you will see in the former, groups of tradesmen standing idly, and showing by their hollow cheeks, their despairing looks, and wasted, broken-spirited appearance, that poverty has followed want of employment, and that wretchedness is the only portion they can bestow on their starving offspring. In our factories you will see looms that are not used because our manufacturers are unable to keep them going; wheels that are seldom turned except to preserve them from rotting through disuse; and window-sashes in which there is no glass, for a necessity does not exist to keep the wind and the rain from places that are unoccupied. Things were not thus before the effects of the Union had time to take place. *Then*, our tradesmen were employed, our factories never empty, and our fellow-citizens prosperous and comfortable, if not happy. And yet, sir, Mr Spring Rice made a statement of our prosperity, a statement which was totally untrue, and the motive for making which his country will not forget. With the fact in contradiction to his falsehood, and that fact easy to be maintained, a man who had expressed a desire to have the very name of his country blotted from history, was believed, when he asserted that our trade was in an improving condition!! Thus, sir, has Ireland ever been the victim of misrepresentation, and it was only when men like yourself were possessed of an enlightened understanding, liberal feelings, and a desire to know, and to publish the truth, came over from England, and saw our real state, and perceived that our complaints were not groundless; that Englishmen who only require to know the truth that they may be guided by it, began to feel that Ireland was labouring under wrongs which justice called on them to redress.

From your visit to our country we expect with confidence that both England and Ireland will derive the utmost advantage. The information which your lectures will spread among all classes in this country will, we hope, have the effect of rendering us unanimous in favour of at least one question, a provision for the poor of Ireland.[1] We trust that you will return to your place in the Senate armed with such an abundance of facts and other information, as may decide the legislature on at once passing some law by which the poor population of this country will be relieved from all future danger of the ills attending hunger and poverty; and by which the cold-hearted beings who at present, at home and abroad, are living in luxury, regardless of the misery in every shape which their poorer fellow-countrymen are enduring, may be forced to contribute a portion of that wealth which God did not give them for their own use exclusively, to the support of those who are reduced to depend on others for subsistence. If, sir, you and your countrymen will assist in passing such a measure, you will deserve, and you may rest assured you will obtain our gratitude.

After the fatigue of your travelling hither today, we shall not detain you by a further expression of the pleasure your presence gives us; but you must allow us to breathe a wish for your personal welfare, and can hope that you may live in unbroken health and spirits to see the day when your exertions, and those of the other great men who are labouring with you in the cause of freedom, may be crowned with triumphant success.

NOTES

[1] 'Daniel O'Connell admitted that. Cobbett had convinced him of the advisability of applying the poor laws to Ireland,' see Spater, op.cit. p.594. A limited poor-law measure for Ireland was introduced in 1838.

APPENDIX VI

Political Register, 11 October 1834.

Address of The Manufacturing and Operative Weavers of Kilkenny, Presented to Mr Cobbett MP, 30 September 1834

DEAR SIR, We, the manufacturing and operative weavers of Kilkenny, beg leave to approach you with feelings of mingled exultation and regret; of exultation at the arrival amongst us of one of the most useful, indefatigable, and enlightened public characters, and one of the most generous and sympathizing friends to our afflicted country; of regret, that the depressed and almost ruined state of our trade renders us wholly unable to offer to so distinguished a man tht reception which his long and useful services to Ireland so eminently merit. But, sir, the consciousness of doing good is its own reward, and there is no man more entitled than you are to the felicity arising from such a conviction. Permit us, sir, to offer to an *Englishman*, conspicuous alike for impartiality and love of justice, a brief but genuine statement of facts relating to our trade, which has been represented as in a flourishing and prosperous condition, by the Right Hon. SPRING RICE, with that unblushing effrontery and indecent disregard to truth which characterized the greater portion of that gentleman's speech in the House of Commons during the last session of Parliament.

The facts, sir, are these:

1. That the manufacturers of the city of Kilkenny, before the passing of the Act of Union, were able to employ 3,000 operatives with families in comparative ease and comfort, until the system of absenteeism and the withdrawal of capital,

consequent on that baneful and ruinous measure.

2. That the taking off of the protecting duties in 1821, the leaving of a poor and impoverished country destitute of the fostering aid of a parental legislature, are the prime and sole causes of the misery and destitution of our native manufacturers, and not any combination of tradesmen, as the member for Cambridge has falsely asserted.

3. That out of the 3,000 individuals alluded to, but 350 are now employed whose average weekly wages have suffered a diminution of three fourths, the average weekly wages amounting to but eight shillings, whereas, originally the same average amount was thirty-two shillings and upwards; that even this employment is wholly partial, inasmuch as that 3,000 stone of wool was originally the weekly average amount.

4. That heretofore, and before the passing of the Act of Union, the spinning mills and factories of LACKEN, BLACK-MILL, BLEACHGREEN, and MOUNT-EAGLE were in full and active employment; that since the passing of that destructive measure, employment in these establishments has totally failed.

5. That a CARPET MANUFACTURE has been attempted in Kilkenny about four years since, and that also wholly failed.

6. That more than one-half of the operative weavers are at this moment in a state of destitution; and out of forty manufactories, but *five* at present exist, and these exhibiting but the mere semblance of employment; and out of forty master manufacturers, but *eight* at present exist, three of whom have been long since obliged to throw them selves on the eleemosynary bounty of their fellow-citizens, and are at this moment the wretched inmates of a poor-house.

Such, sir, are the *facts* relative to the *woollen*, once the *staple* trade of Kilkenny. Your stay amongst us, sir, though short, will enable one of your vast and capacious mind to weight the authenticity of these statements against the unfounded assertions of the Right Hon. member for Cambridge.

That Providence, sir, may long continue to you *a life* so valuable in the diffusion of general enlightenment and so advantageous to Ireland, is the heartfelt wish and prayer of the

Manufacturing operatives & weavers of Kilkenny.

APPENDIX VII

Political Register, 8 November 1834.

Garden and Field Seeds

I could sell some now; but I am so circumstanced as to render it very inconvenient for me to do it before the 1st of January, which is quite soon enough. One great object in my having a farm was to have the means of raising genuine seeds; and to have them in such quantities as never to be tempted to sell any seed that I was not sure would grow, and not disappoint the purchaser. To raise perfectly good seed; to have extraordinary produce from plants of all sorts, has been the great delight of my life, and it sticks to me to the last. Never was schoolboy more eager to get from school to play than I am to get from the Parliament House to the fields of my own corn, cabbages, turnips, mangel-wurzel, and beds of all sorts of seeds. This is no harm, but good, even to the politics. The contrast is so great that to move from one to the other seems like a complete new creation of faculty: at any rate, I drive both the concerns on at some rate or another. The maxim that, 'if the devil find a man idle, he is sure to set him to work', has no terrors for me; being always at one or the other, and coming *fresh* at each; so that; in spite of age, the vigour always remains.

To speak as a seedsman, I shall have, on the 1st of January and thereafter, until the next June,[1] Swedish turnip seed, red and white mangel-wurzel seed, cabbage seed, carrot and parsnip seed, and all other garden seeds, which I shall sell at Bolt-court in bags of two sizes, the large ones for a pound, the small ones for ten shillings. Those who dislike the seeds on account of the politics, must go elsewhere and take their L U C K; those who are not quite fools enough for that will, if they choose, buy my seeds, and if they do not choose, they will let it alone. I reckon *cabbage seed* amongst field seeds. I have, perhaps, about two hundred weight, saved this year. I will sell none of it under eight shillings a pound. One pound is enough for any farm in England; and if two hundred sensible farmers could see my cabbage-fields, and see the troops of cattle and of hogs that are kept upon them, they would, if I were so unreasonable as to demand it, freely give five pounds for every pound of the cabbage seed. It is now more than seven years since I began to bestow the infinite pains which I have bestowed in the raising of these seeds.

In coming to Ireland I stopped two nights at BIRMINGHAM, and went to see the farm of MR WILLIAM MARTIN, at KING'S NORTON; and there I saw seven acres of ground, which I saw a sort of swampy meadow three years before; but which has since been trenched on my plan, as directed in my gardening book, and my book called the 'WOODLANDS';[2] a larger crop of vegetables than I think I ever saw on any one seven acres in my life. A part of this crop consisted of cattle-cabbages, which were planted at four feet apart each way; and the main part of which, I am satisfied, weighed *twenty pounds each*. Upon a statute acre there would be two thousand seven hundred and twenty cabbages, which, at twenty pounds each, would weight twenty-three tons and about seventeen hundred weight. I am against these large cabbages. They were sowed in August, 1833; they were planted out in February or March, 1834. They are fit to use now. I planted out comparatively small garden cabbages in the middle of March; I began feeding with the white loaves on the 1st of June. In some part of the ground I pulled up the stumps, and in other parts of it I cut off the heads and left the stumps standing; and I kept feeding with the loaves until about the 24th of August. Now, mind, my rows were four feet one inch and a half apart, in order to bring four of them within a rod; so that, the cabbages being at fifteen inches apart in the row, here were fifty-three cabbages upon a rod, instead of *seventeen* cabbages upon a rod. The average weight of my cabbages was five pounds. There were many that weighed ten; but also many which did not weigh five. I do, however, understate the weight, when I say an average of five pounds. Here, then, were 8,480 cabbages upon the acre, which, at five pounds a cabbage, make 42,400 pounds weight; or *nineteen* tons, all but sixteen pounds.

Now, observe, while cabbages are in the seed-bed they take up no room and cost nothing; when planted out they occupy ground. Mine went out at the time that Mr MARTIN's did; but mine were ripe and consumed before his could be touched; and what followed upon this same ground? My plough was constantly going as fast as weeds appeared between my cabbages. When the first rows were cleared off, the plough went again and reformed the ridges, and other plants came and supplied their place; and before I left home, which was on the 9th of September, this new plantation was loaved, white fine cabbages, ready to be begun upon, from plants which were actually *sowed* on the 24th of May. Being short of plants I did not follow up throughout the piece, but left the stumps, as I said before. Those stumps have now, I hear, plenty of white loaved cabbages upon them, some of them three or four upon a stump. The young plantation is following regularly on; and this second crop upon the same ground in the same summer will be, I believe, full as large as the first. This crop will be followed by plants which will have loaves *by the latter end of April*; so that the next year there will be four crops of cabbages upon the same piece of ground, or upon any other piece of ground that I choose to select for the purpose; and, at the very lowest estimate, the acre of ground will produce sixty tons of cabbages, without a weed or a bit of grass ever being seen in the ground.

I ordered two rows, the stumps of which to be saved, of this second crop of cabbages. Each row contained about five hundred plants. I had seen them twice every day for a month or six weeks; but after I was ready to come away, I went a quarter of a mile to take one more look at them, and I could not discover one single plant which, whether in stump, height, form, hardness of loaf, or any other point, differed from any other one in the whole thousand plants, though the plants had been taken promiscuously out of the bed in which they were sowed. I was very proud indeed of this. I had saved the seed at KENSINGTON[3] with pains, and with a degree of care and anxiety such as no one could conceive; but it is worth all the pains and all the care. And it is an encouragement for any other man to do the same. When I get upon these subjects I am what the French call a *bavard*; but these are matters that we ought to talk of; and at any rate the talking of them can do my readers no harm.

The cattle-cabbage, besides its yielding but one crop in the year, on the same land, comes only in November and the winter; and it is the summer that you want cabbages much more than in the winter, when you have Swedish turnips and mangel-wurzel. The cabbages come in *summer*, as well as spring and fall, and keep your cattle out of the meadows: and, besides all this, there is the superior quality of the small cabbages; which, I believe, is very nearly two to one, though the half-drunken, laudanum-drenched, and quarter-part-insane Scotch may, perhaps, messing up politics with agriculture, think that reducing the cattle even to a *coarser sort of food* will tend 'to save the estates of the landlords'!

NOTES

[1] Cobbett was to die on 18 June 1835, at his farm near Farnham.

[2] Written in 1825, *The Woodlands*, the most valuable of Cobbett's agricultural works, has never been reprinted.

[3] The house in Kensington, where the Cobbetts lived from 1821 to 1833, had four walled acres of clay ground. It was here that Cobbett grew fruit trees, maize and a wide variety of flowers and garden vegetables.

Index

Addington, Lord, 88, 91n, 99, 237
Alexander I, Tsar, 155
Alfred the Great, 144n, 255
Althorp, Lord, 27, 84, 90n, 109, 112, 114-16, 138, 155, 173, 199, 218, 227, 269
Alton, 38
America, 170n; American War of Independence, 19, 77n, 194; American War 1812, 106, 203; American volunteers, 279
Anglesey, Marquis of, 269, 283n
aristocracy, English, 27, 126, 139, 143, 234-5, 277
Ashley, Lord, 251
Australia, 251

Baker, the Revd Richard, 78n
Bank of England, 155, 277, 283n; charter, 189, 206n
Bankes, MP for Dorsetshire, 197
Barrett, Richard, 163, 170n, 276, 279
Bathurst, Lord, 204
Benett, John, 75n
Bible for Poor Men, Cobbett's projected, 213, 228n
Birkbeck, Morris, 37, 48n
Blackstone, William, 228n
Bloody Buoy, The, 23
Bolt Court, 36, 48n, 243n
Bonaparte, Napoleon, 197, 207n, 218
Bone to Gnaw for the Democrats, A, 19, 23
Botany Bay, 221
Botley, 47n, 78n, 90n
Brighton Gazette, The, 231-2
Bristol Riots, 223
Broadway, Sir Thomas, 197
Broderick, see Middleton
Brook Mountain, Revd. Henry, 137
Bourne, William Sturges, 107, 119n, 136, 155, 170n, 240
Bourne Mill, 38, 48n
Brougham, Lord Henry, 27, 88, 91n, 98, 101-2, 107, 112, 115, 117, 118n, 129, 138, 141, 154-5, 169, 171-2, 176, 179-80, 218, 221, 228n, 233, 246-7, 252
Burdett, Sir Francis, 77n, 205n
Burns, Lizzy, 19
Buxton's anti-slavery petition, 84, 219
Byron, 112

Cabbage seeds and cultivation, 292-297
Canada, 69, 96, 202-3, 208n
Canning, George, 93
Carlow, 93
Caroline, Queen, 153
Cartwright, Major, 223, 229n
Catherine of Aragon, 286n
Castle Comfort, Abington, 147
Castlereagh, Lord, 79, 99, 153-4
Catholic Association, The, 47n, 77n, 285
Catholic Emancipation, 16, 31, 47, 70 72, 77n, 268, 281; Relief Act, 25, 47n Relief Bills, 77n, 90n, 168, 249
Catholic religion, 70, 71-2, 77n, 88, 143 193, 206n, 263-4
Chadwick, Edwin, 100-01, 104, 107, 115, 118n, 129
Champlain, Lake, 204
Charleville, 129
Chartist movement, 20, 25, 119n, 206n
Church of England, Cobbett's view of, 267, 269; Church of England clergy, 187
Clarence, Duke of, 170n
Clonmell, 120, 122, 163, 199
'Coarser-Food Ministry', 27, 247-254
Cobbett, Mrs Anne or Nancy, 21-2, 24, 243n
Cobbett, George, grandfather, 76n; George, father, 19, 76n
Cobbett, William, *passim*
Cobbett, William, junior, 243n
Cobbett-corn, 37, 39, 119n
Cobbett's Weekly Political Register, 19, 27
Cobbettites, The, 227
Cockburn, Sir George, 47n, 119n
Cochrane, Lord Thomas, 172, 205n
Cole, G.D.H., 11, 48n, 206n; Cole,

Margaret, 11, 48n
Coleshill, 132-4
Combination Act, 91n
Congress, United States, 277
Connolly, James, 25, 90n
Cork, city of, 147, 162; county, 176, 182, 218; working people of, 126
Crochan, Major, 204, 208n
Cromwell, Oliver, 25, 52
Curran, J.P., 16, 19

Dean, Mr John, 36, 45, 47n, 61-3, 65, 95, 122, 125, 151, 214, 234, 257
Denman, Tom, farm-boy, 43, 48n, 60
Derrynane, 49, 50, 285
Dissenters, 47n, 248-9, 253
Dorsetshire Men, The, 155, 250 (see Tolpuddle)
Doyle, Dr, Bishop of Carlow, 32
Drennan, Dr William, 23, 118n
Dublin, 24, 34, 43, 59, 73, 78n, 81, 93, 162, 205, 209; Parliament, 24, 73, 196, 206n, 266, 268
Durham, Lord, 253-4
Dwyer, Edward, 49, 284

Easter Rising, The, 25
education, 79, 90n; children's, 75n
Edward VI, 143
Egremont, Earl of, 149, 195-6, 202n
Elizabeth I, 143, 206n
Elston, friar, 286n
emigrants, 275, 279; emigration, 27, 159, 201, 204, 222
Evans, Thomas, 118n
Examiner, The, 167

Fagotten, farmer, 66, 231; Mrs Fagotten, 93
famine, 25, 28, 271-2
Farnham, 11, 36, 38, 44, 48n, 60, 65, 76n
Farr, Tom, 60, 151
Fell, Revd T.C., 137
Fenianism, 25
Fermoy, 122
Fielden, John, MP for Oldham, 11, 229n
Finnerty, Peter, 16
Fires, The, 223-6, 230
Fitzgerald, Lord Edward, 16, 20
Fletcher, Colonel, of Bolton, 227
Foley, Catherine, 78n
Folkestone, Lord, see Radnor
'Forty-Shilling' freeholders, 47n, 90n
Fox, Charles, 280

France, 207; peace with, 197; war with, 274; Frenchwomen, 207; French hospitality, 22; ideas, 23; peasantry and artisans, 207; republicanism, 25, 277; French Revolution, 282n
French, Daniel, 16
Friends of Ireland Society, 170n

Game Laws, 144, 154, 240, 266, 282n
George III, 19, 77n
George IV, 102, 154, 178, 283n
George, Prince Regent, 204
Ghent, Treaty of, 207n
Girondist *émigrés*, 23
Globe, The, 167
Godwin, William, 76n
Goldsmith, Oliver, 15, 40
Graham, Sir James, 158, 170n
grape-vines, English, 37, 39
Grey, Lord Charles, 52, 75n, 90n, 101, 107, 176, 180, 248, 253, 269; Grey's Whig ministry, 170n, 228n
Grogan, Major, see Crochan
Grote, George, historian, 221, 252
Guildford, Earl of, 269, 283n
Guerrière, frigate, 207n
Gumbleton, Owen, 124
Gutsell, James, 48n, 228n

Habeas Corpus, suspension of, 75n, 77n
Hale, Judge, 116, 131
Hamilton, Alexander, 23, 276, 283n
Hanover, House of, 153, 187-8, 193
Harvey, Daniel, 280, 283n
Heathorn, Mrs, 93
Henry V, 96
Henry VIII, 269, 285
History of the Protestant Reformation, 16, 32
Hog's-back, The, 36, 65
Horne, farmer, 66, 76n, 148-9, 183, 214, 231-3
House of Lords, 106-7; reform, 107
Hunt, Henry, 47n
Huskisson, William, 88, 90n

Ireland; absentee landlordism in, 195, 198; Church of, 72, 270; English working-class policy towards, 170n, 279; food exports from, 69, 273; injury to, 262; great landowners of, 90n, 159; Poor Laws for, 65, 74, 291n; 'present state of', 289; projected American invasion of, 274; taxes paid by, 192; war with America,

France, 194; *Ireland's Woes: A Warning to Englishmen*, 11
Irish: Catholic religion, 70, 71-2, 77n, 88, 193, 206n, 263n; Catholic hierarchy, 90n, 206n; Coercion Acts, Bills, 26, 49, 75n, 154-5, 168, 170n, 186, 250; emigrants, emigration, 275, 279; famines, 28, 271; national Parliament, legislature, 73, 198, 205, 273; peasantry, 52, 90n; poor laws, 27, 31, 65, 74, 80, 291; poor-rates, 93, 125; Protestant hierarchy, 17, 263, 268-9; Protestant parliament, 268; 'renegades', 166-8; republicanism, 23; sailors, 203; soldiers, 52, 204; woollen trade, 293; Irish Yeomanry, 250, 258n

Jackson, Andrew, General, President, 96, 118n, 204, 207n, 274-9; *Life of, Cobbett's*, 260n
James I, 206n, 263
James II, 179, 269
James, William, historian, 203, 207n
Jews, 111, 220, 228n
John Bull, 167
'Jolly Farmer', The, 77n, 244n
Johnson Samuel, 48n
Jordan, Mrs Dorothea, 156, 170n
'Juverna' letters, of Judge Robert Johnson, 16

Kenner, George, 43-4, 69; Mary Kenner, 44, 48n
Kensington house, Cobbett's, 243n, 296
Kick for a Bite, A, 23
Kildare, 93
Kilkenny, 79, 93, 120, 163; citizens, 289; weavers, 86, 292-3
Kilmallock, priest and inhabitants, 145-6, 170n
Kugelman, 170n
landlordism, absentee, 94, 123, 148, 159, 262, 266-7, 271, 287-8, 290, 292
Leeds, 168; petition, 253; *Leeds Mercury, The*, 167
Leech, John, 63, 76n, 83, 94
Legacy to Labourers, Cobbett's, 11, 91, 119n, 114n, 233-5, 244n, 254, 257
Lidiard Tregoose, 41
Limerick, 11, 145, 149, 163, 202
Liverpool, Lord, 153
local government, abolition of, 116
Locke, John, 236

London Corresponding Society, The, 118n
London 'Mob', 142; newspapers, 246
Lord High Chancellor, see Brougham
Louis XVI, 22
Lowe, parson, 104, 108, 115, 129, 217

Macdonough, Commodore, 204, 208n
Magna Carta, 187
Mahon, O'Gorman, 166
Malthus, T.R., 64, 76n, 91n, 98, 103, 132, 179, 243, 252
Marshall, Charles, 11, 17, 21, 27, 43, 59, 81, 92, 120, 147, 159, 182, 212, 216, 230, 257; Marshall Dick, 43, 48n
Manchester massacre, without inquiry, 153; Manchester petition, 253
martial law, 26
Martin, William, Cobbettite, 295-6
Martineau, Harriet, 117, 119n, 17, 129
Marx, Eleanor, 19, 25; Jenny, 19, 25; Karl, 19, 27, 76n, 170n
Mary Tudor, 143
Mason, Joseph, 119n; Robert, 110, 119n
Mayo, County, 191
McCulloch, J.R., 75n, 266
Meath Club, 64
Melbourne, Lord, 247
Middleton, Co. Cork, 123
Middleton, Lord, 123-4, 148, 199
militia, conscript, 117, 130-2
Moor Park, 263, 282n
Morning Advertiser, The London, 167
Morning Chronicle, The, 100, 246, 262, 280-1
Morning Herald, The, 142, 156, 167
Morning Post, The London, 167
Morning Register, The, 164-5
Moscow, 170n
Mullinahone, 78n
Mullinavat, 94
Museum, The British, 90n

Napoleonic wars, 20
National Debt, 26-8, 155, 174, 206n, 269
National Political Union, 170n
Nevin, Mr, 52-3, 218-19
New Brunswick, 20, 69
New Orleans, Battle of, 274
New York, 71, 170n, 276; *New York Evening Post, The*, 280
Newcastle, petitions, 168, 253
Newgate, 16, 206n
Newtownbarry, 78n, 250
Ney, Marshal, 154

Nore mutiny, 22, 127
Norman conquest, 144n
Normandy Farm, 11, 36-7, 47n, 48n, 60, 65, 151, 243n; Normandy common, 39, 66
Nottingham Riots, 223; petition, 168
Nova Scotia, 69, 77n

Oastler, Richard, 106, 119n
Observer, The, 166-7
O'Callaghan, Revd J, 16
O'Connell, Daniel, 16, 25-6, 47n, 49, 57, 144n; and Catholic Emancipation, 281-2; Coercion Bill, 75n, 155, 157-9; Poor Laws for Ireland, 291n; Repeal agitation, 186-7, 279; the 'O'Connell tribute', or 'Catholic rent', 161-68
O'Higgins, Mr, 93
Oldfield, Mr Jesse, 11
Oldham, 27, 47n, 58, 86, 146, 168, 223; people of, 245

Paine, Tom, 23, 77n, 118n, 274-5, 283n
Paper Against Gold, 206n, 283n
paper-money, Cobbett's view of, 87, 189, 275
Parkes, Joseph, 110, 119n, 249-50, 253-4
Parliament House, Burning of, 142-4, 153-6, 178-9
Parliaments, annual, 17, 254; triennial, 187, 206n, 254
parliamentary reform, 47n, 55, 174, 206n, 241
Parliamentary Debates, Cobbett's, 229n
Peel, Sir Robert, 77n, 96, 144n, 155, 168, 205, 228n, 229n, 234, 241, 268
Penal Codes, 143, 206n
Peter Porcupine, The Works of, 23
Peterloo, 170n
Peto, William, 285, 286n
Phillips, Sir Thomas, 137, 197
Pilot, The, 11, 186, 283n
Pitt, William, 25, 77n, 78n, 90n, 194, 272
Pole, Margaret, Countess of Salisbury, 286n
police: 'Bourbon-like', 154, 241, 247, 262, 269-70; metropolitan, 283n; 'rural police', 238-240
Poor Law Amendment Act, Bill, 11, 27, 76n, 91n, 98, 102, 106-7, 108-10, 112, 116-17, 128-9, 130, 136, 144n, 155, 171-2, 179, 217, 221, 233, 240, 245, 252; Poor Law Commission, 109, 116, 119n, 139, 136-7, 179, 197, 239
Poor Law, Elizabethan, 48n, 65, 101, 103, 221, 233, 240, 245, 252; Poor-Book, 104; Poor-rates, 27, 46, 93-4, 112-14, 137, 148-9, 151, 230
Popay, 154, 170, 247, 252
Portland, Duke of, 194
Potatoes, 82, 93-5, 109-11, 114, 118n, 125, 145, 147, 151, 184-5, 213, 246
Press, the English, Cobbett's views on, 167, 210, 246
Priestley, Joseph, 23
proprietorship in land, 220-21, 267

Quarterly Review, The, 167, 169

Radnor, Earl of, 27, 98, 118n, 129, 141, 171-2, 180-1, 216, 238; Lady Radnor, 216
Rathcormack, 78n
'Reckoning Commission', 140, 144n
Reform Bill, 242, 249, 253
Reformation, The, 263-4
Regency and Reign of George IV, 197, 207n
Reid, Ann, or Anna, 77n
Relief Acts, see *Catholic Emancipation*
Rents, 62, 83, 106-7, 112-14, 123, 148, 200, 230; rack-rents, 27, 124, 145, 149, 174, 200, 290
Repeal, agitation for, 25, 73, 78n, 186-7, 190, 204, 261, 273, 280
Riot Act, 143; Riots of 1830-1831, 224, 240
Rose, George, 88, 90n
Rush, Dr Benjamin, 23-4

Saint John, New Brunswick, 77n
Salisbury Journal, The, 167
'Scotch Mentor', see Brougham
Scotland, Cobbett's Tour in, 93, 118n
Scotland, people of, 46; 'Scotch vagabonds' 81, 148, 257, 228n
Scott, Sir William, 188
Secret Service, funding of, 154
Senior ('Last Hour') Nassau, economist, 136
Septennial Act, 143, 251
Sherman, Colonel Roger, 194, 206n
Sidmouth, see Addington
Slievenamann, Mount, 52
slavery, 68-9, 84, 91, 176-8, 218-9, 205n, 250-1
Soldier's Friend, The, 15, 21

Spain, war with, 106
Spater, George, 144n, 205n, 228n, 243n
Spithead mutiny, 20
Spence, Thomas, 98, 118n
Spencer, Earl, 194
Spring Rice, Thomas, 25, 86, 90n, 156, 190, 272, 290, 292-3
St. Martha's Hill, 257, 258n
Stanhope, Lord, 222, 239
standing army, 87, 122, 269
Swift, Jonathan, 15, 20, 77n, 90n, 262-3
Swing, Captain, 142, 144n

taxes; beer, 155; food, 232; hops, 224; Malt Tax, 61, 154, 224, 170n, 230-2, 241-2, 252
Temple, Sir William, 263, 282n
Thomastown, 78n
tithes, 31, 47n, 70, 72, 78n, 113, 131, 143-4, 159, 194, 213, 248-9, 267, 274, 290; Tithe War, 26, 258n, 283n
Thompson, William, 258n
Times, The, 157, 160, 163-6, 167-8, 170n
Tipperary County, 120
Tolpuddle Martyrs, 170n, 250
transportation, penal, 154, 240; Special Commissions for, 236, 238, 242, 250
Troubridge, Sir Thomas, 155
True Sun, The, 167, 283n

Union, Act of, 25-6, 70, 73, 78n, 90n, 170n, 190, 192, 290, 292-3; Union with Ireland; 73, 86, 170n
United Irishmen, 19; Rising of 1798, 78n, 118n, 194
United States of America: danger of war with, 274-6
universal suffrage, 254

Vansittart, Nicholas, 88
Vaughan, Judge, 119
vestry votes, 107-8, 110, 114, 138, 155, 170n

wages, 61, 82, 109, 112-3, 138, 148, 224-5, 230-1, 293
Wales, journey through, 39, 40-1; Welshwomen, 41; men, 236
Wallscourt Farm, 78n
Walsingham, Lord, 269, 283n
Walters, John, editor *The Times*, 170n
Washington, George, 194, 274, 276, 283n
Waterford, 84, 92-3, 163; citizens of, 88
Waterloo, 52, 118n, 255
Wellington, Duke of, 52, 77n, 168, 170n, 247, 249, 255, 268
West, farmer, 66, 231; Mrs West, 93
Westminster, 24, 78n
Wey, River, 48n, 258n
Wheeler, Anna, 258n
Whitlaw, Mr, Cobbettite, 65
Wicklow, County, 93
Wilberforce, William, 17, 88, 91n, 176, 218, 260
'Wild Irish, The', 19, 35, 262
William Cobbett Society, The, 11
William III, 193, 206n, 282n; William and Mary, 153
William IV, 228n, 242
William of Normandy, 144
Wood, Alderman John, Preston candidate, 222, 251

Year's Residence in America, Cobbett's Journal of a, 23
Young, Arthur, 38, 48n, 206n